Policing the Great Plains

Published in cooperation with
the William P. Clements Center
for Southwest Studies, Southern
Methodist University.

ANDREW R. GRAYBILL

Policing the Great Plains

Rangers, Mounties,
and the North
American Frontier,
1875–1910

University of Nebraska Press   Lincoln & London

Library of Congress Cataloging-in-Publication Data

Graybill, Andrew R., 1971–
Policing the Great Plains : Rangers, Mounties, and
the North American frontier, 1875–1910 / Andrew R.
Graybill.
p.   cm.

"An earlier version of chapter 2 appeared as "Rangers,
Mounties, and the Subjugation of Indigenous Peoples,
1870–1885," Great Plains Quarterly 24, no. 2 (Spring
2004): 85–99. Reprinted by permission.

An earlier version of chapter 4 appeared as "Rural
Police and the Defense of the Cattleman's Empire in
Texas and Canada, 1875–1900," Agricultural History 75,
no. 3 (Summer 2005): 253–80. Copyright 2005 by the
Agricultural History Society. Reprinted by permission.

An earlier version of chapter 5 appeared as "Texas
Rangers, Canadian Mounties, and the Policing of
the Transnational Industrial Frontier, 1885–1910,"
Western Historical Quarterly 35 (Summer 2004):
167–91. Copyright by the Western History Association.
Reprinted by permission."

Includes bibliographical references and index.
ISBN 978-0-8032-6002-3 (pbk. : alk. paper)
1. Police—North America—History. 2. Texas Rangers
—History. 3. Royal Canadian Mounted Police—
History. I. Title.
HV7909.G73 2007
363.209764'09034—dc22
2006037640

Set in Minion by Bob Reitz.

For my family, with love and thanks

Contents

Illustrations

Maps

Acknowledgments

I became an inveterate reader of acknowledgments when I started graduate school, and at that time I was struck by the number of people and institutions who were thanked by the various authors I read. I marveled that anyone could possibly need so much help in writing a book. Experience has taught me just how naïve I was back then, and I would like to thank those individuals and organizations that have given generously to me of their time and expertise.

This book began as a dissertation at Princeton University, where I had the good sense and great fortune to work with Andrew Isenberg. Drew gave me enormous amounts of direction and support, allayed my anxieties, and affirmed my belief in mentorship. When I told him once that he was the "Shaquille O'Neal of advisers," he warmed to the sports metaphor but corrected my analysis, writing that "if I'm trying to do anything as an adviser, in basketball terms I'm a point guard: [I] dish off to my teammates (i.e., advisees) so they can score. And [I] help out on defense so that my teammates don't get beat." I guess that makes him the Tony Parker of advisers. I would like also to thank the other members of my PhD committee, Jeremy Adelman and James McPherson, as well as John Murrin, whose formidable mind is exceeded only by his thorough decency.

My graduate school experience was much richer for the friends I made at Princeton, who provided a constant source of support and inspiration. Thanks especially to Denver Brunsman, Bill Carter, Genelle Gertz-Robinson, Holly Grieco, Drew Levy, Jarbel Rodriguez, Jenny Weber, and Amanda Wunder. Alec Dun and Nick Guyatt made my years in central New Jersey more fun than I could ever have imagined when we first met in the fall of 1997.

I spent the 2004–5 academic year as a fellow at the Clements Center for Southwest Studies at Southern Methodist University, where I had time to revise and extend the manuscript in an incredibly collegial and stimulating environment. I was humbled by the generosity of the Center's faculty and staff, and I thank Andrea Boardman, Ruth Ann Elmore, Sherry Smith, and David Weber for making my smu sojourn so rewarding. Brian Frehner, Ben

Johnson, and Michelle Nickerson brought about the unlikeliest of personal transformations in me: a deep, abiding affection for Dallas, Texas. And special thanks to Sarah Carter, Elliott West, and the other participants who critiqued my manuscript in a workshop held at smu in September 2004.

I finished the book at the University of Nebraska–Lincoln, and I would like to acknowledge the support of my friends and colleagues in the history department at unl, who have made the Cornhusker State an exceptionally pleasant place to work. I offer special thanks to the department's chairman, Ken Winkle, who has been most supportive and who helped arrange for my leave. In Lincoln, thanks also to the folks at the University of Nebraska Press, particularly my editor, Heather Lundine; her assistant, Bridget Barry; and also Elizabeth Demers, who acquired my project during her tenure at the Press. And I am most grateful to geographer Ezra Zeitler for preparing the maps, and to copyeditor Ruth Melville for cleaning up the text considerably.

I couldn't have written the book without the assistance of numerous archivists and research librarians scattered throughout North America. In the United States, I'd like to acknowledge the assistance of the following individuals and institutions: the Center for American History at the University of Texas–Austin; the Howard Payne University Library; the Johns Hopkins University Library, especially Agnes Flannery-Denner; the libraries of the University of Nebraska–Lincoln; the Panhandle-Plains Historical Museum, especially Betty Bustos; the Princeton University Library, especially Alfred Bush and Mary George; the libraries of Southern Methodist University; the Southwest Collection at Texas Tech University; the special collections division at the library of the University of Texas–Arlington; the Texas Ranger Hall of Fame and Museum, especially Judy Shofner; the Texas State Library and Archives, especially John Anderson; the Trinity University Library; and the Western History Collections at the University of Oklahoma, especially John Lovett. In Canada, thanks go to the staffs of the National Archives of Canada and the Glenbow-Alberta Institute, especially Jim Bowman and Doug Cass.

I am also grateful for the financial assistance that made my research trips possible in the first place, which was provided by the following: the history department and the graduate school at Princeton University; the Center of International Studies and the Council on Regional Studies, both at Princeton; the Canadian Embassy (through a graduate student research fellowship); the Clements Center for Southwest Studies; and a Rawley Fund Grant from the history department at the University of Nebraska–Lincoln. On the ground, thanks to Karen Dinitz, John Greenman, Dianne Hardy-Garcia, and Martin Jones for putting me up (and putting up with me) while I was away from home.

Along the way, I have benefited enormously from the suggestions of many fellow scholars. In the United States, thanks go to Steve Aron, Gregg Cantrell, Mark Ellis, Laura Ehrisman, James Gump, David Gutierrez, Pekka Hämäläinen, Carol Higham, Fran Kaye, Pete Maslowski, Karen Merrill, Marilyn Rhinehart, Alan Taylor, Sandra VanBurkleo, Richard Voeltz, and John Wunder. In Canada, thanks to David Breen, Warren Elofson, Simon Evans, Sterling Evans, Max Foran, Walter Hildebrandt, Greg Kealey, Bob Macdonald, Kent McNeil, and Jeremy Mouat. I am particularly grateful to several historians of the Texas Rangers, who—though they might disagree with some of my conclusions—nevertheless responded generously to my questions and pointed me in the direction of helpful primary and secondary material. Thanks to Harold Weiss and the late Frederick Wilkins, and especially to Bob Utley, who went so far as to e-mail me copies of his voluminous notes on Ranger efforts to combat fence cutting and labor agitation, saving me countless hours of toil. When I expressed my gratitude a few years ago, Bob stated simply his belief that established scholars had a responsibility to assist young and struggling ones. Consider it duly noted.

Several chapters from the book appeared as articles in slightly to significantly different form, and I would like to acknowledge the journals and their editors that published those pieces and to extend my thanks for permission to reprint them here: Claire Strom at *Agricultural History*; Chuck Braithwaite at *Great Plains Quarterly*; and David Rich Lewis at the *Western Historical Quarterly*.

Of course my biggest debts are to my extended family. I'm truly blessed to have the Ebingers in my corner, and I consider Chuck, Lynn, Sara, Brad, and Margaret nothing less than blood. My sister Lisa has helped immeasurably to keep my feet on the ground. And my mom and dad are simply the finest people I know, without whom this project—and frankly anything else I've ever done—would not be possible. But where would I be without Jennifer Ebinger? She alone knows how much I owe to her. I am privileged to be her husband, and I look forward to sharing with her and Fiona all the joys and challenges that lie ahead.

Policing the Great Plains

Introduction

"Similar Organizations in Other Parts"

In April 1919 a novice instructor at the University of Texas named Walter Prescott Webb wrote to a government official in Ottawa inquiring about the history of the Royal North-West Mounted Police (RNWMP).[1] Webb was looking for information on the Mounties that might add depth to the master's thesis he was writing at Austin, a study of another famed North American rural constabulary, the Texas Rangers. Webb had been inspired to undertake the project by the controversy roiling the force that spring, when the Texas state legislature had launched an investigation into alleged Ranger atrocities committed against Mexicans after a failed uprising in South Texas.[2] For his part, the Canadian official promised Webb his assistance and—attempting perhaps to allay the young historian's concerns about the spread of Ranger notoriety—added amiably that the Texas constabulary still enjoyed "considerable reputation in [Canada] and it would be too bad should they be allowed to fall into disrepute."[3]

Whatever Webb made of the dusty, fire-damaged annual reports sent to him that fall from the RNWMP's headquarters in Regina, Saskatchewan, he did not say; the Mounties do not receive even a passing mention in his sprawling 1935 study of the Texas state police. Maybe the prospect of extensive archival research in Canada (in the dead of winter) did not appeal to him; or perhaps Webb was simply conserving academic energy for his massive study of the Great Plains, which appeared in 1931. To be sure, in the years since the publication of Webb's book on the Rangers, scholars of each constabulary have often noted the parallels between what Webb's Canadian correspondent termed "similar organizations in other parts." But such comparisons have usually been fleeting and superficial, merely reminding readers that the Rangers and Mounties are likely the two best-known police forces in the world.[4]

The absence of a sustained analytical comparison of the Rangers and Mounties is surprising, both because such a project seems so obvious and also because insights can be gleaned by juxtaposing the two forces. On the most fundamental level, measuring the constabularies against each other challenges the notions of historical exceptionalism that animate most histories of the Rangers and Mounties and also of the regions they policed. The forces were created at almost the same moment in the early 1870s, for a strikingly similar reason: to extend the power of the state to outlying regions. More broadly, looking through the institutions themselves to the areas they patrolled undermines the tendency among scholars to describe nineteenth-century Texas and the Canadian prairies in singular terms. The myth of the sui generis North American frontier runs especially deep in both places, but collapses when one realizes, for instance, that the Lone Star State's cattle kingdom had a robust counterpart in southern Alberta, or that the "last, best West" so heavily promoted by Ottawa in the 1890s looked just as bleak to Canadian Indians as the West lying to the south of the 49th parallel appeared to their American counterparts.

Beyond this challenge to exceptionalism, a comparison of the Rangers and Mounties offers fresh perspectives on the Great Plains. Writers and scholars have long confined their studies to either one side of the 49th parallel or the other, imposing intellectual parameters seemingly no less arbitrary than the international border itself.[5] The very existence of these rural constabularies at opposite ends of the region, however, as well as the remarkable overlap between their missions emphasizes the transnational reach of the Great Plains. That the two forces policed nearly identical populations—including Indians, peoples of mixed ancestry, homesteaders, and industrial workers—reinforces the notion that Texas and the Canadian North-West were bound by conditions of ecology, economy, and demography that transcended North American political boundaries. Moreover, because the enforcement of international borders was so central to the work of each force, comparing such efforts by the Rangers and Mounties establishes that the Great Plains belong in any academic discussion of the "borderlands," which for many decades has served as a sort of shorthand referring exclusively to the American Southwest.[6]

Most importantly, linking the histories of the Rangers and Mounties brings into sharp relief the common process by which states incorporated their frontiers during the late nineteenth century. The first step involved the

confinement or removal of indigenous peoples in order to prepare the hinterlands for occupation by white farmers and entrepreneurs. In Texas, the
Rangers—who were driven by decades of brutal native-white conflict within
the region—secured the state's borders by forcing Kiowas and Comanches
north across the Red River into Indian Territory (present-day Oklahoma)
and by pushing Apaches westward into New Mexico, where the Indians
then became the responsibility of the federal government. Though employ-
ing far less violence, the Mounties were no less effective in the North-West,
since they confined Blackfoot and Crees to reserves, where (it was hoped)
the First Nations could then be assimilated into broader Canadian society.

Next came the dispossession of peoples of mixed ancestry, whose communal resource use threatened the privatization of valuable natural resources. For the NWMP, this meant breaking the grasp of the Métis on the
river valleys of Saskatchewan, which were coveted by Eurocanadian farmers
moving west from Ontario. The Mounties imposed Ottawa's decree that
lands throughout the North-West would be divided into square tracts (and
not the oblong lots with narrow river frontage favored by the Métis), and
then the police worked to quell resistance to federal surveys and land sales.
The Rangers, on the other hand, used terrorism and lethal force to protect
the cattle of Anglo ranchers from Mexicans (who for their part insisted that
many of the animals had been taken from them by whites in the years following the Mexican-American War). The Rangers also suppressed Mexican
resistance to the privatization of communal salt deposits in far West Texas,
which for decades local residents had used for their livestock or to generate
extra income in times of want.

The police then defended cattlemen and ranching syndicates from the
protests of the rural poor. With the spread of barbed wire throughout Texas
during the 1870s, farmers and smaller ranchers found their access to the
free water and grass of the public domain under siege by the wealthy, who
enclosed their lands (legally and otherwise) in order to feed their animals
and provide for selective breeding. When an intense drought hit the state in
1883, angry nesters retaliated against their more powerful neighbors by destroying fences and stealing livestock. The state government responded by
sending out the Rangers, whose primary mission in the mid-1880s involved
the eradication of fence cutting. At the other end of the Plains, the Mounties faced the inverse problem: keeping the poor from erecting enclosures
(usually along river bottoms) on public lands that had been leased by Ot-

tawa to Alberta's biggest stock growers. The NWMP thus drove off squatters whose shacks and fences impeded the access of fine-blooded animals to water and forage.

Lastly, the police defeated the threat to nascent industrial development by intervening in strikes at the largest collieries in Texas and the North-West. Mountie involvement at the Alberta Railway and Coal Company helped that corporation through more than a decade of labor disturbances, and saw the police evolve from relatively honest brokers between the two sides to—what many strikers considered—little more than company muscle. The Rangers enjoyed a nearly identical relationship with Colonel Robert D. Hunter's Texas and Pacific Coal Company, with some members of the force even serving in Hunter's private security detail in order to gain more leverage over the dissidents. Over the course of their fifteen years in Thurber, however, the Rangers became less enthusiastic (and consequently less effective) in defending management from the strident efforts of labor activists to unionize the T&PCC workforce.

The convergence of the constabularies' work frames the political objectives and economic imperatives shared by authorities in Austin and Ottawa at this moment, while illuminating police strategies for facilitating the absorption of the hinterlands. While the methods of the police may have diverged sharply—contrast the Rangers' enthusiastic dispensation of violence with the relative restraint of the Mounties—the goals and the net results of their efforts were virtually indistinguishable. Beyond merely linking together the Rangers and the Mounties or the geographical extremes of the Great Plains, such a discovery serves to integrate the frontiers of North America into a global story of economic transformation in the industrial age.

1 Instruments of Incorporation

In September 1878 the *Saskatchewan Herald* published a poem by an author identified only by the initials W. S. titled "The Riders of the Plains," the piece celebrated the valor of the North-West Mounted Police (NWMP), who had arrived on the prairies four years earlier to establish Canadian authority in the region. After describing the myriad challenges met and overcome by the constabulary during its famed march to the West in 1874, the poem reaches its crescendo in the final stanza:

> Our mission is to plant the right
> Of British freedom here—
> Restrain the lawless savages,
> And protect the pioneer.
> And 'tis a proud and daring trust
> To hold these vast domains
> With but three hundred mounted men—
> The Riders of the Plains.

The poem soon became the best-known verse about the Mounties, and inspired later writers to add their own stanzas to the original.[1]

Although W. S. no doubt believed the Mounties were peerless, just six years later a Texas woman named Mary Saunders Curry drafted a paean to the Texas Rangers that echoed the tributes heaped by the Canadian poet upon the Mounted Police. Of the typical Ranger, Curry wrote in 1884:

> He stands our faithful bulwark
> Against the savage foe;
> Through lonely woodland places

Our children come and go.
Our flocks and herds untended
O'er hill and valley roam;
The ranger in the saddle
Means peace for us at home.[2]

While Curry's poem seems to have been intended only for the amusement of Captain L. P. "Lam" Sieker and the men of Ranger Company D, it, too, enjoyed broad circulation, suggested by its reprinting in a state periodical some eight years later.[3]

The parallels between the verses are striking. For instance, both writers evoke the forbidding landscapes of their respective Great Plains frontiers, and each identifies the chief responsibility of the police as protecting (white) settlers from "savage" Indians. And yet even a passing glance at the poems uncovers some revealing differences. W. S. emphasizes the Old World traditions undergirding the NWMP, as well as the aim of the force to "plant the right of British freedom" in the West—in other words, to bring justice to areas then beyond Ottawa's control. There is no mention of such high-minded duties anywhere in Curry's poem; rather, she stresses throughout the importance of Ranger vigilance in keeping Anglo-Texans safe from the terrors of murder and theft.

Though of dubious literary quality, the poems are useful in opening a window onto the Rangers, Mounties, and the transnational Great Plains frontier they policed during the late nineteenth century. For one thing, the verses attest to the powerful resemblances linking the two constabularies, which were formed at virtually the same moment, for nearly identical reasons, and to patrol similar environments. Moreover, the authors' unabashed celebrations of the police underscore the intensive process of mythmaking that has surrounded the constabularies from the moments of their inception right up to the present. But no less than such similarities, the poems also call attention to the significant differences between the conditions faced and the means employed by the Rangers and the Mounties as they incorporated the hinterlands of Texas and the North-West. If in the end their efforts produced overlapping results at the far edges of the Plains, Ranger violence contrasted with Mountie restraint reveals much about the forces themselves and the societies that deployed them.

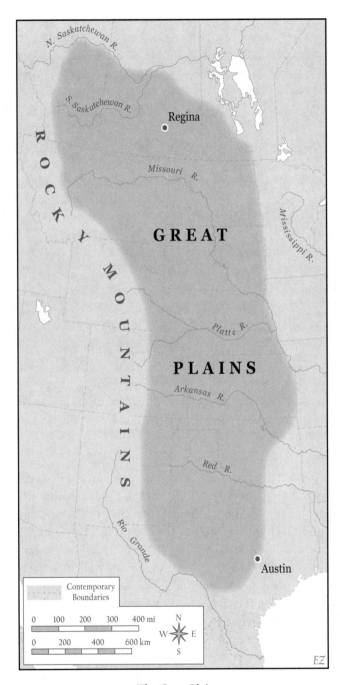

1. The Great Plains

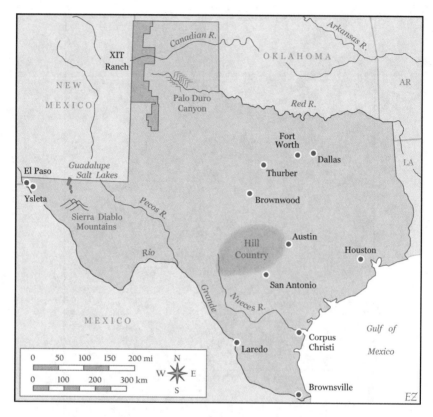

2. Texas

The Plains

Though separated by more than 2,000 miles (plus an international boundary), Texas and the North-West Territories of Canada had much in common during the last third of the nineteenth century. For one thing, as the southern and northern extremes of the Great Plains, they were linked by the environmental conditions of the vast North American grasslands, characterized by a semiarid climate, a flat or slightly rolling landscape, and a wide variety of plant and animal species of which the bison was the most famous.[4] For another, they resembled each other in size: at 261,000 square miles, Texas is roughly equal in area to the lower halves of Alberta and Saskatchewan, which made up the heart of the North-West Territories.[5] Moreover, the composition of their human populations was analogous, consisting of natives, peoples of mixed ancestry, Anglo settlers, and European industrial workers.

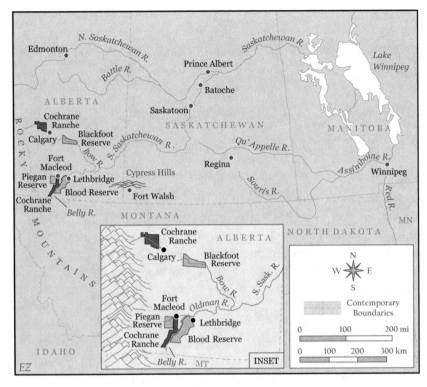

3. Western Canada

Texas and the North-West Territories were related in this period in more complex ways as well. Both were borderlands regions of larger state entities actively engaged in the process of state building, and as such, officials in Austin and Ottawa placed the highest priority on bringing these hinterlands under their political and economic control. The North-West, for instance, lay beyond the grasp of the federal government at the time of Canadian Confederation in 1867. For the previous two centuries, the area (known as Prince Rupert's Land) had existed under the jurisdiction of the Hudson's Bay Company (HBC), established in 1670 by King Charles II of England to exploit the abundance of fur-bearing game in the region north and west of the Great Lakes. After Confederation, however, Ottawa moved quickly to acquire the territory from the HBC in order to extend the reach of the new nation but also to deny the United States the opportunity to annex it, a legitimate concern given America's territorial pretensions of the nineteenth century. Thus it was that Ottawa purchased Rupert's Land in 1869 from the British for £300,000.

Likewise, Texas in the late 1860s and early 1870s was in political and geographic transition. As part of the United States, the Lone Star State was mired in the throes of national reconstruction following a bitter civil war, and Texas experienced its own rebirth in this period, as control of the state shifted back to the Democrats after nine years of postwar Republican rule.[6] Moreover, as in Ottawa, officials in Austin sensed a keen need to shore up the borders surrounding their outlying regions, and so set about strengthening the human and physical boundaries between Mexico to the south and Indian Territory to the north. While of course neither Mexicans nor Indians sought the annexation of Texas, their continued presence within the confines of the state imperiled Austin's plans for the absorption of the region, in much the same way that prospective American interlopers threatened the fragile dream of a transcontinental Dominion of Canada.

Even more broadly, Texas and the North-West were both located on the peripheries of an expanding system of international capitalism, one marked in late nineteenth-century North America (as elsewhere) by the rapid movement of people and investment capital to the frontier and the ensuing development of natural resources for commercial exchange.[7] While the Great Plains was among the last parts of the continent integrated into the global market economy, industrialization swept across it with transformative power between 1870 and 1900. For instance, this period witnessed the massive extension of rail networks in Texas and the Canadian West, as the Lone Star State added nearly 9,000 miles of track and Ottawa oversaw the hurried construction of the transcontinental Canadian Pacific Railway. These infrastructural improvements facilitated the migration of white settlers—many of whom harbored entrepreneurial ambitions—to resource-rich but previously inaccessible places such as the Texas Panhandle and the Bow River Valley of present-day Alberta. Their new ventures in ranching and mining attracted great sums from domestic and overseas investors and served to bind the hinterlands to more developed urban areas in Texas and Canada.

Despite these powerful resemblances, several features nevertheless distinguished Texas and the North-West from one another. Most fundamental was the issue of political status. Though Texas had existed briefly as an independent republic from 1836 to 1845 (and thus entered the United States in possession of most of its territory), in 1870 it was merely a state within a larger nation, one that had formally separated from England nearly a century before. The Canadian prairies, by contrast, were—for the most part—portions of an unorganized federal territory belonging to a union that retained strong political and social ties to Great Britain, even after the Dominion's Confederation in 1867. Additionally, the capitals that administered the two regions stood in opposite geographical relationships to the areas in question: Austin is situated near the center of Texas, while Ottawa lies some 2,100 miles east of the Rocky Mountains, which mark the western edge of the Plains. State officials in Texas could thus respond more immediately to settler concerns—and often faced more pressure to do so—than their federal counterparts in Ottawa.

Moreover, the incorporation of these borderlands regions took place against starkly contrasting backdrops of peace and turmoil. Although some Americans had long spoken of annexing portions of Canada—especially the territory west of the Great Lakes—to the United States, these proposals attracted only casual support and never blossomed into the filibustering expeditions so often directed at nations lying to the south of the United States.[8] Thus Ottawa's expansion onto the Plains in the 1870s was of a primarily defensive nature, meant to quench any lingering American hopes of seizing the Canadian West. The northern and southern boundaries of Texas, on the other hand, were sites of brutal violence, where for decades Anglos had battled Indians and Mexicans, respectively, for control of land and resources. The bloodshed of the 1870s stemmed directly from the attempts of state officials to solidify the conquest of nonwhite peoples within the borders of Texas, a process that was necessarily more offensive than the preventative measures taken by the Canadian government.

The differing levels of violence in the borderlands of Texas and the North-West suggest another essential schism between the two locations: the size and timing of white settlement. Racial friction in the Lone Star State derived in large part from the penetration of Anglos into the central, southern, and western portions of Texas throughout the mid- to late nineteenth century. For example, in 1870 Anglos accounted for more than 550,000 of the state's 818,000 people. White settlement to the Canadian prairies, by contrast, was delayed by the presence of the Canadian Shield, an expanse of rocky soil stretching onto the Plains from eastern Canada. Because it was largely unsuited to agriculture, the Shield slowed the westward migration of farming families until the 1880s, at which point migrants used the railroad to traverse it and reach the more fertile prairies. Thus in 1870 there were likely fewer than 2,000 white people scattered among the estimated 25,000 to 35,000 indigenous peoples in Canada's western interior, and thus they constituted a much less immediate threat to nonwhite peoples than did their counterparts in Texas.

The Police

The similar (though not identical) conditions prevailing in Texas and the North-West led officials in both locations to devise a common solution to the problem of frontier incorporation: the formation of mounted constabularies. As with the northern and southern edges of the Plains themselves, the parallels between the forces are striking and extend to circumstances as basic as the dates of their creation. Ottawa established the North-West Mounted Police by an act of Parliament passed in May 1873, following several years of planning by Canadian prime minister Sir John A. Macdonald.[9] The Texas Rangers—though tracing their history as far back as 1823—were formally institutionalized as a police constabulary by the state legislature of Texas in April 1874, less than a year after the founding of the NWMP.[10] Moreover, the missions of the two forces were essentially the same: to bring frontier regions of Texas and the Canadian North-West under the political control of Austin and Ottawa in order to promote white settlement and economic development in these resource-rich hinterlands.

The institutional infrastructures of the two forces also resembled one another: each was under the command of a single appointed official—the adjutant general of Texas and the commissioner of the NWMP, respectively—and consisted of six companies lettered A to F. Officers directed the units, which counted fifty men each for the Mounties and seventy-five for the Rangers.[11] As suggested by such an organizational schema, the forces were decidedly military in their orientation; although both constabularies were invested with typical law enforcement responsibilities (including the power to arrest and incarcerate alleged lawbreakers), the primary objectives of the police involved the occupation and absorption of outlying lands. The men who served in the forces understood as much. Famed Mountie officer R. Burton Deane insisted in his memoirs that "the N.W.M. Police, if not a military body, are as nearly military as it is possible for an armed body of constabulary to be."[12] For his part, Ranger James B. Gillett explained that the Texas Rangers had constituted "the nucleus of a national standing army" during its formative years and retained that purpose throughout the nineteenth century.[13]

Notwithstanding these likenesses, the Rangers and Mounties were hardly mirror images. For one thing, the constabularies derived from very different martial traditions. In the case of the NWMP, the close ties between England and Canada (which until 1867 was a British colony) led Macdonald to look to the mother country for inspiration in developing his force. However, rather than using the London Metropolitan Police (LMP) as his model, the prime minister took his inspiration instead from the Royal Irish Constabulary (RIC), which had been established in 1822. There were several reasons for this. In the first place, the RIC had developed within the context of extreme social unrest in Ireland during the early nineteenth century, conditions Macdonald feared might emerge in the North-West. Moreover, unlike the LMP, members of the RIC were authorized to carry weapons, were trained within a system of military discipline, and were directed by central (and not local) officials. Macdonald sought to replicate precisely these features of the RIC, to the extent that he dispatched the first NWMP commissioner, G. A. French, to Ireland in the hopes of shaping his new force in its image.[14]

The Texas Rangers, by contrast, had firm North American roots, inheriting a ranging tradition that stretched back to the frontier of the colonial period and the early U.S. republic. Farmers and small businessmen by trade, these early rangers had banded together in the face of acute adversity—such as Indian raiding in the Appalachian backcountry during the Seven Years' War—and supplied their own horses, weapons, and rations. This was the model that Stephen F. Austin—the leader of the Anglo colony in Texas—had in mind in August 1823 when he explored the possibility of enlisting a small company of men to "act as rangers for the common defence."[15] Specifically, Austin and other Anglo-Texans recognized an urgent need for protection from groups of Indians such as the Karankawas and Tawakonis, who challenged the northern and western edges of white settlement. Austin's plan languished for more than a decade, during which time the colony relied on a volunteer militia, but Anglos never abandoned the idea and formally established the Texas Rangers in 1835 in response to the needs of their rapidly growing colony. For the next four decades the Rangers served as citizen soldiers, until they were institutionalized by the state legislature in 1874.

The divergent origins of the two forces—seen in Macdonald's careful plans for the implementation of the NWMP in comparison to the ad hoc deployment of the Rangers throughout much of the nineteenth century—were reflected in the constabularies' contrasting levels of professionalism. Even after 1874 members of the Texas Rangers still furnished their own weapons and mounts, wore largely what they chose, and did not carry their famous badges (a five-pointed star) until 1900. Though each company was led by a captain and two lieutenants, relationships within the units were characterized by a comfortable informality, and enlistees signed up to serve not for a set term, but rather until state funds ran out.[16] While the chief qualification for a Ranger leadership position appears to have been military service of one form or another (usually in the Confederate army), most Ranger recruits hailed from the South and had worked on farms or ranches before joining the force.[17] Many of them had imbibed the racial prejudices common in their home states, which—when combined with the long Anglo-Texan history of conflict with Indians and Mexicans—lent an especially brutal dimension to their subjugation of nonwhite peoples in the Lone Star State. Once in the constabulary, they spent the majority of their time in the field and slept under the stars; camps were only slightly more comfortable, consisting of canvas tents and cooking fires.[18]

Conditions in the NWMP were different in most every way. First, Mountie officers usually came from eastern Canada's "governing elite," and their training in legal and military affairs distinguished them from their less educated Ranger counterparts.[19] Once in the West, they sought to re-create the East's familiar social and cultural norms, entertaining themselves with formal balls, sporting events such as cricket and polo, and subscriptions to periodicals like *Punch* and the *Illustrated London News*. Likewise, NWMP recruits differed from their Texan equivalents by virtue of their diverse national origins and their previous occupations. Fully half of NWMP enlisted men in 1890 were British-born (though that figure dropped sharply later in the decade), and while some were farmers, others had served as clerks, policemen, or skilled workers before joining the force.[20] Also unlike the Rangers, NWMP recruits signed three-year service contracts (fulfillment of which earned a free grant of 160 acres of land) and were outfitted by their government with horses, arms, and bright scarlet uniforms.[21] In contrast to the racial prejudices of the Rangers, members of the NWMP (especially the officer corps) imported strong, class-based notions about the settling of the West. They tended to view the region's aboriginal inhabitants as well as its poorer homesteaders and industrial laborers with condescension rather than animosity. Though such a perspective may have facilitated the work of keeping Indians on reserves or evicting squatters from ranch lands, it very rarely led to bloodshed. Furthermore, the Mounties built a series of forts in the North-West, complete with barracks, stables, field hospitals, and quartermaster's stores, all organized around a central square, thus providing—along with the outposts scattered throughout the region—a sense of permanence and stability for its members.[22]

Most significantly, the incorporating missions of the Mounties and Rangers were not interchangeable. Having acquired the North-West from Britain, Prime Minister Macdonald wanted to secure it for development and white migration, but as peacefully and inexpensively as possible. Given his reluctance to use the unreliable and poorly trained Canadian militia, Macdonald proposed the creation of the NWMP as a key component of his Conservative Party's National Policy, a general development plan for Canada based on tariffs, state-sponsored immigration, and especially western expansion. The Mounties would facilitate these goals by establishing governmental authority in the North-West, at once placing it beyond the reach of grasping Americans while preparing the diplomatic and structural groundwork necessary for the smooth absorption of the territory into the new nation. The Mounties were vested by federal authorities with a broad range of powers: beyond their traditional law enforcement duties, the police served as mailmen, justices of the peace, and even as magistrates.[23] This last duty meant that, in addition to apprehending alleged lawbreakers, the police were empowered to prosecute, judge, and sentence them as well, creating what one historian has (admiringly) termed "a legal tyranny in the West."[24]

In stark contrast to the NWMP, the Rangers were not sent ahead of survey and settlement in order to pave the way for Austin's firm but orderly annexation of the Texas frontier. Rather, the Rangers were revived in the 1870s to take by brute force those portions of the state where conflict between Anglos and nonwhites was historical and endemic. While officials in Austin did not endow them with the same legal powers that Ottawa had granted the Mounties, lawmakers nevertheless gave the constabulary free rein to dispense violence as needed in order to extend white hegemony to regions beyond Austin's control. The Rangers seemed like just the right men for the job, considering their lengthy experience in frontier warfare against Indians and Mexicans, as well as the fact that the state's other military organizations had obvious shortcomings. For instance, as in Canada, the militia (also known as the Texas National Guard) was inexperienced and intended primarily for quelling civil disturbances. The U.S. Army units stationed in Texas, on the other hand, were largely distrusted by the state's white population, which had bitter memories of its Reconstruction-era occupation and thus doubted the willingness of federal soldiers to respond to Anglo-Texan needs.

The Mythologies

The verses by W. S. and Mary Saunders Curry highlight one more parallel between the Rangers and Mounties: both constabularies were swaddled in mythology even during the process of frontier absorption. Journalists helped reinforce the heroic image exemplified in the poems as they reported on police missions and adventures during the 1880s and 1890s, but after the turn of the century retired policemen themselves picked up and embellished these triumphal narratives. The memoirs of Mounties such as R. Burton Deane and Sam Steele and Rangers like James B. Gillett and N. A. Jennings conformed to the same basic model, beginning with brief autobiographies, followed by short histories of the forces, and then an extensive narration of the author's exploits (sometimes recounted in breathless self-admiration).[25] These favorable representations facilitated the very work of incorporation by suggesting that the police were tough but fair, a notion further projected by the mottoes developed by each constabulary during its formative period. The Mounties' promise to "maintain the right" is similar—if much less colorful—than Ranger captain Bill McDonald's assertion that "no man in the wrong can stand up against a fellow that's in the right and keeps on acomin."[26]

The first major histories of the constabularies adopted these uncritical perspectives of the police, and—varnished by the authors' professional credentials—the myths were thus preserved beneath a veneer of historical legitimacy. Walter Prescott Webb's *The Texas Rangers: A Century of Frontier Defense*, and John Peter Turner's massive, two-volume *The North-West Mounted Police, 1873–1893* are perhaps better described as hagiographies, for they lavish praise on the institutions and largely avoid even passing mention of the constabularies' missteps (which, as later historians have established, were hardly unknown). As both books—but especially Turner's—draw heavily on the authors' interviews with former policemen, the volumes often give the last word to participants in the events they describe. Weaknesses such as these led author Larry McMurtry to conclude several years after Webb's death that *The Texas Rangers* "is a flawed book," especially in terms of the author's uncritical attitude toward his subject. "Webb admired the Rangers inordinately," McMurtry wrote, "and as a consequence the book mixes homage with history in a manner one can only think sloppy."[27] A later historian of the NWMP offered a similar (if less caustic) assessment of *The North-West Mounted Police*.[28]

Whatever effects these volumes may have had in building the fame and establishing the heroic reputations of the Rangers and Mounties, it was in the realm of popular culture that the constabularies became truly iconic. For instance, more than 150 dime novels about the NWMP appeared between 1890 and 1940, published by companies in Toronto but also in New York and London, suggesting the broad popularity of the force. The books, which were aimed mostly at young men, "constructed a quintessential Mounted Policeman: a chivalric, self-abnegating hero whose motives and methods were always beyond question."[29] This stereotype was replicated in the radio broadcasts of the 1930s and 1940s, including programs such as *Renfrew of the Mounted* (1938–40) and *Challenge of the Yukon* (1947–55). The latter, known during its final season as *Sergeant Preston of the Yukon*, then became a hugely popular television show that ran from 1955 to 1958 (and was later rebroadcast in the 1960s). Starring Richard Simmons in the title role, the program—which was set at the turn of the century—popularized for American audiences the image of the gallant and unimpeachable Mountie, as Sergeant Preston tracked various lawbreakers across the frozen North.[30] Although declining interest in the Western genre during the 1970s meant fewer portrayals of the NWMP on television, the force returned to prime time in 1994 with *Due South*, a comedy centered on the adventures of a contemporary Mountie and a Chicago police detective.

The Rangers followed an almost identical path into the popular imagination, beginning with their frequent appearance in print during the pulp fiction boom of the early to mid-twentieth century. One of the more significant books to lionize the lawmen was Zane Grey's *The Lone Star Ranger*, published in 1915 and dedicated to John R. Hughes, a storied Ranger captain who had retired from the force that year. The book was made into a movie three different times, twice during the silent era.[31] Like the NWMP, however, the Rangers achieved their widest renown via the airwaves. The *Lone Ranger* first appeared in 1933 as a radio broadcast on a local Detroit station (the same one that produced *Challenge of the Yukon*) and then moved to television from 1949 to 1957, where it featured Clayton Moore as the masked man and Jay Silverheels as Tonto, his Indian sidekick. While the force also disappeared from the television lineup in the 1970s, the Rangers made a comeback on the small screen in 1989 with the TV miniseries *Lonesome Dove*, based on Larry McMurtry's novel about a pair of aging ex-Rangers driving a herd of cattle from Texas to Montana. Most recently, the force was represented from 1993 to 2001 in *Walker, Texas Ranger*, featuring Chuck Norris as a modern-day lawman who dispenses justice to evildoers with an arsenal of martial arts techniques.

Hollywood played perhaps the largest role of all in elevating the constabularies to mythic status, as movie studios churned out a staggering number of films depicting the two forces during the cinematic golden age of the 1930s and 1940s. The NWMP appeared in more than 250 movies during the twentieth century, including Metro-Goldwyn-Mayer's classic 1936 production of *Rose Marie*, a romance starring Nelson Eddy as a Mountie officer who falls in love with the title character (played by Jeanette MacDonald) while pursuing her fugitive brother in the Canadian wilderness.[32] Like countless celluloid Mounties that followed, Eddy's dashing and proper Sergeant Bruce embodied the "Victorian manliness" celebrated earlier in the Mountie dime novels, and exported that image to moviegoers in the United States.[33] The Rangers were also a highly popular subject for filmmakers, as—by one count—the Texas lawmen were featured in no less than 118 movies between 1910 and 1995.[34] These pictures tended to depict the Rangers as brave and indefatigable in their efforts to clear the Lone Star State of miscreants, by violence if necessary. And though the two constabularies carried on their cinematic struggles against evil separated by the great expanse of the Plains, they did join forces in Cecil B. DeMille's 1940 epic *North West Mounted Police*, which starred Gary Cooper as Dusty Rivers, a Ranger who—having tracked a criminal from Texas all the way to Canada—arrives just in time to help the overmatched NWMP thwart the 1885 North-West Rebellion.[35]

Notwithstanding a 1999 film version of *Dudley Do-Right* and a 2001 movie about Leander McNelly's Special Force of Rangers, the constabularies' best days on the big screen have long since passed.[36] Their grip on

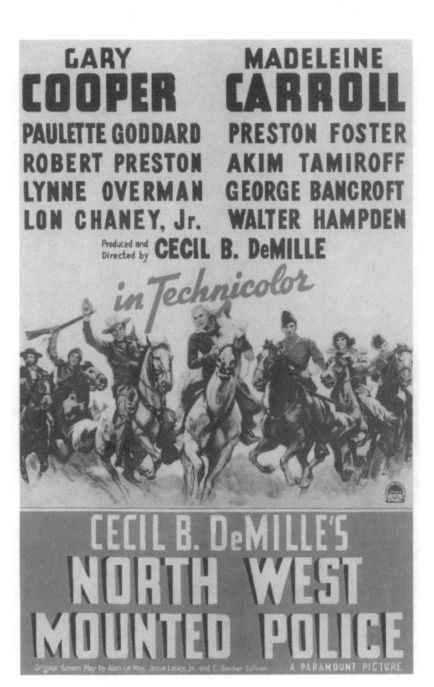

1. Movie poster from *North West Mounted Police*, 1940. Courtesy of Universal Studios Licensing LLLP.

the imagination, however, seems as tight as ever. Consider, for instance, the enduring popularity of the Mounties' Musical Ride, a publicly performed production dating to 1901 that serves to showcase the equestrian skills of select members of the force. The 2005 tour had stops throughout North America, from Prince Edward Island to Colorado. More telling, perhaps, was the Walt Disney Company's 1995 purchase of licensing rights to the Mountie image, which now appears on products ranging from stuffed animals to men's underwear.[37] Meanwhile, the Texas Rangers have lent their name to a Major League Baseball team, and airplane passengers arriving in the main terminal at Love Field in Dallas are greeted by *Legend in Bronze*, a large statue of a Texas Ranger. The RCMP Centennial Museum in Regina and the Texas Ranger Hall of Fame and Museum in Waco attract visitors from every corner of the globe, as do some of the smaller institutions dedicated to preserving their histories. For example, at the Texas Pioneer, Trail Driver and Texas Rangers Museum in San Antonio, one visitor to the United States from London wrote in the guestbook that his visit was "certainly one of the highlights of my trip." Another guest noted that "it makes one feel small to be in the presence of such great men."[38]

Yet even as the Rangers and Mounties are bound by the fact of their celebrity as well as by the multiple media through which their reputations have been created, the images of the constabularies in the popular imagination are not identical. On the one hand, the NWMP are esteemed for their gallantry; "they always get their man," as the saying goes, but usually through perseverance and a scrupulous dedication to duty. From the role model Mounted Policeman of dime novel fame to the movie era's singing Mountie clad in scarlet and Stetson, representations of the NWMP have emphasized romance, manners, and the preservation of justice through fair play. Portrayals of the Rangers, by contrast, have featured violence as a key ingredient, starting with the legend of the Lone Ranger. As the only survivor of an ambush that leaves five of his fellow lawmen dead, the masked man thereafter enforces the law with his six-shooter (though he aims only to injure—and not to kill—his desperado prey). The constabularies themselves have reinforced such divergences: whereas the RCMP Centennial Museum attempts to set the history of the force in the context of the Canadian West and thus showcases a wide range of artifacts, much of the display area at the Ranger Hall of Fame is given over to firearms and weaponry.

The gap between the cautious, determined Mountie and the gun-toting

Ranger is grounded in the actual histories of the two forces, as well as in the incorporating aspirations projected by the state entities they served. The NWMP did, in fact, resort to violence far less frequently than did their Texan counterparts, for a host of reasons ranging from their elite class background to the timing of Anglo settlement in the Canadian West. Moreover, the image of the upstanding Mounted Policeman memorialized by writers and moviemakers corresponded quite closely to Ottawa's own hopes for the NWMP; namely, that the force would peacefully occupy the West and establish a standard for fairness and decency that would differ sharply from the chaos south of the 49th parallel. These are precisely the "visions of order" associated with the NWMP etched into the popular consciousness ever since the late nineteenth century.[39] The Rangers, by comparison, used lethal force with regularity, especially in their struggles against Indians and Mexicans. While Austin officials might have wished for their own process of bloodless frontier absorption, they insisted that armed conquest was the only viable alternative, given the long history of racial violence within the state. So it was that radio, television, and cinema came to celebrate the Rangers' deliverance of justice through the barrel of a gun.

The perception and the reality of Ranger violence contrasted with Mountie restraint may help to explain perhaps the most significant difference between the images of the two forces: the presence of countermyths. In Texas, a tradition of deep skepticism about the Rangers developed among Mexicans in the nineteenth century, and its central features—which emphasized the constabulary's brutality and corruption—were transmitted through folklore to later generations.[40] This black-hat version of the Rangers received a boost from the revisionist historical scholarship of the 1970s, and has reached an even broader audience in recent years with a book and a PBS documentary examining the controversial role of the force in suppressing the Plan de San Diego insurrection of 1915.[41] The antiheroic image of the NWMP, on the other hand, has found little traction over the years. To be sure, the constabulary has come in for its own share of criticism, particularly because of its involvement in a range of political scandals in the 1970s.[42] Still, even at the height of the allegations against the force, a Gallup poll found that fewer than 20 percent of Canadians felt that the Mounties had too much power.[43] The reluctance of Canadians to think ill of the constabulary is owed likely to the fact that the alleged crimes included blackmail and the destruction of private property (as opposed to homicide), and especially to the importance of the force to a shared sense of Canadian national identity. A comparative examination of the Rangers and Mounties during the late nineteenth century confirms the different means employed by the constabularies in incorporating their respective Great Plains frontiers. And yet because the net results of their efforts were nearly identical, to the peoples they policed both constabularies must have seemed to be blunt instruments indeed.

2 Subjugating Indigenous Groups

On a bitterly cold morning in January 1881, a squad of twenty-one Rangers crawled up the crest of a low mountain in the Sierra Diablo Range of extreme western Texas.[1] With the help of their Tigua Indian scouts, the Rangers had located a small band of Apache raiders they had been trailing for nearly two weeks, and were determined now to kill or capture them. Once they had closed to within a hundred yards of the natives' camp, the Rangers rose to their knees and opened fire on the Apaches, who had just gathered for breakfast. The Indians "ran like a herd of deer," and as they were wrapped in blankets the Rangers could not distinguish between men and women. When the shooting stopped a few moments later, six Apaches—including two women—lay dead, with several others wounded, young children among them.[2] As Captain George W. Baylor wryly remarked in his report on the ambush, "[I] dont think [the Indians] will sit down to eat breakfast again without looking around to see if the Rangers are in sight."

There are few instances in the history of the North-West Mounted Police that compare with Baylor's skirmish, save perhaps for the Mounties' pursuit and killing in 1897 of Almighty Voice—a Cree Indian wanted for the murder of a policeman—and his two companions.[3] Such an example became famous in Canada precisely because of its relatively exceptional nature; in Texas, by contrast, Indian killing was an established Ranger duty dating to the informal origins of the constabulary in 1823 and continuing largely unabated for most of the next six decades.[4] In fact, the Mounted Police were far more likely to earn accolades than enmity from the Indians they encountered in the 1870s, as suggested by a speech made by the Blackfoot leader Red Crow at treaty negotiations with the Canadian government in 1877. In endorsing the agreement, Red Crow cited his faith in the NWMP, stating: "Everything that the police have done has been good. I entirely trust [Mountie commander James F. Macleod], and will leave everything to him."[5] Such a statement from a Texas Indian about the Rangers is inconceivable.

Though striking, this divergence between Ranger violence and Mountie benevolence should not disguise the parallels linking the Indian frontiers of Texas and the Canadian North-West during the last quarter of the nineteenth century. For instance, just like the Kiowas and Comanches who hunted buffalo in the Lone Star State, the Blackfoot and Crees who lived on the Canadian prairies faced threats to their existence posed by white expansion and the disappearance of the bison. Moreover, officials in Austin and Ottawa turned to their rural police to manage these beleaguered indigenous populations; indeed, the Mounties were created and the Rangers renewed and reorganized at virtually the same moment in the early 1870s to address the pressing "native question" confronting Texas and western Canada. Though they went about their work dissimilarly—and such differences illuminate a range of variations distinguishing the forces and the states that employed them—the police were bound by the nearly identical results of their efforts, epitomized by the confinement of Indians on reservations at either end of the Plains.

Indian Anxiety in Texas and the North-West Territories

Though fought almost entirely to the east of Texas, the Civil War was nevertheless damaging for the state. For instance, two of its leading antebellum political figures—soldier and congressman Ben McCulloch and Albert Sidney Johnston, former secretary of war for the Republic of Texas—had been killed in the fighting, perishing in Arkansas and Tennessee, respectively.[6] More disturbing was the recession of the frontier, a by-product of the manpower needs of the Confederacy, which had left Texas unable to defend itself from Indian attacks, long a feature of Anglo-native relations in the state. Given the instability of the Civil War era in Texas, the violence of this period was among the worst that the state's white population had yet endured, with one historian estimating that over 400 residents were killed, wounded, or taken captive between 1862 and 1865 alone.[7] Despite the territorial ambitions of many Anglo-Texans, the line of white settlement had stalled west of San Antonio and north of Fort Worth by the mid-1860s, leaving the far western portion of the state largely to the Indians.

With the end of the war, however, Austin turned its attention once again to the nagging problem of native attacks, which, if anything, seemed to be growing worse after 1865. In North Texas, settlers complained frequently of Kiowa and Comanche raids emanating from the Indian Territory (present-day Oklahoma), just across the Red River, as suggested by the following 1868 letter from San Saba County. The writers lamented that "great insecurity is felt generally throughout the country, from the numerous indian raids [that] are being made upon the frontier settlements, and we feel sensibly, and forcibly the necessity for some kind of organization, for internal defence."[8] To the northeast, residents of Parker County, near Fort Worth, reported fourteen citizens killed or captured and 418 horses stolen by Indians in less than two years in the late 1860s, figures not exceptional in any regard. Such attacks, explained one farmer, had left neighboring Montague County practically uninhabitable, with the sad result that "the oldest Settlers are making their arrangements to leave the frontier."[9]

It would be difficult to overstate the anxiety caused in Austin by such missives, since state officials worried that the violence, if unchecked, would halt migration to West Texas, a concern voiced explicitly by a number of Anglo settlers. For instance, Peter Gallagher wrote an 1870 letter to Governor E. J. Davis explaining that "our frontier Countys is constantly Depredated on by the Indians, to the Great Injury of the People, and the utter impossibility of extending the Settlements, and Consequently retards the Progress of the Country."[10] Another Texan, H. Secrest, ended his report to the governor by offering a domino theory of frontier recession for Comanche County, among the areas of North Texas hardest hit by Indian raids. Describing the area's abandonment by white settlers, Secrest noted that "if a few more families leave the rest will be bound to follow . . . and there is no telling where the frontier will then be."[11]

Texans were not alone in their dire assessments of the circumstances along the frontier, as several federal officials dispatched to the region commented on the adverse effects of native violence on white settlers. One such observer was Lawrie Tatum, the Indian agent at Fort Sill in the Indian Territory, who reported regularly to the secretary of the interior. In one letter from 1871 Tatum explained, "Instead of the western portion of Texas expanding with new settlements and thriving villages, as it should, the line of settlement is being contracted, on account of the frequent depredations of the Indians." Tatum, however, sounded a slightly more optimistic note

2. Comanches skinning a buffalo at Fort Sill, Indian Territory. Courtesy of Western History Collections, University of Oklahoma Libraries.

than either Gallagher or Secrest when he added that the Comanche Indians responsible for the raids were "fast passing away," and that unless they soon chose a more civilized path, "it is not likely they will last much beyond the present generation."[12]

Considered with the missives of the worried Texans, Tatum's letter is particularly useful in evoking the climate along the state's northern and western frontiers, for it suggests that white settlers were not the only residents of the southern Plains experiencing great hardships following the Civil War. Indeed, his postscript reveals that the plight of the area's Indians was perhaps even more desperate than the one facing their white victims, as indicated by his frank if unsympathetic prediction of the natives' looming extinction. Like many of the settlers, though, Tatum seems not to have recognized the powerful correlative relationship between the sufferings of both Anglos and Indians at this time. White insecurities stemmed directly from the natives' own dilemmas, and helped to shape official strategies to secure the Texas frontier.

The Comanche Indians who raided in northern and central Texas during the nineteenth century were descendants of the group's eastern branch, which had migrated to Texas from Colorado in the mid-eighteenth century. Although this offshoot—known also as the *Kotsotekas*, or "buffalo eaters"—maintained commercial ties with the trade-oriented western division, the eastern group focused its efforts primarily on raiding horse camps in Texas and northern Mexico. The Kotsotekas hunted elk, black bear, deer, and antelope, but as their name suggests, their principal means of subsistence was the bison, which they killed with great efficiency from horseback. Like other Plains Indian groups such as the Blackfoot and Sioux, Comanches relied upon the buffalo as the staple of their existence, the source of meat, lodging, and tools. With their superb horsemanship, by the early 1800s the Kotsotekas dominated the bison hunting grounds below the Arkansas River, and Comanche bands ranged as far into Texas as the Hill Country, located in the south-central part of the state.[13]

Hunting alongside the Comanches were the Kiowas, who despite cultural and linguistic differences had forged an extremely close alliance with the Comanches during the late eighteenth century.[14] Like the Kotsotekas, the Kiowas had migrated to the southern Plains in order to take advantage of the region's warmer climate and plentiful game. Establishing themselves immediately to the east of their allies, the Kiowas served as a buffer between the Comanches and their Osage rivals, while defending their own territory from the Cheyennes and Arapahos to the north. Like the Comanches, the Kiowas inhabited the grasslands south of the Arkansas River, developing a cultural and economic reliance on the region's bison, whose numbers—estimated at approximately eight million—must have seemed inexhaustible to the Indians during the first half of the nineteenth century.[15] Such was not the case, however.

By the early 1860s a combination of human and ecological factors had reduced the number of buffalo.[16] Compounding matters for the Indians was the fact that white settlement and expansion onto the central Plains had pushed the dwindling herds into Texas, which had expelled the Comanches from their reservation on the Brazos River in 1859.[17] Caught between a scarcity of game and the U.S. Army (sent to defend railroads and settlers), the Kiowas and Comanches—with estimated populations in the late 1860s of 2,000 and 2,500, respectively—met several times with federal representatives to establish peace and chart a course for native survival.[18] Treaty negotiations, however, also provided Indian leaders with a chance to vent their frustrations with U.S. policy, as captured in a speech by Eagle Drinking, a Comanche chief, at the 1865 proceedings on the Little Arkansas River. In response to Commissioner J. B. Sanborn's proposal that the Comanches and Kiowas cede lands north of the Canadian River and accept settlement on a reservation in the Indian Territory, Eagle Drinking replied: "I am fond of the land I was born on. The white man has land enough. I don't want to divide again."[19] Nevertheless, in exchange for a supposedly permanent hunting ground in far northwestern Texas, Eagle Drinking, among others, signed the treaty on 18 October 1865.

As the Comanches and Kiowas were to discover, however, peace negotiations often promised more than they delivered. For instance, while the bands who signed the 1867 Treaty of Medicine Lodge Creek believed that the agreement had guaranteed them exclusive access to the hunting grounds below the Arkansas River, the treaty never expressly forbade Euroamericans from entering the area. Thus the white hide hunters who poured into the Texas Panhandle after 1870 drove to the brink of extinction the very herds of bison on which the Indians had pinned their own hopes of survival. Moreover, those groups opting to accept the government's offers of settlement on a reservation in the southwest corner of the Indian Territory fared little better, since federal promises of schools, dependable rations, and improved housing materialized slowly, if at all. Deepening the aggravations of the reservation-bound was the ridicule heaped upon them by noncompliant bands, usually composed of younger Indians, who chastised their elders for acceding to the government's wishes.[20]

Frustrated by the disappearance of the bison and exasperated by the perceived duplicity of federal officials, as many as two-thirds of the Kiowas and Comanches (including some who had previously accepted treaty obligations) ventured into Texas during the late 1860s. While their primary objectives were buffalo and the horses needed to hunt them, many Indians also increased their attacks on white settlements, with the intent of driving off those who would endanger their access to the diminishing herds. Fueling their anger, as one Indian agent explained, was the natives' deep-seated sense of entitlement to the area. He wrote, "The Comanches claim truly that they never ceded away Texas, which was their original country, and that they therefore have a right to make war there."[21] Although military officials in the area warned the Indians against crossing into the state and threatened them with grave consequences should they disobey, by the early 1870s even some of the more patient native leaders had resolved to defy federal authorities and pursue the herds wherever they might wander. As an agent at Fort Sill reported in 1872, Teakatzchenna, a Comanche chief, explained his hope to avoid conflicts but frankly "stated his desire to roam the plains for the present, his disinclination to enter into any closer connection with the Government, [and] his opposition to any encroachments upon or invasions of the country they claim."[22]

These were the bands of raiders so bitterly described by Euroamericans along the Texas frontier in the late 1860s and early 1870s. While state residents and Austin officials denounced the Indians as "savages" who killed and plundered, the Kiowas and Comanches considered the Anglos no less a threat to their own existence, since Euroamericans impeded native access to the bison. Seeking a definitive end to the conflict and the promotion of further Anglo migration, the Texas legislature passed a bill in June 1870 authorizing the institution of a "Frontier Force." This act had the effect of reestablishing the Texas Rangers, who had lapsed into irrelevance during the Civil War and Reconstruction, replaced with the state police by a Republican administration skeptical of the Rangers. Four years later, this detachment was reorganized into the six companies of the Frontier Battalion and charged with containing "hostile Indians, Mexicans, or other marauding or thieving parties."[23] Their mission was relatively straightforward: to exterminate or drive from within the borders of the state any natives who crossed into Texas.

§

At the other end of the Great Plains, Canadian officials in the early 1870s did not face the same troubling reality of native-white conflict that their Austin counterparts did, for a variety of reasons. First, in contrast to the bloodshed in Texas, interactions between newcomers and the First Nations of western Canada were relatively peaceful, owing in part to the 200-year history of the European fur trade, which developed in the North-West after the founding of the Hudson's Bay Company (HBC) in 1670. Though England's charter had invested the HBC with a broad range of powers in Rupert's Land (the name given to the territory in honor of Prince Rupert, the company's first governor), HBC dominion within the territory derived not from military conquest but rather from the company's mere claim to the area. French-Canadian trappers challenged their English rivals for control of the North-West by heading inland from the bays to the interior, where they developed friendly relationships with Indian peoples, typified by intermarriage with aboriginal women. Such unions produced the Métis, peoples of mixed native and European ancestry.[24]

Moreover, a distinctly different pattern of settlement in the Canadian West reduced the potential for native-white violence there. Whereas by 1875

Anglo-Texans had pushed westward into the farthest reaches of the state and established communities in the heart of Indian country, there were very few permanent Eurocanadian settlers in the North-West at this time. Westward migration from Ontario onto the Plains had stalled at midcentury because of the presence of the Canadian Shield, a vast expanse of land characterized by thin, rocky soil largely unsuitable for farming. Thus it was not until the extension of the transcontinental railroad onto the prairies in the 1880s that significant numbers of white migrants arrived in the North-West. One historian has estimated that the white population of the Dominion's western interior in 1870 consisted of fewer than 2,000 individuals, as opposed to somewhere between 25,000 and 35,000 Indians spread throughout the region.[25]

Though absent a history of native-white violence on the Plains, this demographic disparity nevertheless worried officials in Ottawa, for the august goals of the National Policy—especially the completion of the Canadian Pacific Railway (CPR) and the promotion of white migration—would surely languish if faced with systematic aboriginal resistance. With but little experience in dealing with the native groups of the North-West and knowing also the steady deterioration of their living conditions, marked by the accelerating disappearance of the bison, Ottawa considered Indian opposition to white expansion a distinct possibility, however much federal observers wanted to avoid armed conflict. Before Eurocanadian settlers could establish homesteads and entrepreneurial ventures on the prairies, Ottawa needed assurance that white migrants would suffer no harm from natives.

These official concerns were not entirely unfounded, as suggested by reports arriving in the capital from Eurocanadians already on the Plains. Although the federal government had laid the groundwork for peaceful westward expansion by negotiating treaties in 1871 with bands of Ojibwa and Swampy Cree Indians in southern Manitoba, Ottawa had made few inroads among the First Nations groups farther west who lived between Lake Winnipeg and the Rocky Mountains. These natives, particularly the Cree and Blackfoot peoples, deeply resented the growing Eurocanadian presence in their midst and insisted that whites first obtain permission before venturing onto the lands they claimed as their hunting grounds. Settlers and surveyors, however, sometimes moved more quickly than did the officials charged with treaty making, and so white Canadians encountered mounting opposition on the prairie from distrustful Indians.

Given the importance to Ottawa of pulling the West firmly into the nation's orbit, it is not surprising that many of the Indian-white confrontations on the Plains in the mid-1870s involved teams of government inspectors sent west to conduct geological and telegraphic surveys meant to extend transportation and communications networks. Worried that these crews represented the front line of a permanent Eurocanadian presence, natives resisted by impeding their progress and sabotaging their works. As a magistrate in the Saskatchewan District explained to the lieutenant governor of the North-West Territories in July 1875: "I have just heard that the Indians contemplate turning back the carts that are carrying the materials for the telegraph line from Fort Pelly to Edmonton. I have at once sent an influential person . . . to prevail upon the Indians to remain quiet."[26] Another official wrote later that summer to report that a party of Cree Indians "have objected to the cutting of Poles and Telegraph Construction generally . . . and threaten to burn down poles, etc."[27]

Although such Indian interruptions were rarely accompanied by violence (even native threats of force were unusual) the holdups caused by downed telegraph poles or blockaded routes of travel disquieted federal officials bent on rapid western development. As NWMP commissioner G. A. French reported in 1875 after one such disruption by a band of Crees, "The stoppage of the telegraphic construction is a very serious matter, which not only delays a great and important work, but gives the contractors grounds on which to base claims against the Government." Conceding that physical coercion was impolitic (and probably ineffective, anyway), French urged the minister of justice to expedite negotiations with native bands not yet under treaty. In the absence of such agreements, French explained, Plains Indians were unlikely to submit passively to further Eurocanadian encroachments.[28]

The Cree Indians so vehemently opposed to Canadian expansion occupied the southeastern Plains of the Dominion's western frontier, inhabiting the area on either side of the border separating the present-day provinces of Alberta and Saskatchewan. Their ancestors had migrated to this territory in the late eighteenth century, leaving behind the region between Lake Superior and Hudson's Bay in pursuit of animals they hunted for exchange in the European fur trade. Once on the Plains, however, these woodland Crees acquired horses and gradually abandoned trapping in favor of hunting buffalo, which had become the central element of Cree existence by the early

1800s. Aided by their Assiniboine allies, the Crees developed an extensive horse-raiding network, which they built through forays to points as distant as the Rocky Mountains and the Missouri River. With an 1860 population of approximately 12,000, the Crees were the largest single indigenous group on the Canadian Plains, and they controlled the fertile hunting grounds along the Battle and North Saskatchewan rivers.[29]

The principal rivals to the Crees for both horses and access to the bison were the estimated 10,000 Indians making up the three groups of the Blackfoot Confederacy: the Blood, Peigan, and Blackfoot proper.[30] Described by one historian as "the strongest and most aggressive nation on the Canadian prairies" in the mid-eighteenth century, the Blackfoot claimed the area to the southwest of the Cree hunting grounds, a region that straddled the international boundary between the Dominion and the United States.[31] Given the expansionist ambitions of the Confederacy, conflict with the powerful and proximate Crees became a regular feature of Blackfoot life after the groups' short-lived alliance disintegrated in 1806 following a dispute over horses. Warfare between the Crees and Blackfoot continued until 1870, when several bands of Bloods and Peigans repelled a Cree-Assiniboine attack on their camps at the juncture of the Oldman and St. Mary's rivers, with the Blackfoot killing between 200 and 300 Cree warriors. Exhausted from decades of thefts and reprisals and weakened by a recent smallpox epidemic, the groups treated for peace the next autumn.[32]

By that time, both the Blackfoot and the Crees faced greater problems than the horse-raiding expeditions launched by one people against the other. In the first place, in 1869 the HBC had transferred the vast territory of the North-West to the recently confederated Dominion of Canada, leaving the status of the region's Indians in doubt.[33] More distressing to the natives, however, was the rapid decline in the area's bison population. As at the other end of the Great Plains, the lucrative trade in buffalo robes and hides—greatly facilitated by the extension of the American transcontinental railroads and the advent of repeating rifles—lured increasing numbers of white commercial hunters onto the Indians' subsistence grounds. Already pressured by the natives themselves, as well as by the Métis, the once great herds had been pushed to the extreme western edge of the northern Plains by the early 1870s.[34]

Keenly aware of the threat to their existence posed by the land transfer and the disappearance of the bison, the Crees and Blackfoot looked upon white newcomers with great skepticism. As one HBC trader communicated to a territorial official in 1871, a deputation of Cree chiefs had come to see him at Edmonton, where they sought "to ascertain whether their lands had been sold or not, and what was the intention of the Canadian Government in relation to them." The trader enclosed a message from Sweet Grass, a Cree chief, that began in part: "We heard our lands were sold and we did not like it; we don't want to sell our lands; it is our property, and no one has a right to sell them."[35] Several years later, George McDougall, a missionary stationed in the Rocky Mountains, reported a testy exchange between a Cree chief and a land speculator who wished to take a claim on the Battle River. According to McDougall the Indian barred the settler's way and insisted that until the "great white man" (the Canadian government) had come and established fair terms with the Indians, "I caution you to put up no stakes in our country."[36]

The Blackfoot were no less concerned by the growing white encroachment. As explained by Constantine Scollen, an oblate priest traveling among the Indians in the mid-1870s, "The Blackfeet are extremely jealous of what they consider their country, and never allowed any white men, Half-breeds [Métis], or Crees to remain in it for any length of time." Moreover, the priest noted that Blackfoot resistance was likely to intensify in the near future, because increased settlement around forts Calgary and Macleod had driven the remaining buffalo southward into Montana, still further from the Indians' traditional hunting grounds. Compounding Blackfoot anxieties, Scollen explained, was the advent of the NWMP among the natives, for they believed that the police had come not only to establish law and order "but also to protect white people against them, and that this country will be gradually taken from them without any ceremony."[37]

Fueled by these anxieties, the Crees and Blackfoot sought to defend themselves by challenging the white outsiders who arrived in their territory without native consent and who killed or scared off the dwindling game on which Indian survival depended. Ottawa, on the other hand, was no less resolved to promote its own agenda for the area, and turned now to the NWMP for help in resolving the impasse. Unlike the Rangers, however, the Mounties' mission—as described by Minister of Justice S. A. Darion—was essentially a nonviolent one: "to give confidence to peaceable Indians and intending Settlers."[38] This the Mounties would do by smoothing the way for treaty negotiations to take place, which would in turn ensure a basis for "cooperative coexistence" between natives and whites.

Rangers, Mounties, and Indians

Considering that after the Civil War the U.S. government had committed significant military resources to Texas for the purposes of frontier defense, including one artillery, three cavalry, and four infantry regiments, one wonders why state administrators felt it necessary to resuscitate the Rangers.[39] There are two answers: Ranger history, and Anglo-Texan distrust of the U.S. Army. In the first place, white residents of the Lone Star State revered the Rangers as Indian fighters par excellence, a reputation that dated back to their campaigns against the Comanches in the 1840s. One storied battle took place in June 1844 at Walker Creek, north of San Antonio in present-day Kendall County, when Captain John Coffee Hays led a Ranger squad of only fourteen men against more than seventy Indians who had come south to hunt bison and raid Anglo settlements. Armed with the Paterson Colt—a five-shot .36-caliber pistol—the Rangers killed twenty-three Indians and wounded another thirty, while suffering only one dead of their own.[40] Fierce Ranger-Indian warfare persisted into the next decade, earning accolades for men such as William "Big Foot" Wallace and John Salmon "Rip" Ford.

Faced now with a level of Indian violence not seen since the early 1850s, Texans of the post–Civil War period looked to the Rangers once more to deliver them from "the many tribes of savages" along the frontier, a job for which they seemed uniquely qualified.[41] One judge in central Texas wrote in 1874 to commend Frontier Battalion commander Major John B. Jones for the efforts of his men, adding that "we all feel that your service among us has demonstrated the superiority of these organizations over all others for this peculiar warfare." Another Jones partisan lionized the Ranger's father as an "old-time Indian fighter" and credited Jones's own success in that regard to a frontier upbringing in which he had "learned by experience much of the character and habits of the Indians."[42] In the eyes of many admirers, these attributes included indefatigability and relentlessness in combat. Or as Rip Ford had put it, Rangers could "ride like Mexicans; trail like Indians; shoot like Tennesseans; and fight like the devil."[43]

The reality matched the reputation, for the Rangers were indeed well prepared for the task of Indian fighting, a fact deriving in part from their broad (and historical) mandate from Austin to subjugate the state's native peoples. Such discretion in its administration of Indian affairs distinguished Texas from other western states, where a legacy of territorial jurisdiction empowered the federal government to determine Indian policy. Texas, on the other hand, had entered the Union in 1845 as a formerly independent nation and thus retained full possession of its public lands, thereby reserving a large measure of control over the management of native concerns within its borders. The importance of this sovereignty became clear in 1859, when Austin effectively canceled the two Texas reservations that federal officials had urged the state to create just five years before. Although the Indians on these parcels had lived mostly in peace with their white neighbors—with some even accompanying the Rangers on a raid against the Comanches in 1858—intense Anglo hostility to the concept prompted the local Indian agent to lead the natives across the Red River to safety.[44]

Armed with directives from Austin—as well as powerful firearms—the Rangers were an enthusiastic and highly effective anti-Indian force, as suggested by a brief comparison of their efforts with those of the U.S. Army in Texas after 1865. Although there were approximately 4,500 federal troops in the Lone Star State at any given time following the Civil War, the Rangers (whose numbers fluctuated between 450 and 700 men) engaged Indians in battle on more than one-third as many occasions as their army counterparts between 1865 and 1881.[45] During the final, bloody stages of Indian removal beginning in the mid-1870s, Ranger-Indian battles actually outnumbered army skirmishes, thirty-two to thirty. Still more significant from the perspectives of a state administration bent on total victory and an Anglo populace thirsty for vengeance was the body count, and here, too, the Rangers excelled. Though usually possessing only one-tenth of the army's manpower in Texas, the Rangers killed half as many Indians as the federal troops did over the same period (82 to 163, respectively) and managed to wound two more (26 to 24).[46]

The background of most Rangers had readied them for such work, since the overwhelming majority of recruits hailed from rural parts of Texas, the Plains states, and the South, and thus likely harbored the virulent anti-Indian prejudice characteristic of those sections of the country.[47] Others, like Ranger Captain G. W. Arrington—a Confederate army veteran who before coming to Texas had lynched a black man in his native Alabama and "was quite a leader of the Ku Klux Klan"—were hardened, garden-variety white supremacists.[48] Moreover, the long history of Anglo-Indian conflict in Texas had brutalized the state's white people, making them—in the words of one anthropologist who studied a similar phenomenon in frontier Mexico—"specialists in violence," where men earned social status as Indian fighters, as with Big Foot Wallace and Rip Ford.[49] Such conditions may help explain why the Rangers regularly scalped the bodies of Indians they killed in combat, but never the corpses of Mexicans or other adversaries.

Whereas the well-deserved reputation of the Rangers as ruthless Indian fighters had earned them lasting admiration from Anglo-Texans, profound white suspicion about the U.S. Army was the second reason why Austin reestablished the Rangers in the 1870s to counter native raids. Texan misgivings about the army stemmed from a number of sources, but chief among them was the prominent and controversial role played by the U.S. military in establishing law and order in the Lone Star State during the Reconstruction era. Federal troops in Texas after 1865—whose numbers at one time exceeded 50,000—served as a constant reminder of the South's defeat in the Civil War and infuriated Anglo residents by protecting the state's sizable population of freedmen from white violence.[50] Moreover, U.S. military commanders often intervened directly into Texas politics, as when General Philip H. Sheridan removed Governor James Throckmorton from office in 1867, insisting that he was hostile to federal Reconstruction efforts.

Although the mere presence of the U.S. Army in Texas was irritant enough, white residents were convinced that the troops were also ineffective in defending them against Kiowa and Comanche raiders. Much of the problem, they believed, lay in the fact that authorities in Washington DC habitually underestimated the Indian dangers along the state's frontiers. As a Bexar County judge complained in an 1867 letter to Governor Throckmorton, "The general Government in doing something in the premises will fall in the old error to adopt half measures . . . as they in Washington generally judge our Indian affairs to be analog with them in the Northern part of the Union."[51] Federal officials did in fact have their doubts about the dire conditions reported in Texas, as exemplified by an 1871 visit from William T. Sherman to Fort Richardson, which the general made with the express purpose of debunking the Texans' anxieties. Sherman believed the hysteria little more than a ruse intended to distract federal troops although he changed his mind after narrowly escaping a mixed party of Kiowa and Comanche raiders near the Salt Creek Prairie.[52]

More vexing than the army's apparent inability to defend them, however, was the sense among many Texans that the federal government was simply not committed to a policy of total Indian removal from the state, which in fact it was not. While Anglo-Texans clamored for the complete eradication of native peoples from within the borders of Texas, authorities in Washington had settled on President U. S. Grant's so-called Peace Policy, a less confrontational plan that sought diplomatic solutions to the Anglo-native conflicts raging throughout the West. This federal strategy produced agreements like the 1867 decision at Medicine Lodge Creek that allowed Indians the right to hunt buffalo in the Texas Panhandle (although lax federal enforcement coupled with unchecked white migration often rendered such treaties meaningless). Residents along the state's frontier denounced such concessions as representing an unnecessarily "soft" approach to Native Americans, considering lenience a virtual invitation for future Indian raids into the state. As one angry San Antonian rhymed in an editorial: "'Let us have peace' means peace to the Indian and oppression to the South; the quiet of the grave and the peace of the charnel-house."[53]

This federal moderation, Texans believed, had infected the military detachments stationed on the southern Plains. Though capable of striking with indiscriminate ferocity—as seen in engagements at the Washita River and Summit Springs—the army seemed just as likely to display a peculiar quality of restraint. For instance, soldiers in Texas rarely followed up their minor victories with decisive engagements, belying the genocidal bent often ascribed to them by modern historians.[54] Limited perhaps by the tenets of the Peace Policy or preferring instead to wage a war of attrition, the U.S. Army did not attempt the complete removal of Indians from the state during the 1870s, and on occasion even allowed natives to remain within its borders. Such decisions drove Texans nearly to distraction, like the citizens of Donley County, who in 1878 complained to Austin that "the few United States troops stationed in the Pan Handle are totally inadequate to cope with the present danger." Instead of asking for more U.S. soldiers to come to their relief, however, the people of Clarendon begged for a Ranger squad to "aid us in our present distress."[55] State officials heeded these requests, relying increasingly on the Rangers to accomplish that which Washington could—or would—not do.

§

If the Rangers appealed to Austin as the perfect instrument for securing the Texas frontier from Indians, Ottawa likewise considered its rural constabulary ideally suited to the task of protecting white migrants from the First

Nations of the North-West. The Mounties' initial job with regard to native peoples, however, was exactly the inverse of the Rangers' duty: rather than exterminating or expelling Indians from the prairies, the NWMP sought to make peace with aboriginal peoples and thus lay the groundwork for Ottawa's nonhostile absorption of the region. Although the mostly tranquil history of native-white relations in the North-West seemed to recommend such a course of action, basic financial considerations left Ottawa little choice but to pursue a nonaggressive strategy on the Plains. For example, while in the 1870s the United States spent a yearly total of nearly $20 million on its Indian wars, Canada's entire annual budget during the same period was only $19 million.[56]

As the Dominion's principal representatives in the North-West, the Mounties were the obvious choice to assume the responsibility of establishing friendly relations between the federal government and the First Nations. By the time such efforts began in earnest, the force already enjoyed a solid reputation among the natives, for a handful of reasons. Most important, perhaps, was the central role of the NWMP in eradicating the liquor trade in the Canadian West. Whites had introduced alcohol to the Indians of the northern Plains as early as the late eighteenth century, and by the 1830s liquor had become a critical component of the bison-robe trade.[57] However, the exchange of animal hides for whiskey and rum experienced explosive growth above the 49th parallel only after 1869, when the HBC ceded its lands to Canada. With no legal injunctions against the sale of alcohol in the North-West, white traders from Montana poured across the international boundary and did brisk business at the forts of southern Alberta, places with such names as Whoop-Up, Slide-Out, and Standoff.[58]

The liquor trade had a devastating effect on the peoples of the First Nations. Only five years after the so-called invasion of the free traders, Father Constantine Scollen reported on the deteriorating conditions among the Blackfoot, writing, "It was painful to me to see the state of poverty to which they had been reduced. Formerly they had been the most opulent Indians in the country, and now they were clothed in rags, without horses and without guns."[59] Natives intoxicated by vast quantities of whiskey died in scores, with one missionary estimating that forty-two otherwise healthy Blackfoot men had perished in drunken brawls or by freezing to death in the winter of 1873–74 alone. Especially unsettling to government officials was the Cypress Hills Massacre of June 1873, in which a party of Montana wolf trappers searching for some stolen horses crossed into Canada and attacked a group of Assiniboines. The wolfers descended on the drunken and largely defenseless camp, murdering at least sixteen men, women, and children and mutilating their corpses.[60]

Such events horrified native headmen like Crowfoot, a prominent Blackfoot leader, who in 1874 described to a Protestant missionary the destruction wrought by the liquor trade on his people. He explained: "The whiskey brought among us by the Traders is fast killing us off and we are powerless before the evil. [We are] totally unable to resist the temptation to drink when brought in contact with the white man's water. We are also unable to pitch anywhere that the Trader cannot follow us."[61] Many native chiefs therefore applauded the vigilance of the police in arresting and prosecuting whiskey runners, actions that—by one NWMP account—had suppressed the trade by the end of 1876, little more than two years after the constabulary's arrival in the West.[62] Of course there was a practical side to these NWMP efforts, too. Considering that, in the words of one federal official, alcohol "has had the effect of demoralizing the Indians and retarding all efforts toward civilizing and quieting them," eradicating the liquor trade was a key first step in promoting white migration to the Plains.[63]

Romantic relationships between Mounted Policemen and native women may also have smoothed the NWMP's efforts to build diplomatic links between Ottawa and the First Nations. While many of these liaisons were no doubt affairs of convenience for young, single men far from their homes in eastern Canada, a number of such relationships led eventually to marriage. For example, a Lakota historian asserts that six members of the Mountie post at Wood Mountain, in Saskatchewan, married women from Sitting Bull's band during the time that the Sioux leader took refuge in Canada between 1876 and 1881, with most of the couples remaining together for the rest of their lives.[64] However, though some such relationships—for which no parallel existed among the Texas Rangers—may well have forged tender ties between the Mounties and native peoples, others clearly compromised the prospective goodwill of the Indians, as when the police physically or sexually abused aboriginal women.

One last factor that helped the police earn a measure of trust from the First Nations was the distribution of federal aid by the NWMP to bands of native peoples. This largesse took a number of forms. Most common were material gifts such as blankets, tobacco, tea, and ammunition.[65] But the

3. Mounted Police with a group of First Nations chiefs, including Red Crow (back row, center) and Crowfoot (front row, left), ca. 1875.
Courtesy of Glenbow Archives, NA-13-1.

Mounties also made their doctors available to natives who needed medical attention, "as this course would not alone be productive of cordiality between our men and the Indians, but impress the Indians with the belief that the Government really meant to deal fairly with them."[66] This was an important gesture, for both the Blackfoot and the Crees had suffered population losses of between 10 and 15 percent during the smallpox epidemic of 1869–70, and with the evaporation of the bison economy during the 1870s the "diseases of poverty" began to ravage their communities.[67]

The basically favorable relationship between the police and native peoples of the North-West helped to facilitate the negotiation of two vitally important treaties made by the Canadian government with the Indians.[68] By virtue of these agreements—Treaty Six with the Crees in 1876, and Treaty Seven with the Blackfoot in 1877—Ottawa claimed legal title to large portions of what became Saskatchewan and Alberta, opening the West to the extension of the transcontinental railroad and the eventual migration of white settlers. In fact, some native leaders cited Mountie benevolence as the pivotal factor in their decision to make treaties with the Dominion, none more famously than Crowfoot. At the completion of the negotiations for Treaty Seven, the Blackfoot chief said:

> If the Police had not come to the country, where would be all now? Bad men and whiskey were killing us so fast that very few, indeed, of us would have been left to-day. The Police have protected us as the feathers of the bird protect it from the frosts of winter. I wish them all good, and trust that our hearts will increase in goodness from this time forward. I am satisfied. I will sign the treaty.[69]

It seems safe to assume that no Texas Indian ever heaped such praise upon the Rangers.

There was another side to the Mounties' role in the negotiations, however. To be sure, the First Nations held some individual members of the force in the highest esteem, like Colonel James F. Macleod, whom the Blackfoot so revered that they called him *Stamikkso'tokaani* (Bull Head), the same name of a renowned Peigan warrior. And yet oral histories from Treaty Seven suggest that the net effect of the NWMP's attendance at the deliberations was coercive. For one thing, their scarlet uniforms gave the Mounties the appearance of a "military colour guard for the government officials," an impression probably enhanced by their position atop well-trained horses. Still less subtle were the cannons the NWMP had brought along to the proceedings and which they allegedly directed at the Indians in menacing fashion. This prompted one Assiniboine chief to remark: "You talk of peace while there are guns pointing at me. This is not peace . . . lay down your guns." Other natives remembered the negotiations as "scary" and believed that the NWMP was ready to launch an attack, if necessary, from the defensive positions they had established at the campground.[70]

As it turned out, the intimidating presence of the Mounties was a portent of events to come. Part of the problem for native peoples was that they un-

4. James F. Macleod, pictured during his tenure as commissioner of the North-West Mounted Police, 1876–1880. Courtesy of Glenbow Archives, NA-23-2.

derstood the agreements quite differently than did Canadian officials, and believed that by making treaties with Ottawa they were merely consenting to share the lands in question with newcomers, not surrender them, as the Dominion insisted.[71] Moreover, federal negotiators did not explain to the Crees or Blackfoot that native acceptance of the treaties bound them to the provisions of the Indian Act of 1876, legislation described by one scholar as a "formidable dossier of repression." This law made the First Nations wards of the state, with a legal status equal to that enjoyed by children, felons, and the insane, and—among other things—barred Indians from voting, practicing law, or taking up homesteads.[72] The Indian Act would later justify the imposition of a host of repressive measures—such as the pass system, the circumscription of religious practice, and compulsory school attendance for indigenous children—that Ottawa called on the NWMP to enforce, bringing police and natives into conflict and weakening their relationship.

Rural Police and Indian Subjugation

By 1874 the situation facing the Kiowas and Comanches had reached a crisis point, as a "spasm of industrial expansion" had driven the bison to the verge of extinction. With the discovery that buffalo hides served as an effective source of the leather belting required by machinery in the factories of the East, white hunters descended on the southern Plains with increasingly deadly weapons, determined to cash in on the bonanza.[73] For their part, the Indians were not content simply to witness the destruction of their most important resource, and they resisted further Anglo encroachment into western Texas, especially the Panhandle region that the government had supposedly promised to them by the Treaty of Medicine Lodge in 1867. As the Indian agent at Fort Sill reported in 1874, a mixed group of Comanches and Southern Cheyennes had met that spring in a war council and resolved "to go and kill the buffalo hunters who had been slaying their buffalo by thousands."[74]

The ambush of a group of Dodge City hide hunters at Adobe Walls on 27 June by a party of 700 Comanche, Kiowa, Cheyenne, and Arapaho warriors was the first major battle of the Red River War. Federal officials responded by ordering the U.S. Army into action. General Philip H. Sheridan devised a strategy in which five separate army columns would advance from different directions on the Indian redoubts in the Texas Panhandle, forcing the natives to choose between surrender (and confinement on reserves) or death. Although the conflict lasted into the spring of 1875, Colonel Ranald S. Mackenzie effectively delivered the coup de grâce in September 1874 at Palo Duro Canyon, when he led several companies of cavalry and infantry in a daring advance against a much larger Indian force. Although Mackenzie's troops killed only a handful of natives, they burned the Indian encampments and destroyed more than a thousand of their horses, scattering the Indians onto the Plains at the outset of an unusually cold winter.[75] The Indians were unable to mount a concerted offensive thereafter, and most of them retreated permanently to their reservations.

The Rangers, who had been institutionalized by the Texas legislature only ten weeks earlier, played no role in the U.S. offensive in the Panhandle. They did, however, engage at least one native war party that entered the state during the conflict. In early July, Major John B. Jones, commander of the Frontier Battalion, and some thirty Rangers struck a large Kiowa trail in present-day Jack County, northwest of Fort Worth.[76] Led by chiefs Ma-man-ti and Lone Wolf, the Indians—whose numbers Jones later estimated at between 100 and 150 men—had murdered a cowhand from Oliver Loving's ranch two days before. A small Kiowa detachment lured Jones and his squad into a narrow valley, where the Rangers then encountered the rest of the Indians. The ensuing fight lasted nearly three hours, during which time Jones lost two men killed and another two wounded, along with thirteen horses shot down by the Indians. In a message to Adjutant General William Steele, Jones claimed that the Rangers had killed or wounded six natives and forced the others to retreat, leading Steele to proclaim that "the loss of life and property, prevented by this timely and gallant action, can only be imagined."[77]

In the wake of the Red River War, federal observers believed that Indian resistance on the southern Plains had come to an end. With most of the natives having returned to their agencies in the Indian Territory by the summer of 1875, officials in the region declared that peace (if perhaps an uneasy one) reigned in the area, as suggested by a letter sent later that year from Fort Sill. The Indian agent there wrote that "the clouds of trouble which were lowering around us at the time of making my last report have happily about all passed away," adding that the Indians had surrendered their stock and allowed their children to begin school on the reservation.[78] As an indication of federal confidence, Washington reduced troop strength in Texas, diverting extra forces—including Mackenzie's Fourth Cavalry—to the northern Plains, where the United States faced stiff opposition from groups of Sioux, Northern Cheyennes, and Northern Arapahos resisting the same white encroachment that had triggered the Red River conflict.

Texans, however, were not nearly so sanguine about conditions along their northern and western frontiers, since reports of Indian sightings continued unabated. In 1875—the same year that the Indian agent at Fort Sill reported on the favorable developments among the natives there—the Rangers killed twenty-four Indians in Texas and wounded eight more.[79] Major Jones and a squad of about twenty men drawn from three different companies were responsible for five of the Indian dead, whom they dispatched at almost exactly the same location where Jones had skirmished with the party led by Lone Wolf and Maman-ti the year before. Having learned that Indians had stolen horses from the oft-raided Loving Ranch, Jones set off after the thieves the next day and soon overtook them. According to his report, the Indians—who were armed with shotguns and six-shooters—"fought desperately, three of them continuing to fight after they were shot down." Superior Ranger numbers and mounts proved decisive, however, and the police "did not stop to scalp and plunder the Indians that were killed, as is too often done in such fights, but continued the rout until the last Indian in sight was killed." Jones suspected that they had come from a reservation, because they were well clothed and carried blankets bearing the initials of the U.S. Interior Department, which had assumed control of native affairs from the War Department in 1849.[80]

Discoveries such as these convinced Texans that, beyond failing to solve the problem of native incursions into the state, the federal government was in fact largely to blame for the continued Indian presence south of the Red River. Emanuel Deibbs of Wheeler County captured the frustrations of many when he wrote to Governor O. M. Roberts in 1879: "These Indians are allowed by their Agents to leave their reservations with passes . . . and as a consequence, they are continually crossing the Texas line to the terror of settlers."[81] As it happened, Deibbs was correct: many of the native bands that traversed northern Texas had passed into the state with the consent of Indian agents or army officers stationed in the region. Complaining of starvation on their reserves, Indian chiefs sought permission for small hunting parties to cross into the area beyond the Red River, which by that time was the last refuge of the bison on the southern Plains. Moved in part by expediency—reducing starvation could alleviate the tensions posed by native confinement—but also by compassion, the officers and agents sometimes complied with these requests.[82]

Texans, predictably, complained bitterly about this practice, believing that the presence of the native hunting parties was merely the prelude to another major conflict in the region. One citizen in Brown County explained to Governor Roberts in February 1879 that "there was now on Texas soil over one thousand 'Indians,' pretending that their mission was 'hunting,'" and added that there was "great danger of an outbreak, in the Spring, on our frontier."[83] Such threats presented dire implications for the nascent stock-raising industry of West Texas, which residents hoped would bind the area to more developed parts of the state. Seeking redress, officials in Austin transmitted their concerns to the state's federal representatives in Washington, who joined the growing chorus of indignation.[84]

For their part, military officials defended their actions, insisting that settlers greatly exaggerated both the size and frequency of such Indian forays, while flatly dismissing as unfounded Anglo claims of alleged "outrages" committed by the natives.[85] This attitude stemmed from the beliefs of many army officers that white settlers deserved much of the blame for the Indian "problem" in the West because of their invasions of native territory and their aggression toward Indian people.[86] Although some officers promised to send military escorts along with Indian hunting parties, others explained that troop reductions made this practice infeasible. General John Pope, commander of the Department of the Missouri and a noted advocate of fair treatment for the Indians, evinced less patience for the Texans' complaints. In a sharp letter to Governor Roberts, Pope declared his intention to allow continued Red River crossings, and suggested that Austin take up the matter with federal officials, explaining that "insufficient subsistence" by the government made bison hunts "absolutely necessary." Tweaking the Texans' fears, however, Pope added mordantly that "no man can tell when a party of Indians starts out equipped for hunting, whether they will hunt game or people."[87]

Feeling abandoned by the federal government, Austin called upon the Rangers to settle the state's Indian question once and for all. The police did not disappoint, resolving, it seems, to pursue with ferocity every native band trespassing in the state. Such grim determination emerges in an 1878 letter from Ranger Lieutenant G. W. Arrington, the former Klan leader, who wrote to Major Jones—now the adjutant general—that he had heard rumors of several Indian bands camped just south of the state line in Wilbarger County. Volunteering to intercept them, Arrington added that he was "satisfied we can bring scalps back with us."[88] Further south, Lieutenant D. W. Roberts reported that he and a detachment from Company D had spotted a group of Lipan Apache Indians suspected of murdering three settlers and stealing numerous horses. Frustrated by the natives' escape, Roberts explained that "I hate it all the more that I couldn't kill them," but added that with a company of seventy-five men he was confident that he could locate and break up all Indian bands in that part of the state.[89]

5. Captain D. W. Roberts's Ranger camp in Menard County, Texas, 1878. Courtesy of Western History Collections, University of Oklahoma Libraries.

More significantly, the Rangers aimed to cut off the Fort Sill Indians from any access to the state's remaining bison, believing that this tactic would deter natives from entering Texas and cause the federal government to seal the borders. Jones went so far as to claim in an 1879 letter that there were no buffalo and few game of any kind in northwest Texas—likely an exaggeration—in the hopes that Pope and his men might put a stop to the crossings.[90] When this failed to solve the problem, the Rangers adopted more radical measures, which brought them into direct conflict with Washington and the military establishment. One such encounter took place in June 1879 when Arrington traveled to Wheeler County—on the border between Texas and the Indian Territory—with a squad of twenty men to investigate complaints by local ranchers about cattle poaching by Indians from Fort Sill. Upon Arrington's arrival in the vicinity of Fort Elliott, General John W. Davidson accosted him and demanded to know whether the Rangers planned to kill any Indians, to which Arrington replied that he "most assuredly would if they were armed."[91]

Perhaps the most serious collision between Captain Arrington and soldiers of the U.S. Army took place earlier that year. Moved by the hardships facing a band of Kiowas and Comanches who had left Fort Sill in search of food—the Indians having already killed and eaten many of their own horses—Captain Nicholas Nolan of the Tenth Cavalry arranged for the group to cross into Texas with an escort. Arrington's squad encountered the party and promptly attacked the Indians, killing Sunboy, a Kiowa chief, whom the Rangers then scalped. Soon afterward the police found the natives' camp and charged it, only to discover the small detachment of U.S. troops sent to accompany the Indians. A quarrel erupted between the two groups, and before leaving Arrington scornfully returned Sunboy's rifle, which, as he noted, had been loaned to the Indian by a U.S. Army corporal.[92]

Ranger vigilance doubtless played a large part in driving Indians from North Texas, but the force received substantial help from an unlikely source: the U.S. Congress. Troubled by the continuing violence in the state and persuaded by the impassioned appeals drafted by local representatives, both houses in Washington approved House Resolution 5040 in March 1880. It stated that "all officers and agents of the Army and Indian Bureau are prohibited, except in a case specially directed by the President, from granting permission in writing or otherwise to any Indian or Indians on any reservation to go into the State of Texas under any pretext whatever." Most telling, perhaps, was the sentence that concluded section 1 of the act, which mandated that "any officer or agent of the Army or Indian Bureau who shall violate this law shall be dismissed from the public service."[93] With the passage of the bill, the border between Texas and the federally administered Indian Territory closed definitively for Native Americans.

Even as these efforts secured the Red River country against native crossings, another frontier of Ranger-Indian combat opened in the late 1870s in West Texas, which experienced a rash of incursions by Mescalero and Chiricahua Apaches. As in northern Texas, the Indians of the Trans-Pecos defied the political boundaries marking the borders of the state, and raided into Texas from the New Mexico Territory and northern Mexico. Federal Indian policy deserved much of the blame, since Washington's attempts to concentrate numerous—and sometimes mutually hostile—Apache bands on the San Carlos Reservation in eastern Arizona had generated intense native discord. Especially resentful of these initiatives was Victorio, a Chiricahua chief who had lived quietly for most of a decade near Ojo Caliente, in eastern New Mexico. Shortly after his removal in 1877 to the bleak Apache reserve, however, Victorio abandoned San Carlos and with several hundred Indians began raiding into Mexico, New Mexico, and West Texas.[94]

A variety of military organizations pursued Victorio over the course of the next three years, including the African American Ninth and Tenth

6. Ranger sergeant James B. Gillett in 1879, the year that he and other members of Company C crossed into Mexico in pursuit of Victorio. Courtesy of Western History Collections, University of Oklahoma Libraries.

U.S. cavalries as well as private and state militias from northern Mexico.[95] The Rangers became involved in October 1879 when one of their scouts struck an Apache trail southeast of El Paso, heading toward the Rio Grande and across the river into the state of Chihuahua. At that point, Lieutenant George W. Baylor, commander of Ranger Company C stationed at Ysleta, sent a scout into the nearby Mexican town of Guadalupe to ask permission for his ten-man Ranger unit to cross into Mexico.[96] Given the frequency and brutality of Apache raids in his area, the mayor happily consented, and went so far as to gather his own posse and join up with the Rangers, making a combined force of about twenty-five men. The group tracked the Apaches nearly a hundred miles into Mexico, where they engaged the Indians in an all-day fight in a canyon. Sergeant James B. Gillett killed one Apache and the Mexicans shot another, but the natives could not be dislodged and so the group called off the scout, with the Rangers returning to their camp at Ysleta after five days and more than 220 miles of travel.[97]

The Rangers did not remain at Ysleta for long. In November, Victorio and his warriors slaughtered two separate parties of Mexicans, totaling nearly thirty men. The organizers of what Gillett called a "punitive expedition" wrote to Lieutenant Baylor a few days later, inviting the Rangers to join the mission and offering him command of the entire 110-man group; Baylor thought it best to decline the leadership position, as he would be on Mexican soil. In the end, because the Apaches had left the area, the only work for the Rangers and Mexican volunteers was to bury the dead, which was a wrenching experience according to Gillett. He wrote: "The saddest scene I ever witnessed was that presented as we gathered the bodies of the murdered men. At each fresh discovery of a loved friend, brother, or father, a wail of sorrow went up, and I doubt if there was a dry eye either of Mexican or Texan in the whole command."[98] The Rangers made one last foray into Mexico in the fall of 1880, but after a month tracking the Apaches they were ordered back across the river by Joaquín Terrazas, leader of the Chihuahua state militia. Just days later, Terrazas and his troops cornered Victorio at a mountainous redoubt called Tres Castillos and killed him, along with sixty-two warriors and eighteen women and children.[99]

On the night before the battle with Terrazas, however, a band of twelve warriors and their families left Victorio and crossed back into Texas. During the next two months, the Indians ambushed a pair of U.S. cavalry patrols, an emigrant train, and a stagecoach, killing a total of least fifteen people. In mid-January 1881, Baylor (since promoted to captain) set out after them with a small squad of fourteen Rangers from Company A (formed when Company C was mustered out), and was joined later in the month by Lieutenant C. L. Nevill and nine men from Company E. On 29 January the Rangers located the Apaches high in the Sierra Diablo, some seventy-five miles east of El Paso. Leaving five men behind to guard their horses, the other Rangers crept to within a hundred yards of the natives' camp before opening fire, killing several Indians and wounding most of the rest, who left trails of blood leading away from the campsite. Two children and a woman were also taken captive. Baylor reported that the hungry and exhausted Rangers then ate breakfast around the Apaches' fire, "the beauty of the scenery only marred by 'man's inhumanity to man,' the ghostly forms of the dead lying around."[100]

This skirmish marked the last fight in the bitter history of Anglo-native encounters in Texas. With the Kiowas and Comanches barred by law from entering the state and the Apaches driven permanently from the Trans-

Pecos, Adjutant General W. H. King declared that the Indian raids had come to an end.[101] To be sure, there were sporadic reports of Indian sightings by rail crews in West Texas during the early 1880s, but when investigated by the Rangers—who would stop by the camps for a day or two—such scouts usually turned up very little.[102] In the end, it was this much less violent Ranger assignment (the supervision of rail camps) that delivered the final blow to native resistance in Texas. By keeping a close watch on track and grading crews in the Trans-Pecos, the Rangers facilitated the extension of the all-important iron roads, which brought with them into even the farthest reaches of the state the white settlers of Austin's aspirations.

§

At first glance, the efforts of the NWMP to control the Indians of the Canadian North-West seem to diverge so much from the Rangers' policing of indigenous peoples in the Lone Star State as to make the two examples appear incomparable. After all, while the Rangers slaughtered scores of Apaches, Kiowas, and Comanches in the process of closing the borders of Texas, the Mounted Police approached the Blackfoot and the Crees as Ottawa's diplomatic vanguard on the prairies. A closer look, however, suggests that the Mounties' role in facilitating treaties and especially in enforcing their dictates served to control the First Nations in much the same way that dogged Ranger pursuit brought Texas Indians to heel. In the end, the main difference between the work of the Rangers and the Mounties in subjugating indigenous peoples was one of method: instead of exterminating or expelling the Blackfoot and Crees, the Mounties sought to subdue them by implementing Ottawa's policy of coerced assimilation.

Fundamental to this strategy was the extension of Anglo-Canadian law to Indians, an approach designed to end objectionable or inconvenient native customs and, most importantly, to force white social mores upon the First Nations.[103] (Such tactics would have been unthinkable in Texas, where after 1859 the only statutes that applied to Indians were those that outlawed their presence within the state.) The Mounties were well positioned for such work, because Ottawa had invested the constabulary with the power to arrest, prosecute, judge, and sentence offenders—a system that one historian of the NWMP has deemed (though not unfavorably) "a legal tyranny."[104] Statistics for the five years after 1878—when such record keeping by the NWMP began—indicate that natives accounted for anywhere from 21 to 32 percent of total arrests for criminal behavior.[105] While these figures may seem small when one considers that indigenous people constituted the vast majority of the region's population, the turmoil they experienced by the abrupt imposition of a foreign legal code should not be underestimated. For the Indians, NWMP jails—complete with shackles and constant police supervision—must have been extremely unsettling.[106]

Among the native behaviors first targeted by the government (and thus the Mounties) was the consumption of alcohol: Indians were prohibited from selling, drinking, or even possessing intoxicating spirits. To be sure, whites faced similar injunctions, and the NWMP cracked down especially hard on smugglers and those who sold liquor to the First Nations.[107] However, the Mounties were often willing to look the other way when they uncovered minor offenses committed by whites. Indians, on the other hand, were not so fortunate, since the police treated all native liquor violations with utmost seriousness. Mountie vigilance in this regard likely derived from a number of sources, not least among them a deep reservoir of white condescension. This attitude held that "Indians were too far down the scale of civilization to be permitted the right to drink, for they could not hold their liquor and were capable of the most outrageous and dangerous behaviour when drunk." Weaning natives off liquor, officials hoped, would help prepare them to become "brown white people."[108]

The NWMP also used the power of law to curtail native horse theft. For bison-hunting peoples like the Crees and the Blackfoot, horses were indispensable to the pursuit of game as well as to the transportation of families and belongings across vast distances on the Plains. Beyond these more practical considerations, horses served a social purpose, too, for the size of a native man's horse herd and the quality of his mounts were critical factors in determining a warrior's status within the community. Wealth in horses was essentially a prerequisite for men with political ambitions, since leadership positions in native bands often depended on the giving of horses as gifts in order to obtain broad support for an individual's candidacy. Because economic and especially ecological factors kept Indians of the northern Plains relatively poor in horses, at least in comparison with their counterparts farther south, the competition among native groups for equestrian supremacy was intense.[109]

In order to build and maintain their herds, small bands of Cree and Blackfoot warriors regularly attacked the camps of rival native groups—preferably by stealth, as opposed to overt warfare—and made off with as many horses as the raiding party could hope to transport. Although they stole from one another, after the arrival of the NWMP the Crees and Blackfoot more often targeted the herds of groups to the south, in contiguous parts of the United States. The Crees, for instance, frequently poached from Mandan and Hidatsa camps located in the Dakota Territory, while the Blackfoot, who considered Cree horses to be inferior, coveted steeds belonging to the Crows and Flatheads, Montana groups who lived to their southeast and southwest, respectively.[110] As with the theft of the horses themselves, these raids served social as well as economic purposes, for success in warfare lent prestige to young men seeking advancement in their communities.

NWMP reports from the late 1870s and early 1880s indicate the extent of horse theft on the northern Plains and the growing international dimensions of the raids during this period. As Superintendent Leif Crozier noted in a letter from 1880, "When the spring opened horse stealing prevailed to a fearful extent," with parties of Crees, Blackfoot and various American groups camped along the border, "all of whom were stealing each from the other."[111] Particularly vexing to the Mounted Police was the fact that Canadian Indians considered areas north of the international boundary as something of a safe haven, referring to the 49th parallel as the "medicine line" and believing that they were immune from punishment once they had crossed it.[112] Such attitudes were common in Texas, too, where Victorio—among others—exploited the jurisdictional limitations posed by the international boundary between the United States and Mexico. Superintendent Crozier expressed his concern that "unless some understanding is arrived at between the American and Canadian Governments that offenders may be promptly and vigorously dealt with . . . the country along the border will be scarcely habitable."[113]

Given that in the majority of such instances Indians stole from other Indians, and with little attendant violence, one wonders why the Mounted Police worked so hard to extinguish the problem. The answer, it seems, turns on the recognition by Canadian officials that putting a stop to native horse theft would circumscribe the movement of the First Nations and thus facilitate their assimilation.[114] So it was that the Mounties addressed the problem of horse stealing with much the same zeal that they brought to the prosecution of alcohol-related offenses, a fact confirmed by NWMP criminal statistics. Horse stealing was among the most frequently prosecuted offenses in the North-West, and Indians made up nearly half the number of those arrested on such charges between 1878 and 1889. Moreover, the majority of cases concerning the importation of stolen property across the international boundary and into Canada involved natives apprehended with horses they had taken illegally from Indian camps on the U.S. side of the line.[115] Police vigilance steadily reduced horse stealing after it peaked in the early to mid-1880s.[116]

Beyond merely applying the law to native peoples, the NWMP played a crucial role in Ottawa's more direct efforts to assimilate aboriginal groups. A key step in this process was inducing Indians to move onto the reserves guaranteed them during treaty negotiations, a goal of paramount importance to federal officials for a variety of reasons. First and perhaps most pressing was the matter of Indian subsistence. By the end of the 1870s, the bison economy upon which the First Nations of the Canadian prairies depended had collapsed, pushing native people to the edge of starvation.[117] Concentrating Indians on reserves would allow the government—at least in theory—to feed them, while providing Indian Department officials with leverage (in the form of withheld rations) when dealing with recalcitrant bands. Moreover, the rapid extension of railroads across the Plains promised an influx of white laborers and migrants whom the government wanted to protect "from Indian depredations of all kinds."[118] Finally, as in the United States, federal officials in Canada viewed the reservation system as a device through which Indians could be persuaded to eschew their own culture and adopt white social and economic practices.

In light of these imperatives, Ottawa called on the NWMP to assist in settling Indians on designated lands, a duty that often involved police compulsion. Such was the case with the Mounties' removal of various Cree bands from the Cypress Hills in the early 1880s.[119] Though the Indians had lived and hunted there for years, Dominion officials worried about their proximity to the international boundary and thus decided to relocate them to northern reserves. When the Indians resisted, the Canadian government instructed the Mounties to apply pressure. For example, NWMP commissioner A. G. Irvine resolved in the spring of 1882 to drive off those Indians who refused to leave the vicinity of the Mountie post at Fort Walsh.[120] Irvine also employed coercive methods the following year when another band of Crees refused to head north to their reserve, which was more than 400 miles distant from the 49th parallel. The natives finally gave in after the commissioner threatened their chief with arrest, although for good measure Irvine "escorted the Indians some eight miles on their way northward . . . making use of the detachment of police to prevent any stragglers either returning to Maple Creek or travelling southward."[121]

Of course, forcing Indians onto reserves was of little consequence if they could not be made to stay there, and so the government enlisted the police to enforce the so-called pass system. First proposed in 1883, this measure required Indians to obtain permission—in the form of a permit signed by an Indian Department official—before venturing off their reserves. Like the Mountie crackdown against horse theft, the pass system was meant to curb Indian movement and thus reduce the potential for native interference with construction crews, ranchers, and farmers, while preparing them for a sedentary existence. It aimed also to limit the access of native women to urban centers, where some of them worked as prostitutes in a desperate bid to feed themselves and their families.[122] Although some NWMP officials expressed concern about the fairness of the system—which had no legal standing—they had little choice but to implement their orders, and a senior Indian Department official sketched out a possible plan for police intervention. He explained that enforcement might be achieved "in a very simple manner by the Mounted Police . . . requiring that the owners of any tepee [off a reserve] produce a permit . . . and should there be no permit . . . the tepee should be at once broken up by the Police and the occupants warned off."[123]

Annual reports from the 1880s make frequent mention of such duties, such as the NWMP commissioner's 1887 account of a fifteen-man squad patrolling south of the Blood Reserve "in order to intercept any small parties of Indians leaving their Reserve for Montana without the written permission of their Agent."[124] His report for the following year explains, "It has been our endeavor to keep [the Indians] as much as possible on their reserves, and we have succeeded to a great extent."[125] For their part, although they recognized that the pass system was illegal and something to which they had never consented during the treaty negotiations, Indians complied because they knew from past experience that the NWMP or especially the Indian Department would otherwise withhold their rations. Still, this did not stop them from complaining bitterly about the situation. As North Axe, a Peigan chief, protested to Mountie superintendent P. R. Neale in an interview in 1888: "Since you came here the Indians are afraid to go off their Reserves. Before you came, they went where they liked."[126]

Once it had confined the First Nations to their reserves, Ottawa—through the Indian Department—waged a vigorous assault on Indian culture, in the hopes of eradicating native customs and replacing them with white social mores. To this end, Parliament amended the Indian Act several times after 1885 in order to criminalize various native religious ceremonies, including the Potlatch and the Sun (or Thirst) Dance.[127] The latter was especially important to aboriginal groups of the Plains, because it drew diffuse communities together once a year and served to reinforce kinship ties. However, the Sun Dance horrified white reformers with its communalistic gift sharing and especially its rituals of self-mortification, characterized by extensive piercing of the flesh. Hoping to stamp out the ceremonies and in the process to force upon the natives the importance of accumulating private property, the Indian Department asked for assistance from the Mounties to prevent such native gatherings.

Records show that federal officials called on the Mounted Police in the 1880s and 1890s in order to control or outlaw the Sun Dance, as suggested by a representative case from the File Hills Reserve in 1896. That May, Indian Commissioner Hayter Reed contacted Lawrence Herchmer, commissioner of the NWMP, to ask for police assistance in preventing a rumored Cree and Assiniboine ceremony. Although Reed conceded that it was difficult to stop Indians from congregating on their own reserve, he expressed his hope that the Mounties might be able to turn away any other Indian bands traveling to the area to take part, thus limiting its attendance and potential impact. Herchmer pledged his readiness to Reed, and then instructed Mountie inspector E. Brown to investigate the situation. By the time Brown's squad arrived from Regina several days later, the visiting Indian bands had returned to their own reserves, causing the headmen of the File Hills "to give up all intention of having a Sun Dance." For his part, the Indian agent credited the work of the police, but added that the Indians "feel very much hurt that they were not allowed to keep up their old customs and think they have sacrificed a great deal in acceding to the wishes of the Department."[128]

While many Mounties shared Ottawa's concerns about the Sun Dance—for instance, Superintendent R. B. Deane felt that it had "the effect of bringing out all the bad qualities of the Indians"—some officers expressed their reluctance to enforce the law.[129] Several policemen (Deane among them) even allowed similar dance ceremonies to proceed on occasion, provided that the Indians removed all objectionable behaviors, like the piercing of

7. Mounted Policemen and Peigan Indians at a Sun Dance, 1886.
Courtesy of Glenbow Archives, NA-2928-53.

flesh, and did not consume alcohol.[130] Indian protests may have cultivated such police equanimity, especially when natives pointed to the hypocrisy of allowing Christian clergy to promote their beliefs on the reserves but outlawing non-Christian religious observance by the First Nations.[131] However, police leniency disappeared after a testy exchange in 1901 between NWMP comptroller Fred White and a federal official, who insisted that "the purpose of the police is . . . to prevent rather than encourage any violation of the law in regard to 'Sun Dances' and other unlawful or dangerous festivals."[132]

More distasteful to the NWMP than their work in getting rid of the Sun Dance was the role of the police in enforcing the removal of Indian children from their families and their placement in residential and industrial schools. Convinced that the First Nations would perpetuate harmful native traditions by teaching such customs to succeeding generations, the Indian Department developed the schools beginning in the late 1870s as a vehicle for aboriginal social control. Or, put more bluntly by one historian, the idea was "'to kill the Indian' in the child for the sake of Christian civilization."[133] Indian youths were thus sequestered in boarding schools throughout Manitoba and the North-West Territories, where they received the basics of formal education as well as extensive vocational training in fields such as carpentry, gardening, and blacksmithing. Some children were also "planted out," or placed in white families in order to facilitate their instruction but also to perform menial labor.[134]

No less important to the church leaders and government officials who managed the system was the eradication of native customs, a process that involved refashioning—by force if necessary—all aspects of native life, from dress to speech.[135] Backsliders faced stiff punishment, including physical or verbal abuse and the withholding of rations. Reinforcing these austere conditions were the school facilities themselves, many of which were hastily and poorly built, thus serving as fertile breeding grounds for epidemic disease. One doctor who studied fifteen schools for the period between 1888 and 1905 found that nearly 25 percent of the students enrolled at those institutions had died, almost exclusively from tuberculosis.[136] Facing such circumstances and suffering from severe alienation, many children opted to leave the institutions and return to their parents, prompting Indian Department officials to enlist the NWMP to pursue the runaways and return them to the schools.

As with the pass system, the legal basis for compulsory Indian education was scant (though it was later codified by amendment to the Indian Act), and members of the NWMP—from the top down—expressed grave misgivings about police intervention in such matters.[137] In the end, it was determined that the Mounties could only apprehend runaways intercepted before they reached their homes; once reunited with their families, it was up to the parents to determine whether their children would stay on the reserve or return to school.[138] Even after the establishment of these guidelines, Indian Department officials quarreled with Mountie brass over police involvement in truancy cases, as indicated by an incident from 1894. In December of that year, Inspector C. Constantine refused to arrest a runaway Indian boy whom Constantine believed to be suffering from tuberculosis. Despite the exhortations of the school's headmaster to seize the child, the inspector demurred, explaining that "it would have been an inhuman act to have taken the boy away."[139] Notwithstanding their objections, however, members of the NWMP often returned runaways to the schools, and provided a further service to the Indian Department by dispersing or arresting Indian parents seeking to remove their children illegally from the institutions.[140]

By the turn of the century, Dominion control of the North-West and Ottawa's assault on native freedoms had thoroughly conquered the First Nations. In facilitating the first objective and enforcing (however reluctantly) the second, the Mounted Police played an indispensable role in the subjugation of Canada's Plains Indians. And ironically, it was the very success of such Mountie efforts that compromised Ottawa's stated goal of Indian assimilation. By herding the First Nations onto reserves and then supporting federal measures to erode native culture, the NWMP had so divided western Canada's aboriginal inhabitants from its white newcomers that most natives could not imagine a future lived entirely on terms set by Ottawa. Such Indian resistance to assimilation emerges in a telling statistic: between 1857 and 1920, only 250 Indians elected full Canadian citizenship, with the overwhelming majority of those who qualified choosing instead to remain on the reserves.[141] Any regrets federal officials might have experienced about this system of apartheid were not likely shared by European immigrants, who after 1900 poured into the region and cultivated the Indians' former hunting grounds.

On 10 June 1881 a Caddo Indian named Tinah addressed an assembly of natives who had gathered at Anadarko in the Indian Territory in order to register their dissatisfaction with the proposed U.S. policy of allotment. Delegates from several Indian groups that had been expelled from Texas attended the meeting, including representatives for the Comanches and the Kiowas. Tinah told his audience: "We know this is our country. Our Father gave us this land to live on. . . . At that time we thought we had a large country, but since then our country has become smaller. But we still remember the talk and ask our Father to have mercy and not cut up our country."[142] Though eloquent, Tinah's speech—and others like it—were ultimately of little use, since the federal government implemented the Dawes General Allotment Act six years later, breaking up reservations in the Indian Territory and throughout the West and thus further eroding the natives' land base.

The First Nations of western Canada witnessed a similar assault on their shrunken homelands after 1900, although such efforts were less successful above the 49th parallel than below it, in large part because Dominion officials insisted upon obtaining native consent to any proposed reductions to the reserves. Still, Plains Indians in Canada experienced significant land loss, especially the member nations of the Blackfoot Confederacy, whose reserves were situated on some of the best lands in the region. During the first decade of the twentieth century, various Blackfoot groups bowed to intense federal pressure and surrendered sizable portions of their territory, with the *Sik-sik-a* alone selling 115,000 acres (or half of their reserve) to the federal government in 1910. Ottawa's attempt to resell these lands to white newcomers took longer than anticipated, during which time the government sought to offset its financial shortfall by reducing the natives' promised beef rations.[143]

Such austerity on the reservations in Indian Territory and Alberta linked the experiences of southern and northern Plains Indians at the turn of the century, just as these native hardships bound the Rangers and Mounties, who, after all, had expedited the Indians' confinement in the first place. Indeed, officials in each capital attributed the very fact of native subjugation and attendant white prosperity in frontier areas to their rural police. For example, Texas adjutant general W. H. King remarked in 1882, "Practically, there is very little use for any Rangers so far as danger from Indian raids is concerned."[144] NWMP commissioner A. G. Irvine struck a similar chord the next year in praising the Mounted Police for their assistance in extending the Canadian Pacific Railway, writing, "Fortunately, the Indians were so kept in subjection that no opposition of any moment was encountered from them."[145]

Of course there is more than merely the self-interested proclamations of their commanders to indicate the extensive overlap between the constabularies and their efforts to control Indians. On the most fundamental level, the Rangers and Mounties were charged at almost exactly the same moment in the early 1870s with the responsibility of securing frontier portions of Texas and the North-West. The NWMP made its famed Great March to the West in 1874, the very same year that Texas lawmakers ratified an act creating the Frontier Battalion of the Texas Rangers. Central to each development was a desire shared by officials in Austin and Ottawa to settle whites along the periphery of their territories and then to exploit the vast natural resources found there. The constabularies were to serve as the vanguard of this process, eliminating any threats posed by indigenous peoples.

Once established, the Rangers and Mounties found their work made much easier by a subsistence crisis facing the Indians of the northern and southern Plains in the 1870s, marked by the disappearance of the bison. The collapse of the buffalo economy in Canada and the U.S. West derived from similar causes: namely, the pressures of white expansion, which eroded the winter habitats of the bison and drove the animals to the geographical extremes of the grasslands, where they were then slaughtered by commercial hide hunters. Pushed to the brink of starvation by the decline of the herds and weakened by the diseases of poverty, Indians in Texas and the North-West were less able to withstand increased white incursions, whether the interlopers were settlers, surveyors, or police. This constellation of circumstances eased Ranger efforts to expel the Kiowas and Comanches from Texas, just as it smoothed the treaty negotiations with the Crees and Blackfoot facilitated by the NWMP.

Most significantly, the work of each force resembled that of the other in terms of the outcomes for both native and white people at either end of the Plains. Indians in both locales witnessed the eclipse of their autonomy and a growing dependence upon federal largesse for food, health care, and education. Their alienation from the mainstream of Anglo society cemented their status as second-class citizens and justified their inequality in the workplace and before the courts. Whites, on the other hand, filled the physical and economic space created by the removal or confinement of Indians, in almost identical ways. Anglo settlers and entrepreneurs migrated to North and West Texas, where they started mining ventures and established large cattle ranches. Likewise, Eurocanadians began to move in greater numbers to the lands that became the provinces of Alberta and Saskatchewan, where they, too, founded ranching empires and hatched plans to dig coal and provide it to the railroad companies hurriedly extending their lines across the prairies.

And yet even as the net results of their efforts may have been powerfully similar, the means used to achieve those ends differed considerably, seen most vividly in the Rangers' liberal use of violence as compared to Mountie restraint. This schism grew from a host of factors, beginning with the sharply contrasting histories of native-white relations at the opposite ends of the Plains. In Texas, a legacy of conflict between Anglos and Indians dated back to the earliest days of white settlement there during the 1820s. Anti-Indian factions within the republic received a boost in 1838 when Mirabeau Lamar was elected as the second president of Texas and set about removing or exterminating native peoples, a strategy that continued as state policy after Texas was admitted to the United States in 1845. A strong current of white racism undergirded these efforts and led many within Texas to press state officials on the matter of Indian subjugation, a responsibility that fell primarily to the Rangers.

In the North-West Territories, on the other hand, the cooperative nature of the fur trade had produced a largely peaceful history of native-white interaction for two centuries, epitomized by networks of kinship and intermarriage that had no parallel in Texas. The pace of white settlement to the region was also a critical factor in reducing the potential for interracial violence, since the Laurentian Shield had delayed the arrival of Eurocanadian newcomers long enough for Ottawa to develop a coherent (if not unproblematic) plan for the future administration of the North-West. Central to this strategy was an emphasis—motivated in part by financial expediency but also by a desire to demonstrate the superiority of the Canadian approach to Indian affairs in contrast to that in the United States—on maintaining cordial relations with the aboriginal people of the prairies. No such option existed in Texas (or in large portions of the U.S. West, for that matter), where Anglos had consistently settled ahead of survey, provoking Indian defensiveness and initiating an unending cycle of bloodshed.

The early duties of the constabularies illustrate both the fact and the significance of this divergence. The Mounted Police arrived in the West in 1874 ahead of surveyors and settlers, and worked to create optimum conditions for Eurocanadian newcomers well in advance of their migration from the East. Unencumbered by a history of native-white conflict, the police had the opportunity to earn the goodwill of the First Nations, which they achieved in part by controlling unscrupulous whites, such as liquor traders. Furthermore, the Mounties sought to allay native suspicions and confirm Ottawa's goodwill through the distribution of presents and the promises of treaty negotiations. If the advent of the NWMP spelled the end of Plains Indian existence as the First Nations had known it, the more coercive features of incorporation did not emerge all at once but rather appeared throughout the 1880s and 1890s after the Dominion had strengthened its grip on the North-West.

In Texas, by contrast, the Frontier Battalion inherited a tradition of Ranger service based on the armed protection of a continually expanding frontier, one marked by violent encounters between Anglos and Indians. Rather than entering remote portions of Texas in order to lay the physical, legal, and diplomatic groundwork necessary for Euroamerican occupation, as the Mounties had done in Canada, the Rangers traveled to flashpoints of conflict along the lines of white settlement in a fashion resembling a game of catch-up. Given the insecurity of Texas's scattered outposts and the violence that had usually attended their creation, the Rangers' use of lethal force to shore up Anglo territorial gains does not seem surprising. The founding of Charles Goodnight's cattle-ranching empire in the Panhandle, for instance, carried a heavy price tag for the region's Comanche and Kiowa Indians. Goodnight, along with many of his West Texas counterparts, depended on the Rangers not to serve as the precursor to his entrepreneurial ambitions but rather to defend what he had already tried to conquer.

Perhaps the central feature in explaining Ranger brutality as compared to Mountie nonviolence hinges on the fact that one was a state force and the other a federal one. The Republic of Texas gained admission to the United States in full possession of its lands, and after the failure of its Indian reservations in the 1850s was free to handle its native population as deemed fit by Austin officials. This entailed driving Kiowas and Comanches across the state's borders, into present-day Oklahoma or New Mexico, where the Indians then became a "problem" for Washington to solve. The Mounted Police, on the other hand, as agents of a federal government committed to larger, national goals, did not have such an aggressive option at their disposal. They could not simply push the Crees and Blackfoot across the 49th parallel into Montana, nor did officials want them to; Ottawa's goal was to assimilate—not exterminate—Canada's indigenous peoples.

Even when acknowledging the coercive dimensions of NWMP duty involving aboriginal peoples, Canadian historians have mostly celebrated the gentle treatment afforded the First Nations by the Mounted Police.[146] No doubt the speeches of Crowfoot and Red Crow have bolstered such an interpretation. One scholar of the NWMP has even offered an explicit (if passing) comparison of Mountie and Ranger interaction with natives, insisting that the Texans "were the antithesis of the Mounted Police."[147] Such a statement rings true on several levels, especially when considered from the vantage point of the historian. After all, the Rangers were racist, violent, and beholden only to the demands of a narrowly self-interested state government. The Mounties, on the other hand, rarely used lethal force, were prone to moments of circumspection about their orders, and served as the face of the Dominion itself throughout the vast North-West Territories. But from the imagined perspective of the reservation-bound Kiowas and Comanches or Blackfoot and Crees, the differences would no doubt have seemed much smaller.

3 Dispossessing Peoples of Mixed Ancestry

In December 1887 the exiled Métis leader Gabriel Dumont sent a letter to George Demanche, a French journalist who had written several articles for a Paris newspaper about the failed North-West Rebellion of 1885.[1] As Dumont explained, he wished to thank the editor for his attention to the plight of the Métis—the offspring of native women and French or British fur trappers—whose insurrection had been crushed by Ottawa two years before. While the tone of Dumont's note was measured, he lapsed nevertheless into a recapitulation of the wrongs done to the Métis by Canadian officials. Most egregious, he insisted, was the fact that "the English Government will never pardon those who frightened them and they have given the proof in having burnt on 30th May 1431 the heroine Joan of Arc—that young inspired one who attempted to throw terror into the English army."[2]

Dumont's missive provides valuable insight into the frustrations and predicaments faced by peoples of mixed ancestry at both ends of the Great Plains during the last third of the nineteenth century. Just as the Métis of Manitoba and the Canadian North-West believed that they had been severely mistreated by Eurocanadian settlers and government officials, Texas Mexicans—who were descended from Spaniards and the indigenous peoples of Mexico—chafed under the oppressive rule of an Anglo-dominated regime.[3] While both groups had enjoyed some degree of inclusion in the social hierarchies of the French and Spanish empires in North America, the transition to Anglo hegemony in Texas and on the Canadian prairies between the 1860s and 1880s resulted in their exclusion.[4] Given the new order on the Plains—which was characterized by Anglo antipathy toward the mixed-race remnants of the French and Spanish colonial systems—it is

8. Gabriel Dumont at Red River, Alberta, ca. 1880s.
Courtesy of Glenbow Archives, NA-1063-1.

little wonder that Dumont identified with Joan of Arc, another individual of French descent persecuted by English invaders.

As with the Plains Indians, the cultural and racial differences of mixed-race groups worried government observers. No less problematic, however, was Mexican and Métis control over the territory and resources of Texas and the North-West, which—in contrast to Anglo conceptions of private property—they tended to hold in common, regulating the terms of their use at the local level.[5] Put simply, Anglo settlers and political officials wanted the lands, animals, and minerals claimed by peoples of mixed ancestry, nonwhites whom they viewed as inferior and as clear impediments to the economic integration and development of the hinterlands. White Texans thus migrated to communities situated near the Rio Grande, while Eurocanadian newcomers pushed westward from Ontario and elsewhere into present-day Manitoba. When each mixed-race group took up arms to challenge white encroachment—Mexicans in the so-called Cortina War of 1859 and the Métis ten years later in the first Red River insurgency—these gathering tensions erupted into full-blown battles for resource control.

In the wake of these conflicts, officials in the two capitals turned increasingly to their rural constabularies to help control and monitor peoples of mixed ancestry. The Special Force of Rangers was created in 1874 with a specific mandate to bring order to the trans-Nueces region of Texas, while the Mounted Police marched west that same year, charged with asserting federal sovereignty on the prairies. To be sure, the police went about their work quite differently: while the Mounties rarely resorted to force, the Rangers unleashed such violence that one twentieth-century critic described them as "the Mexican-Americans' Ku Klux Klan."[6] Still, a consideration of the Rangers' actions in South and West Texas and Mountie efforts in the Canadian North-West reveals that the police were bound by a common purpose: to break the hold of mixed-race peoples on the resources at either end of the Great Plains.[7] In the process, the constabularies played an essential role in the proletarianization of Mexicans and the Métis, who having been driven off their lands and deprived of their traditional economies turned increasingly to wage labor.

Historical Roots of the Métis and Tejanos

Ottawa's plans for the economic development of the newly acquired North-West Territories faced stiff resistance from the Plains Métis.[8] These peoples of mixed ancestry traced their beginnings to the second half of the eighteenth century, when French (and later British) contracted servants took wives among the bands of Cree, Assiniboine, Ojibwa, and other First Nations peoples with whom they had wintered during the hunting season.[9] Such unions à la façon du pays—"according to the custom of the country"—usually took place on terms set by the natives. Upon their release from company service, some of these freemen opted to remain with their families on the prairies, hunting buffalo and serving as middlemen between indigenous peoples of the interior and European traders, with whom they maintained ties of kinship and commerce, respectively. Their offspring became the Plains Métis, a group that numbered approximately 15,000 by the early nineteenth century.[10]

Following the union of the North-West Company and the Hudson's Bay Company (HBC) in 1821, the confluence of the Red and Assiniboine rivers—the site of present-day Winnipeg—emerged as the center of Plains Métis society. Typically, the Catholic and French-speaking Métis settled south and west of the junction, while the Protestant and Anglophone Métis, known also as the "Country-born," claimed lands to the north of the forks. Although divided at times by language and religion, common social and economic patterns united the Red River community. Métis families typically lived on oblong lots with narrow river frontage that ran to a depth of one or two miles, where they cultivated spring wheat. Given the short growing season and harsh northern climate, the Métis supplemented their subsistence agriculture by offering freighting services to the HBC and, more importantly, through a twice-yearly buffalo hunt.[11]

For the spring hunt, which was the larger of the two expeditions, virtually every able-bodied man and his family loaded their Red River carts and traveled south to a regular meeting point on the U.S. border, near Pembina, in what is now North Dakota. There the community would elect a series of leaders to coordinate the hunt, establishing a hierarchy akin to that of the European colonial militias found to the east (but modeled also on hunting organizations of Plains Indian groups). Following the leaders' explicit instructions and with punishment awaiting those who failed to comply, the mounted hunters would descend on a herd of bison, riding right into the midst of the buffalo and firing at the animals from point-blank range. Skilled hunters could take as many as ten or twelve animals each, and the collective slaughter could be staggering; during the famous summer hunt of 1840, Red River Métis killed nearly 1,400 bison in a single day. After the hunt, the men butchered the carcasses, and the women prepared the meat as pemmican for community use or for sale to trading posts throughout the North-West.[12]

The increased demand for buffalo robes and hides after 1850 brought changes to the socioeconomic structure of the Red River settlement. With the advent of new trade opportunities in the United States and eastern Canada, a handful of Métis families pursued mercantile careers, while many others—particularly those of French descent—became *hivernants*, or "winterers." The latter spent the period between November and February at hunting sites on the Plains in order to kill bison when their robes were thickest and thus most valuable. One historian offers compelling evidence of the growing Métis involvement in the robe trade after midcentury, explaining that the number of Red River carts arriving in St. Paul, Minnesota—a major fur-trading center—grew from only 6 in 1844 to 1,400 two decades later. By that time, however, the Métis faced the same crisis experienced by the Plains Indians in the mid-1860s, as growing pressure on the bison drove the herds to the west.[13]

A greater threat to the Métis, perhaps, was taking shape in the East. After 1850 the scarcity and expense of pastoral land in southern Ontario had led some Eurocanadians to move westward, where they established farms in areas occupied by both First Nations and Métis peoples. Although this development was of significant concern to the Métis, it was the 1869 transfer of Rupert's Land (the name originally given to the territory claimed by the HBC) to the new Dominion of Canada that brought their anxieties to a crisis point. Not only had the negotiations leading up to Confederation taken place without input from area residents, but the advent of federal sovereignty in the North-West promised a flood of white newcomers. The Métis worried especially that government surveyors would disregard claims to their riverine lots and the communal hay fields behind them and instead carve the area into uniform tracts, to say nothing of the expected assault on Métis cultural independence, marked by their Catholicism and use of the French language. Combined with frustrations caused by several years of poor harvests and the increasing scarcity of the bison, such conditions led some of the estimated 12,000 Red River Métis to challenge the tide of white encroachment in 1869.[14]

§

The earliest Mexican settlements in Texas predated the advent of the Plains Métis by several decades, since groups of colonists began arriving in Texas from the northeastern states of present-day Mexico during the first quarter of the eighteenth century. Although some of the newcomers were Tlascalan Indians, most were *castas*, or peoples of mixed ancestry, who were descended from Spaniards and the indigenous peoples of Mexico. Numbering perhaps as many as 3,000 individuals by the end of the century, these immigrant groups built tight, insular communities around missions or presidios, seeking protection from the harsh elements of frontier life: climatic extremes, nomadic war parties, and acute physical isolation. While some found work on *rancherías*, which were owned by the wealthy, most Tejanos relied on subsistence agriculture or their own small cattle ranches to support themselves and their families, carving out a largely autonomous if somewhat austere existence that weathered the changes wrought by Mexican Independence in 1821. The influx of Euroamericans over the next three decades, however, would prove harder to withstand.[15]

Although the Anglo presence in Texas dated to 1821 and the founding of Stephen F. Austin's colony, few whites lived in the area between San Antonio and the Rio Grande before midcentury. U.S. victory in the Mexican-American War of 1848, however, opened South Texas to white settlement, and cities such as Brownsville, at the mouth of the river, began to swell with white arrivals, most of whom were looking to capitalize on the lucrative border trade. Richard King and Mifflin Kenedy—two men strongly associated with the rise of Anglo hegemony in South Texas—purchased decommissioned military boats nearby and quickly monopolized the shipping of goods arriving from ports along the Gulf of Mexico by displacing or buying up their competition.[16] Though vastly outnumbered in the trans-Nueces region (in 1850 there were about 2,500 whites and more than 18,000 Mexicans), Anglo-Texans set about constructing a rigid socioeconomic order that used the power of the state to favor the white population and keep Mexicans "in their place."[17] This official coercion contradicted the guarantees of the Treaty of Guadalupe Hidalgo, which held that Mexicans electing to remain in the United States after 1848 would receive all the rights of American citizens.

It is worth asking why Anglo-Texans felt it necessary to control Mexicans in the first place. On the most basic level, whites in Texas seemed to believe that the two races could not live together peacefully, an opinion no doubt buttressed by the recent war and the unpleasant memories of the Texas Revolution twelve years earlier.[18] Despite the fact that many Mexicans had fought for independence with Sam Houston and other Anglo leaders in the struggle against Santa Anna, after 1836 whites tended to look upon Mexicans as outsiders whose social and political loyalties lay with Mexico rather than with Texas and the United States. Some Tejanos, moreover, were uncomfortable with the rapid postrevolution expansion of slavery in the new Republic of Texas. When Mexican president Vicente Guerrero abolished the institution in 1829, he had bowed to the demands of irate Texas slave owners and exempted them from the decree. Thereafter, many Tejanos worked to undermine slavery in Texas by helping escaped bondsmen seek freedom on the other side of the Rio Grande.[19] Such actions infuriated white Texans and convinced them of Tejano disloyalty.

Reinforcing this profound distrust was a powerful current of anti-Mexican racism, which was practically an article of faith among nineteenth-century Anglo-Texans. As one historian has argued, "Anglos perceived the physical contrasts of Mexicans as indicating mental and temperamental weaknesses" that rendered them unfit for the privileges of equal citizenship.[20] Though whites made some exceptions for individual Tejanos (drawn almost exclusively from the wealthier classes and beyond suspicion in terms of their fidelity to Texas), most Anglos considered their Mexican neighbors socially and intellectually inferior, and—by dint of their Catholicism— slavishly devoted to the pope. Other scholars have noted the southern roots of many of the state's white emigrants and suggested that their animosity toward Mexicans derived from the racist tenets of *Herrenvolk* democracy, characterized by a dim view of those not belonging to the supposed "master race."[21]

White migrants and officials alike also chafed at the simple fact that Mexicans possessed strong legal claims to the lands and resources of South Texas, rights that had been recognized first by the Spanish crown and later by the Republic of Mexico.[22] Though much of the territory belonged to rich Tejanos—which was trouble enough for settlers and entrepreneurs—still other tracts were publicly held (like the communal lands at the Red River settlement), established by Spain for shared use by the population of a given pueblo. After 1848 many Anglo-Texan settlers south of the Nueces River knew that until they had wrested control of the lands along the Rio Grande from their present (and, as they believed, backward) owners, their dreams of profits generated by the commercial development of the valley would never materialize. In this way, Anglo-Texan ambitions and frustrations paralleled those of Eurocanadians who coveted Métis lands.

This combination of prejudice and economic ambition led Anglos in South Texas to create an oppressive sociopolitical system, the promises of Guadalupe Hidalgo notwithstanding. Tight white control of civic institutions—especially the legal establishment—conferred on Mexicans second-class citizenship at best, exposing them to repeated Anglo abuses, including double standards in the courts.[23] One of the most violent episodes of this period, the so-called Cart War of 1857, demonstrated conclusively the adverse conditions facing Mexicans in South Texas and the costs of their political powerlessness. Aggravated by Mexican control of freight lines between San Antonio and the Gulf coast—a dominance achieved by the Mexicans' assessment of lower rates—white teamsters initiated a brutal and largely unchecked campaign of assassination against their Mexican rivals, forcing them to abandon the profession.[24] None of the assailants suffered arrest or incarceration.

Especially worrisome to Mexicans of the trans-Nueces was their accelerating land loss, facilitated by the imposition of an American legal culture foreign to (and often hostile toward) Texas Mexicans. Aided by shrewd Anglo attorneys such as Stephen Powers, a real estate lawyer specializing in Spanish and Mexican law, white merchants and entrepreneurs had weakened Mexican property claims in South Texas with dramatic results.[25] Between 1840 and 1860, for instance, all but one of the original Mexican land grants in Nueces County fell into Anglo hands. This shift suggests the disproportionate wealth and legal influence enjoyed by the small group of whites in South Texas at the expense of their much more numerous Mexican neighbors.[26] The acquisition of vast tracts of territory, coupled with the dominance of commercial trade along the lower Rio Grande by men such as Kenedy, King, and their partner Charles Stillman, had made Tejanos "foreigners in their native land" by the early 1850s.[27]

Mixed-Race Resistance: Louis Riel and Juan Cortina

Métis resistance to the 1869 transfer of Rupert's Land stemmed in large part from the failure of federal officials to consult the Métis ahead of schedule about the timing, conditions, and implications of the transaction. For instance, government surveyors arrived in Red River in the summer of 1869, well ahead of the official transfer date (originally slated for 1 October but for other reasons later pushed back to 1 December). As explained by one historian, most of the surveyors hailed from established Ontario families and had extensive education and training, but they were largely unfamiliar with the peoples and geography of the prairies. Thus they evinced little sympathy for the Plains residents they encountered, including the Métis, whom the surveyors considered ignorant and unreasonable. The insurgency began in mid-October when a group of Métis rebuffed members of a survey party that had encroached on some of their communal lands.[28]

9. A government survey team near Wood End, Saskatchewan, 1873.
Courtesy of Glenbow Archives, NA-249-42.

Led by Louis Riel, a twenty-five-year-old Métis from Red River who had
been educated at Catholic institutions in Montreal, the insurgents quickly
established a provisional government and prevented William McDougall,
the North-West Territories' first lieutenant governor, from taking office.[29]
All the while, Riel issued statements and proclamations articulating Métis
grievances. In one of these resolutions, Riel characterized the terms of the
transfer as unfair and illegitimate and defended the resistance, declaring
that he and his compatriots had "but acted conformably to that sacred right
which commands every citizen to offer energetic opposition to prevent his
country being enslaved."[30] With the seizure of nearby Fort Garry at the outset of winter, timed carefully to discourage Canadian troops from march-
ing west, Riel strengthened the negotiating position of the Métis before
dispatching emissaries to Ottawa the following spring. The delegates carried with them a range of demands concerning protection of Métis lands,
religious practices, and political interests. Leaders of the insurgency also
ordered the trial and execution of Thomas Scott, an Ontarian who—along
with nearly fifty others—had been captured and imprisoned after a failed
attempt to overthrow the provisional government of the Métis.[31]

Ottawa was stunned by the resistance and sought a quick solution to the impasse in the hopes of avoiding any additional complications regarding the transfer and also to undermine any plans by U.S. annexationists to exploit the chaos as a means of acquiring lands north of the 49th parallel.[32] Thus in the spring of 1870 Parliament ratified the Manitoba Act, which established the first new province of the Dominion of Canada. By the terms of the legislation, Manitoba received a constitution as well as allowances for separate schools for Métis children and the continued use of the French language. Most importantly, perhaps, the Manitoba Act addressed Métis anxieties about their land tenure by sequestering a total of 1.4 million acres for allotment to Métis families.[33] Although their new province was only about a hundred square miles—a tiny island surrounded by the federally administered North-West Territories—the Métis had nevertheless exacted a compromise from the government and won a homeland in the process.

Their apparent victory would prove hollow. Ottawa's refusal to grant a general amnesty forced Riel, among others, to flee across the U.S. border into exile.[34] Also, as one scholar has shown, the political clout of the Métis in their own province was short-lived: while in 1870 fully half of the members of the Manitoba Legislative Assembly were of Métis descent, that figure had plummeted to just 17 percent by 1879.[35] Dwindling Métis representation stemmed in part from the erosion of their electoral base; by 1875 some of the poorer Francophone Métis had abandoned the province and moved westward into the districts of Saskatchewan and Assiniboia in pursuit of the rapidly vanishing bison. Additional groups of French Métis left the Red River area because of the racism and cultural bigotry exhibited by many of the Eurocanadian newcomers, who were particularly intolerant of their Roman Catholicism.

Many other Métis who abandoned Manitoba—particularly those who emigrated after 1875—did so because of their concerns about land use and tenure. In establishing guidelines for the province, Ottawa had drafted regulations that provided for individual, but not corporate, settlement. Such a plan, which benefited Ottawa by diluting a potential rebel stronghold in Manitoba, denied Métis wishes to maintain possession of the large blocs of community land that they viewed as essential to their cultural survival. Furthermore, federal officials acted slowly in approving the grants promised to Métis families, raising concerns that Ottawa's pledges might never materialize and that the Métis would do better to seek new homes elsewhere. Still others found that the oblong lots of the Red River settlement were not conducive to commercial agriculture, and chose therefore to sell their acres in the hopes of acquiring larger parcels farther west where they could mix subsistence farming with limited wage work or entrepreneurial ventures.[36] This constellation of circumstances fostered a Métis diaspora, so that in the words of one historian Manitoba had effectively "ceased to be a metis community" less than a decade after its 1870 founding.[37]

§

While the Métis insurgency of 1869–70 erupted shortly after the encroachment of Eurocanadian outsiders within the vicinity of the Red River settlement, tensions in South Texas simmered without boiling over for more than a decade after the end of the Mexican-American War. Accounting for this difference, perhaps, is the fact that—in light of Mexico's military defeat—those Mexicans inclined toward recalcitrance were wary of initiating another conflict so soon after 1848. Moreover, unlike the Métis, who capitalized on the legal and political limbo created by the transfer of Rupert's Land, the firm imposition of Anglo rule in the trans-Nueces left Texas Mexicans with little room to maneuver and no doubt about where they stood: namely, at the bottom of South Texas society. When they took up arms in the summer and fall of 1859, however, their rebellion posed as great a threat to the state as would the insurgency of their mixed-race counterparts to the north ten years later.

In July 1859 Juan Cortina, the son of a wealthy landowning family, witnessed the abuse of one of his former employees at the hands of Brownsville's white marshal, Bob Shears.[38] Apparently, the Mexican ranchero was drunk and had mistreated the owner of a local coffee shop. In the process of arresting the man, Shears began to pistol-whip him, prompting Cortina to interfere. When he offered to take charge of the man, Shears reportedly asked Cortina, "What is it to you, you damned Mexican?" and refused to surrender the ranchero. At that point, Cortina shot the marshal in the torso, threw his friend onto the back of his horse, and rode out of town.[39] With Shears's recovery, the affair—however unsettling to whites of the lower Rio Grande Valley—might have ended without further incident.

But Cortina had apparently reached the breaking point after more than ten years of Anglo rule in South Texas, and he was not content to let the matter rest. He returned to Brownsville two months later with a large party of armed men, killing four city residents, including two whom Cortina alleged had murdered Mexicans but suffered no punishment. From his mother's ranch outside of town, Cortina then issued a proclamation that (except for the threat of violence) bears a striking resemblance to Riel's address of a decade later. Cortina's statement read in part:

> Our object, as you have seen, has been to chastise the villainy of our en-emies, which heretofore has gone unpunished. These have connived with each other . . . to persecute and rob us . . . for no other crime on our part than that of being of Mexican origin. . . . To defend ourselves, and making use of the sacred right of self-preservation, we have assembled in a popular meeting with a view of discussing a means by which to put an end to our misfortunes. . . . *Our personal enemies shall not possess our lands until they have fattened it with their own gore.*[40]

With this resolution, Cortina—whose wealth and stature had insulated him from many of the mistreatments suffered by less fortunate Texas Mexicans and thus made him a seemingly unlikely insurgent—attracted the support of hundreds of aggrieved Mexicans on both sides of the Rio Grande. For the next five months they controlled South Texas, burning the ranches of whites and the Anglos' wealthy Tejano allies.

Such violence constitutes one of several key differences between the Cor-tina War and the Red River Resistance of 1869–70. For one thing, the Métis had specific political goals (centered on some limited form of self-govern-ment) that they sought to press on a Canadian government in the midst of significant transition, when the prospects for such an outcome seemed most favorable. The Cortinistas, on the other hand (a term that here ap-plies to Tejano combatants and sympathizers, but should not be taken to include all or even most Mexicans in South Texas), harbored no such hopes of legal redress, given the prior consolidation of Anglo political hegemony in the trans-Nueces. Motivating their rebellion, it seems, were frustration and revenge, as well as a desire to demonstrate their intent to resist fur-ther Anglo tyranny. These circumstances may explain the bloodshed along the Rio Grande in contrast to the relative calm that prevailed at Red River. Violence in South Texas reflected Tejano rage and perhaps also a belief that the intimidation of the numerically inferior white population could lead to a lessening of Mexican oppression. Conversely for the Métis, the resort to force was counterproductive to the goal of winning concessions from Ottawa, a point brought home quite vividly by the fallout from the execution of Thomas Scott.

Another divergence between the conflicts concerns the involvement of rural police: while the NWMP had not yet been formed at the time of the Red River Resistance, the Texas Rangers played a critical role in the Cortina War (though it is worth noting that Ranger companies at this time served only on a temporary basis). A detachment of fifty men under the command of William Tobin arrived in Brownsville in early November and swiftly complicated matters by organizing the lynching of Tomás Cabrera, an elderly Cortina lieutenant who had been captured and thrown in jail.[41] This action prolonged the conflict by provoking the rebels into further attacks and imbuing them with a renewed sense of purpose.

Another Ranger squad led by the more disciplined John S. "Rip" Ford made a better showing, defeating the Cortinistas at Rio Grande City in late December and La Bolsa in early February.[42] Ford's men then crossed the Rio Grande and by March 1860 had driven Cortina's "foreign horde" away from the border and deep into the interior of Mexico.[43] Such actions met with the approval of Anglo-Texans such as Brownsville mayor Stephen Powers, who several months before had urged the governor to pursue a strategy of "pursuing [the Cortinistas] & hunting them down like wild beasts."[44] (These white perceptions of Mexicans as savages proved useful in justifying their violent subjugation, just as they facilitated Ranger-led Indian removal efforts in the 1870s.) While this campaign effectively ended the war, Anglo losses were staggering: before their retreat, the Cortinistas had depopulated the area, disrupted trade for 240 miles along the Rio Grande from Laredo to Brownsville, and razed virtually all property belonging to whites with damage estimates exceeding $330,000.[45]

The events of 1859–60 terrified white Texans. Major Samuel P. Heintzelman, who commanded U.S. Army troops in the area, captured the popular sentiment of valley Anglos in a report submitted to Congress. He wrote: "It is dangerous for Americans to settle near their boundary. . . . The industrious, enterprising, active race on one side cannot exist in such close proximity with the idle and vicious on the other without frequent collisions."[46] With the Cortina War, whites sensed for the first time since their occupation of the region both their profound vulnerability and the depth of Mexican frustration with their dispossession by the newcomers. Compounding white fears was the participation in the rebellion by a number of

Mexicans from the south bank of the Rio Grande, many of whom considered the river an artificial border separating them capriciously from their family and friends on the American side. Anglo-Texans in the trans-Nueces, on the other hand, felt their own isolation acutely: Brownsville was located more than 150 miles away from Corpus Christi, and nearly 300 miles from the perceived security of San Antonio.

The Aftermath of Insurrection

The Métis who migrated westward into the Canadian interior after the resistance of 1869–70 established permanent communities, many of them located along the banks of the Saskatchewan and Qu'Appelle rivers in the central portion of the North-West Territories, in what is now present-day Saskatchewan. Once resettled, groups of emigrants sought to maintain the largely communal existence they had enjoyed in Manitoba before the late 1860s and to preserve their French and Catholic heritage. They were quite mindful, however, of the disappointments at Red River stemming from their uncertain land tenure, and thus they enlisted the support of their parish priests for help in petitioning Ottawa to survey and recognize their new claims, which in the meantime they occupied as squatters.[47] In September 1874 one Métis community wrote to Alexander Morris, lieutenant governor of the North-West Territories, to request "that the Government allow to the half-breeds the right of keeping the lands which they have taken or which they may take along the River Qu'Appelle." This entreaty was in addition to their pleas for hunting and fishing privileges in the same vicinity, as well as protection for the settlement's Catholic mission.[48]

Morris's reply captures the complexity of federal policy toward Métis lands in the North-West and offers a context for the ensuing frustrations of the Métis. The lieutenant governor explained that while he was confident that the Dominion would protect and recognize Métis lands already under cultivation in the North-West—"because it has always been the custom to regard the rights of actual possessors of the land"—he could offer no definite assurances in the matter. He was more resolute on the question of future claims, however, noting that Ottawa planned to sequester much of the remaining area for First Nations reserves and white homesteads, making such tracts largely unavailable to the Métis. If this message seemed ambiguous, the lieutenant governor left little doubt as to who would serve as the final arbiter, stating politely but firmly, "It is the wish of the Government to establish its authority everywhere in these vast territories of the Queen." He went on to explain that Ottawa was unlikely to grant legislative powers to "such small communities as the half-breeds and others in these remote territories."[49]

The mixed signals offered by federal officials about the security of Métis lands in the North-West were the product of competing, even contradictory, goals. On the one hand, government authorities—some of them sympathetic to the predicament of the Métis—wanted to alleviate their fears of dispossession in order to discourage them from resuming a semi-itinerant existence and also to prevent them from allying with bands of First Nations peoples.[50] On the other hand, many officials firmly believed that the realization of the region's full economic potential hinged on the influx of Eurocanadian farmers, which in turn was thought to depend upon uniform survey practices that emphasized individual property rights. Métis enclaves marked no small obstacle to these plans, not only because they were insular, communal, and irregularly plotted, but also because they were located in fertile river valleys, some of the best lands in the North-West. Such settlements could serve also as an incubator for political resistance.

In the end, Ottawa failed to meet the requests of the Métis concerning survey and title, for reasons that are the subject of intense historical debate. Some scholars have insisted that the Conservative government of Prime Minister John A. Macdonald (which had returned to power in 1878 after defeating Alexander Mackenzie's Liberal Party) was too preoccupied with implementing the National Policy to respond. Others have seen in Ottawa's inaction a deliberate plan to incite the Métis to violence for possible political gain. Whatever the case, in this climate of growing uncertainty a number of anxious Métis—joined sometimes by Eurocanadian squatters—pleaded with officials for redress. One such group explained in an 1878 petition that "many disputes and disagreements are now arising among the settlers, concerning alleged encroachments upon each other's boundaries," adding ominously that conflicts were "certain to increase in number and bitterness with the increase of settlement."[51]

Though stated as a concern rather than a threat, pronouncements of this nature made Ottawa uneasy by raising the specter of further armed resistance by the Métis. If successful, such a challenge to the authority of the Dominion could alienate the land base of the North-West, thus delaying or endangering the peopling of the region with Eurocanadian farmers. Fur-thermore, officials worried that civil unrest in lands near the international border might provide the U.S. government with ample pretext to annex the region on grounds of national security. Given the events of 1869–70, such anxieties found a wide audience, even if at that moment the Black-foot and Cree seemed to pose more immediate and cumbersome obstacles to the incorporation of the area. Just as they had done with regard to the First Nations, federal officials now enlisted the help of the Mounted Police, charging them with preventing Métis opposition to Canadian policies and, in the process, securing the lands of the North-West for private ownership and individual settlement.

§

In some respects, the circumstances facing Mexicans in South Texas after the Cortina War mirrored those confronted by the Métis in the aftermath of the Red River Resistance, since both groups experienced intensifying levels of white prejudice and distrust in the wake of their insurgencies, as well as continued displacement by Anglo newcomers. However, other aspects of the conflicts' outcomes were different, and in some cases even paradoxi-cal. For instance, though the Métis won a seemingly meaningful victory with the passage of the Manitoba Act, Ottawa's failure (or unwillingness) to implement all of its provisions caused many Métis to abandon their home-land in favor of settlements in the North-West Territories. The Cortina War, by contrast, produced no legislative triumph, and yet the overwhelming majority of Tejanos opted to remain in South Texas instead of crossing the Rio Grande into Mexico, where many had family and friends. While a host of factors may explain the high degree of Mexican persistence in the trans-Nueces after 1860, their desire to protect another contested resource—cat-tle—likely figured in their decision to remain.

As whites slowly made their way back to the Rio Grande Valley after the Cortina War and reassumed control of the lands of South Texas, they de-veloped plans to turn a profit from their expansive real estate holdings by raising and selling cattle. Although Anglo-Texan ranching began earlier in the century, the Civil War had prevented cattle drives and thus bottled up a population of Mexican longhorns that had reached an estimated five mil-lion by 1866. Ranchers returning from Civil War battlefields thus searched their pastures, gathering as many animals as possible to claim as their own.[52]

While this practice helped some Texans build vast herds, such acquisitions could not always offset the losses incurred by livestock raids, which became more brazen after the war. When Richard King and Mifflin Kenedy began to count stock in 1866 in order to dissolve their famed partnership, they could account for less than one-third of their estimated 167,000 cattle, charging that the rest—more than 100,000 head—had been driven off by thieves.[53]

Anglos blamed the thefts on Mexicans from both sides of the Rio Grande. Writing in his 1885 memoirs, Ranger Rip Ford recalled that after the Civil War "bad Mexicans who had been engaged with Cortina crossed into Texas and began depredating upon our people. They murdered men, robbed ranches, and were guilty of many cruel and atrocious acts."[54] To a certain extent, the old Ranger was correct; Mexicans had indeed raided Anglo ranches in South Texas, and in the process had no doubt killed a number of white stockmen. In one of the more notorious incidents, Mexican raiders had attacked Anglo settlements within a few miles of Corpus Christi, and a few weeks later had burned five cattle ranches in the town's vicinity. Moreover, there was plenty of evidence to suggest that Cortina, who had returned to the border region after the Civil War, was behind some of the thefts. Even the faraway New York Times declared in one masthead editorial that the state's Indians did not "do half the damage accomplished by the prince of bandits."[55]

The question of theft, however, was problematic, since many Mexicans in the Nueces Strip (the area between the Nueces River and the Rio Grande) believed that the cattle actually belonged to them and had been illegally appropriated along with their land by Anglo settlers. This, to be sure, was the perspective of John Kelsey, an Anglo who had lived in South Texas since the 1840s. Kelsey took issue with the findings of an 1872 U.S. commission sent to investigate alleged depredations on the frontier, which reported extensive cattle theft perpetrated primarily by Mexicans. While conceding that there were some "bad men" among the area's Tejano population, Kelsey explained that such numbers were "in about the same proportion as in other parts of the United States."[56] He insisted that the report of the U.S. commissioners was greatly exaggerated and reflected the influence of wealthy Rio Grande Valley capitalists (such as King and Kenedy) who were in fact the thieves, because they appropriated cattle from poorer whites and Mexicans alike and then blamed the thefts on Cortina. A committee sent by the Mexican government in 1873 to investigate the border troubles reached a similar conclusion.[57] No less a figure than Walter Prescott Webb, an ardent defender of the Texas cattle barons, conceded that men like King and Kenedy had built their herds at least in part by branding the stock of displaced Mexicans.[58]

Clearly, it was difficult to determine in these cases exactly who was stealing from whom, and one's perspective likely depended on ethnicity: whites suspected Mexicans, and vice versa. What is certain is that by the early 1870s the struggle between Anglo ranchers and Mexican "bandits" (a ubiquitous pejorative seemingly intended to discredit Mexican grievances) was at base a bitter contest over resources. Or, in the words of a group of South Texas whites: "On the Rio Grande the decision will consign the country to Mexican bandits, or secure it to American settlers. It is abandonment on one side, and reconquest on the other. It is a contest between savagery and civilization."[59] As their losses exceeded an estimated $25 million, ranchers begged Austin to deliver them from so-called Mexican depredations.

Mounties, Rangers, and the Dispossession of Mixed-Race Peoples

The Métis played a complex role in the early history of the NWMP, both as prospective members of the new force and as objects of its policing. In the midst of the Red River Resistance in 1869, Prime Minister Macdonald suggested to one official that the proposed constabulary "should be a varied one, of some whites and British and French Half breeds, taking great care that the Half breed element does not predominate." Although Macdonald conceded that the costs associated with such a venture would be enormous, he added that "it would be a pecuniary gain of . . . considerable amounts of money in avoiding the necessity [of a war] by buying off the Insurgents."[60] In this way, Macdonald hoped to mediate the natural tensions between the police and the policed, drawing an explicit comparison to the English experience in India, where (except for officers) military personnel were recruited from the indigenous population.[61] With the worsening of relations between Ottawa and the Métis after the events of 1869–70, Macdonald reconsidered this proposal, though many Métis later served the force as guides and interpreters, none more famously than Jerry Potts.[62]

Potts was born around 1840 at Montana's Fort McKenzie to Namo-Pisi, a Blackfoot woman, and her husband, Andrew R. Potts, a Scotsman who served as a clerk for the American Fur Company (AFC). After the untimely death of his father when Potts was still an infant, he was adopted by an-

10. Jerry Potts (center) with an Indian family and two Mounties, ca. 1880s. Courtesy of Glenbow Archives, NA-3811-2b.

other Scot and thereafter divided much of his time between Fort Benton (a major AFC trading post) and various Blackfoot camps throughout the area. Before the arrival of the Mounties in 1874, Potts worked as a guide and hunter, often serving the whisky traders who exploited the absence of law enforcement on either side of the 49th parallel. He found employment with the NWMP shortly after its advent in the West, signing on for ninety dollars per month to serve as a scout and interpreter. He would assist the constabulary until his death twenty-two years later, becoming something of legend in the North-West for his wilderness skills, his laconic speech, and his prodigious consumption of alcohol. According to one biographer, it is difficult to determine whether Potts's allegiance lay ultimately with white or indigenous people, a clear illustration of the tenuous Métis position between two worlds.[63]

As they did with indigenous women, some Mounties also developed romantic relationships with Métis women. According to one story, the site of the NWMP post at Fort Walsh in the Cypress Hills was chosen because of its proximity to the farm of Edward McKay and his Métis family, which included McKay's five daughters. Two of the women were subsequently married to men in the force, and a third was engaged to a Mountie but committed suicide before the wedding took place.[64] More controversial was NWMP subinspector Cecil Denny's relationship with a part-Peigan woman while he was stationed at Fort Macleod, in what became southern Alberta. Their relationship produced a child, which caused a stir because the woman was married to Mountie Constable Percy Robinson, who promptly brought suit against his colleague for causing his wife to desert him. The charges against Denny were later dismissed, however, when the priest who had performed Robinson's wedding ceremony could not be produced to attest to the sanctity of his marriage to the Métis woman. She then moved across the border to the U.S. Blackfoot reservation in northern Montana, where she raised the child.

There was, of course, much more to early Mountie involvement with the Métis than romantic liaisons and service as guides and mediators, especially as peoples of mixed ancestry abandoned Manitoba—which, as a province, imposed jurisdictional limitations on the NWMP—and reentered federal territory by passing into the North-West. Correspondence and NWMP annual reports suggest that initial Mountie-Métis encounters were guided by Ottawa's intent to manage Métis interactions with native peoples. On the most basic level, federal officials understood that both groups, though mired in a stiff competition for hunting grounds, faced a similar predicament with the disappearance of the bison and the encroachment of Eurocanadians, and hoped to prevent the formation of any sort of antigovernment alliance between them. For instance, in 1876 Inspector J. M. Walsh wrote to Secretary of State R. W. Scott to recommend the prohibition of firearm sales to all nonwhites in the North-West. Walsh explained: "I do not wish to omit the Half Breeds [from this provision] as I do not think they are any more to be entrusted with such arms than the Indians . . . if this great population of Half Breeds and Indians were inclined to be hostile and were armed with this weapon (the Winchester Rifle) it would require more than ten times the number of men to keep them in subjection than is now necessary."[65]

With the natives' mostly favorable reception of the police, fears of a joint Métis–First Nations resistance ebbed, only to be quickly replaced by concerns of Métis interference in the treaty-making process. Specifically, Ottawa worried that the Métis, many of whom maintained close ties with various native bands, might appeal to the Indians to resist land cessions to the government. Such anxiety emerges in an 1875 letter from NWMP commissioner G. A. French to the minister of justice concerning Treaty Four, in which the Crees had "sold" (in the commissioner's words) lands technically belonging to several bands of Bloods. French noted that "if Half breeds should accidentally or willingly make known to the Blackfeet that the Crees had ceded their hunting grounds, it would be productive of much mischief."[66] Similarly, A. G. Irvine, one of French's successors, complained of Métis interference in governmental relations with the First Nations, reporting: "A very discreditable half-breed element influenced the Indians to make exorbitant [treaty] demands, and otherwise conduct themselves in a disorderly manner. Much excitement prevailed, and at times serious trouble seemed impending."[67] The presence of Mountie detachments at future treaty payments served to dissuade such Métis intrusions.

By the end of the 1870s federal officials believed that they had solved Canada's First Nations "problem" by extinguishing native title and establishing a system of reserves. To their thinking, the Numbered Treaties had eliminated native claims while providing their peoples with a protected land base. Not so the Métis, who found themselves in an increasingly awkward position. The majority of Métis in the North-West were neither wards of the state (like the First Nations) nor recognized freeholders (like many of the white newcomers).[68] Instead, they were truly a "people in between," determined to preserve some measure of their autonomy on the lands they had settled in the North-West Territories. On occasion, this resolve led them to oppose the arrival of outsiders. Federal and territorial officials, however, saw in these sporadic acts of independence a clear threat to white migration and called on the Mounties to assert Dominion hegemony.

One such episode occurred in the summer of 1875. That July, Lawrence Clarke, justice of the peace for the North-West Territories, sent a confidential letter to Lieutenant Governor Alexander Morris, explaining that a group of 150 Métis families of French descent had founded a settlement called St. Laurent in the north-central portion of the Saskatchewan District. Clarke added with some concern that "two thirds of this population are connected by intermarriage . . . and have assumed to themselves the right to enact laws, rules and regulations for the government of the colony and adjoining country of a most tyrannical nature." Most alarming to Clarke was the fact that the group, led by Gabriel Dumont, had allegedly accosted a party of French Métis and Country-born hunters in the area and accusing them of trespass, had seized their possessions and ordered them to leave the settlement's vicinity.[69]

The community that so concerned Clarke was in fact merely an attempt by the Métis to devise a local government that would provide for their welfare and cultural survival in the absence of recognized Canadian authority. With the assistance of Father Alexis André, an oblate priest, groups of Métis from settlements scattered along the South Saskatchewan River had met on 10 December 1873 at the church in St. Laurent to form a provisional government. The participants took pains not to antagonize Ottawa, including in their resolution the declaration that "the inhabitants of St. Laurent in no way pretend to constitute for themselves an independent state" and would "submit to the laws of the Dominion" as soon as such a framework was in place.[70]

Not surprisingly, the Métis had turned for leadership to the thirty-six-year-old Dumont, who traced his descent to a Montreal fur trader and his Sarcee wife and who was widely regarded as the finest Métis buffalo hunter. As chief, Dumont presided over the passage of twenty-eight basic laws that governed the settlement, including the levying of taxes, the management of labor relations, and the administration of the buffalo hunt. It was this last item that brought on the conflict related by Clarke, since Dumont and forty men had indeed apprehended the party in question in June 1875 for setting out ten days prior to the date selected for the start of the summer hunting expedition. Dumont, however, punished only the French Métis, who—having been present at St. Laurent in December 1873—were familiar with the rules of the hunt and thus could be expected to have known better.[71]

Morris contacted Major-General Sir Edward Selby Smyth, the commander of the Canadian militia who at that time was touring the prairies with the NWMP, and Selby Smyth suggested that a squad of fifty Mounties travel to the area in order to intercept Dumont and evaluate the disturbance. Led by NWMP commissioner G. A. French, the Mounties effected a hasty eight-day march of 270 miles, arriving at Fort Carlton during the first week of August. Although Selby Smyth and French determined that Clarke's concerns were exaggerated (as they had privately suspected), Selby Smyth nevertheless believed that the symbolism of the NWMP's vigilance was of inestimable value in consolidating Dominion control over the Métis. Explaining that Dumont's actions could lead easily to violence if left unchecked, the major-general noted that "the sudden & unlooked for arrival of the first Governmental armed force that has ever crossed the Saskatchewan will be productive of the best possible effect." Before continuing on his journey, Selby Smyth ordered a small police detachment to remain behind in order to arrest Dumont and bring him before Clarke.[72]

In the end, the law came to Dumont, as NWMP inspector Leif Crozier accompanied Clarke to St. Laurent, where the Métis leader made a tacit agreement to dissolve the council as a formal body in exchange for reserving the right to enforce traditional hunting laws.[73] Writing from Saskatchewan, Commissioner French informed the minister of justice that "there is no reason for alarm," explaining that the supposedly "treasonous" organization was in fact just another hunting party that had established a set of rules and regulations in order to manage the bison chase. After a detailed investigation, French effectively vindicated the viewpoint of the Métis, writing that "on the prairie such regulations are absolutely indispensable and invariably enforced in all parts of the North-West," and thus urged the government to take no further action against Dumont. French also noted that such "infractions" by the Métis stemmed from their ignorance of Canadian law, rather than any malicious intent.[74]

Notwithstanding small victories such as these, the bleak situation that faced the Métis peoples of Saskatchewan in the 1870s only deteriorated during the early years of the following decade. By this time the bison had all but disappeared from Canada. The territorial government had also vanished, moving south from Battleford to the more centrally located Regina and taking with it many of the odd jobs performed by the Métis for extra income.[75] Furthermore, Ottawa had decided that it would provide only limited assistance to Métis families attempting to increase their agricultural production, compounding their fears of starvation. Most importantly, steamboats and the expanding rail network of the Dominion had cut deeply into Métis freighting operations and facilitated the arrival of still more settlers from eastern Canada and Europe. This last development exacerbated longstanding Métis fears about their uncertain land tenure.

They had ample cause for concern. Ottawa had finally taken decisive action with respect to land surveys, declaring that the grid system would prevail in the North-West and that federal and territorial officials would no longer consider petitions requesting approval of the traditional oblong lots favored by the Métis.[76] This led the priest at St. Louis de Langevin, near Prince Albert, to write a spirited letter on behalf of his parishioners. Complaining that the survey's "inflexible limits, right lines and parallels, will traverse fields, pass through houses, [and] cut off farm houses from the fields connected with them," he declared angrily, "What serious hardships, what deplorable results must flow from all this!"[77] No less vexing to the Métis was the government's announcement of its plans to charge two dollars per acre for every odd section of surveyed land in the North-West, vacant or otherwise. As one community wrote in a letter to the minister of the interior, "We are poor people and cannot pay for our land without utter ruin," adding that they could hardly bear to lose their farms to strangers whose only qualification was their willingness to meet Ottawa's price.[78]

Father Alexis André, the Catholic priest who had advised Dumont and the other Métis at St. Laurent as they drew up their provisional government in 1873, sent his own complaint to the government. He explained that because of federal inaction, settlers in his district in north-central Saskatchewan had been unable to file any claims on their property, despite the proximity of a land office and the fact that the territory had been fully surveyed more than two years before. To illustrate the gravity of the situation, he related his own personal frustration with Ottawa's lackadaisical approach, which involved a 200-acre tract of land that he had fenced (at his own expense). Although Father André had occupied the land for seven years and the property had always been recognized as the Catholic mission, a settler by the last name of Kelly had "jumped his claim," declared the property his own, and—ignoring the priest's remonstrations—promptly erected the frame of a house. Noting that this was not the only such occurrence in his district, Father André urged Ottawa to intervene, warning that "if not promptly attended to, things may become grave and serious."[79]

The Mounted Police were well aware of this simmering Métis resentment, and members of the force kept a close watch on developments among their communities in the North-West, especially in the summer of 1884 when the situation appeared to become more volatile. That spring, Lawrence Clarke reported once again on some disturbing developments at St. Laurent, although these were of a more alarming variety than Dumont's alleged violations of a decade before. Clarke explained that a number of French and English Métis had proclaimed their refusal "to recognize the right of the government to the North West Territories," and had sent a delegation to Montana in hopes of luring the exiled Louis Riel back to Canada. Clarke noted their hard economic circumstances—including the disappearance of the bison and diminishing freighting opportunities—and insisted that these woes, and not their grievances against the government, were the root cause of their agitation. Concerned that their leader's return could galvanize the Métis community against Ottawa, he urged the NWMP to investigate.[80]

Mountie patrols in the North-West quickly determined that Riel had indeed crossed the border, arriving with his family in the central Saskatchewan town of Duck Lake, near Prince Albert, in early July. Of greater concern to Ottawa was the fact that Riel had conferred with a handful of First Nations leaders, raising the possibility of a coordinated resistance launched by both native and Métis peoples. Superintendent Leif Crozier voiced what must have been the government's worst fears three weeks later, explaining that "these constant 'excitements' must have a most injurious effect upon the country and among those effects, not the least a sense of insecurity among settlers."[81] In an attempt to reassure Eurocanadian farmers of federal control in the North-West, Comptroller Fred White arranged for an increased Mountie presence in Saskatchewan, securing the use of the HBC buildings at Fort Carlton to accommodate the extra policemen during the fall and winter. Meanwhile, Commissioner A. G. Irvine organized an extensive surveillance network to report on any suspicious activities by Riel, natives, or the Métis.[82]

Reports arrived from all corners of Saskatchewan. Sergeant W. A. Brooks reported from Prince Albert that Riel had abandoned the idea of returning to his home in Montana, declaring instead his intent to remain among the Métis in the North-West.[83] Two hundred miles away, near the border with Alberta, Inspector Francis Dickens (son of the English novelist) wrote from Fort Pitt with an assessment of the military preparedness of the First Nations and Métis in his area, estimating their numbers and describing the size and quality of their arsenal.[84] Sergeant G. H. Keenan, stationed in central Saskatchewan at Fort Carlton, noted the uneasy reaction of the community there to the arrival of a Mountie detachment sent to keep watch. Common to many reports was the notion that the Métis had become desperate, with one officer explaining, "There is no doubt but that everyone is hard up, and they thought they must do something to draw [the government's] attention."[85]

The culmination of these grievances was the North-West Rebellion, one of the defining events of nineteenth-century Canadian history and certainly one of the most studied.[86] The conflict erupted on 26 March 1885 when Superintendent Crozier, leading a combined force of 99 volunteers and Mounted Police, attempted to secure a cache of supplies and ammunition abandoned by a white merchant at Duck Lake. Learning of this plan, Dumont led 300 Métis to intercept the police a few miles short of their objective. At first sight of the Mounties, Isidore Dumont, Gabriel's brother, and an elderly native chief named Aseeweyin rode out under a white flag to speak with Joseph McKay, the NWMP's Country-born interpreter. Accounts differ concerning the firing of the first round, but most seem to agree that McKay shot Aseeweyin when the chief attempted to disarm him, which provoked a volley from Crozier's troops.[87] Whatever the case, after a short but decisive skirmish in which he lost twelve men, Crozier gathered the survivors and retreated hastily to Fort Carlton, which the police abandoned later that evening after accidentally setting fire to the post.

Ottawa responded with a massive military call-up, dispatching militiamen by rail to the North-West. The militiamen were joined in the field by concerned white residents of the area to make up a force of some 8,000 men. Early clashes, such as the 24 April battle at Fish Creek—in which General Sir Frederick Middleton led as many as 900 troops against 250 Métis—were indecisive, with both sides sustaining limited numbers of casualties. In the absence of a major military victory, however, the militiamen—inspired perhaps by Middleton's open contempt for the Métis—took symbolic action against the enemy, incinerating a collection of farm buildings abandoned by the outnumbered defenders. Middleton's attack on the rebel stronghold at Batoche two weeks later was much more successful, as the Canadians wore down the supplies and defenses of the Métis, who used make-shift ammunition fashioned from duck shot and melted nails.[88] Their surrender on 12 May 1885 effectively ended the rebellion, although the last of several native bands that had joined the Métis did not lay down their arms for another six weeks.[89]

Noting the relatively small number of combatants involved and a combined death total of less than a hundred people, one scholar has argued that the North-West Rebellion was but a "trifling affair" on a world scale.[90] This perspective, however, overlooks a handful of key considerations. First, the capture and incarceration of most of the rebel leaders, and the execution of Riel that November (despite appeals for clemency from U.S. president Grover Cleveland), demonstrated conclusively Ottawa's intent to resolve with force rather than politics future challenges to Eurocanadian hegemony. Moreover, the decisive white triumph over the Métis led inevitably to feelings of superiority for the victors and resentment among the defeated, a legacy that has colored interactions between the two groups up to the present day.[91] Most significantly, the crushing of the insurrection ended once and for all any vestige of Métis control on the prairies; never again would they constitute a threat to Ottawa's plans for the North-West.

Similarly, the role played by the Mounted Police in the conflict is the subject of some disagreement. One scholar has suggested that the police behaved in a reckless and cowardly fashion, while another has insisted that their contributions were so insignificant that the events should not be emphasized in the history of the force.[92] The second of these two viewpoints is especially problematic. Mountie reconnaissance, after all, had furnished Ottawa with extensive reports on Métis dissatisfactions and preparations for war, which led to sweeping police mobilization in the countryside. Furthermore, it was an action of the Mounted Police—their attempt to protect the arms and supplies at Hillyard Mitchell's store—that initiated the fighting, which was hardly the only campaign in which they participated. Ultimately, the Mounted Police performed exactly the duty for which they had been created: they "protected the white population until the militia put down the Rebellion."[93]

This is to say nothing of the role that the police had played in bringing about the conditions that led to the conflagration. To be sure, the Métis took up arms against Ottawa because of their extreme dissatisfaction with the federal government, especially its refusal to guarantee the recognition and protection of their lands. However, as the most important and visible federal representatives in the West, the Mounties also served to channel Métis resentment. The force had established outposts throughout the 1870s in the heart of Métis communities in the North-West in order to demonstrate Dominion sovereignty in the region. Their presence also thwarted Métis attempts to defend their shrinking hunting grounds from native incursions and the encroachment of Anglo settlers. Of greatest concern was the protection afforded by the NWMP for teams of surveyors, whose mission in the North-West, particularly after 1880, was to impose physical boundaries that the Métis believed posed a threat to the survival of their communities. These police actions, intended to slacken the Métis hold on the lands of the North-West, thus contributed to the very conflict that finally, and decisively, broke their grasp.

§

Just as Ottawa enlisted the NWMP to monitor and control the Métis, Texas officials turned to the Rangers in hopes of ending the cattle raids allegedly perpetrated by Mexicans and also to reassure anxious whites that South

Texas was safe for Anglo settlement and commerce. And just as the Texas legislature had created the Frontier Battalion in 1874, so too did the lawmakers provide for the Special Force of Rangers, a single company charged with bringing order to the Nueces Strip.[94] The decision was an easy one for Austin, since the U.S. soldiers in the state had no authority to make arrests and were thus concerned with Mexicans only to the extent that they posed a threat of armed invasion on the scale of the Cortina insurgency. Moreover, given the constant frictions along the border, officials in Washington were hesitant to risk an engagement using federal troops that might send an overly aggressive message to their counterparts in Mexico City. Meanwhile, local sheriffs along the Rio Grande had no power outside their small jurisdictions and were heavily occupied in their own localities, anyway. The Rangers, who had achieved their greatest success (and notoriety for brutality) as a unit during the Mexican-American War, once again seemed the obvious choice to shore up Anglo gains along the border.[95]

The Special Force was led by Captain Leander H. McNelly, a Virginian who had come to Texas in 1860 and later served with Confederate forces in Texas, New Mexico, and Louisiana during the Civil War. After the end of the conflict in 1865, McNelly joined the Reconstruction-era State Police, a short-lived force that was hated by many white Texans for its efforts to protect African Americans from violence. Short and weakened by tuberculosis, McNelly had nevertheless earned a reputation as a ruthless solider, and he brought this quality to the Ranger company under his command.[96] From the beginning the preferred tactics of the Special Force in dealing with the Mexican population of South Texas featured intimidation, torture, and the liberal use of violence. As George Durham, who served in the unit, later recalled: McNelly "said in so many words that all he wanted was dead bandits. He didn't want prisoners. He didn't want reports. . . . Captain said reports weren't what bandits needed. He held that a well-placed bullet from a Sharps did more for law enforcement than a hundred reports."[97]

McNelly's grim directive suggests the powerful differences between the interventions of the Rangers and Mounties into the affairs of mixed-race peoples at their respective end of the Plains. In Canada, the central mission of the NWMP regarding the Métis (at least until the events of 1885) was essentially a nonviolent one and consisted primarily of "showing the flag," or in other words, demonstrating to peoples of mixed ancestry Ottawa's unquestioned sovereignty in the North-West.[98] This the police achieved by

11. Ranger captain Leander H. McNelly. Courtesy of Western History Collections, University of Oklahoma Libraries.

establishing a conspicuous presence throughout the territories, marked by the construction of permanent forts and outposts, visits (sometimes unannounced) to Métis communities, and attendance at events such as native treaty signings. To be sure, the threat of force lay behind many of these gestures, since policemen were outfitted with firearms, and some detachments even lugged with them pieces of field artillery. Still, it seems clear that the NWMP sought to exert Dominion control on the prairies without unduly antagonizing its Métis inhabitants, who were understandably wary of federal pretensions.

The Rangers, on the other hand, applied no such caution to their intervention in the chaos roiling the Nueces Strip; rather, they approached the struggle with a clear determination to exterminate suspected Mexican cattle thieves. Several factors may explain their unchecked aggression. For one thing, perhaps even more than most Anglo-Texans, the Rangers harbored deep anti-Mexican prejudice, which dated back to their involvement in the Mexican-American War. During that conflict, Ranger companies behaved with such ferocity against Mexican soldiers and citizens alike that they became known as *los diablos Tejanos*, the Texan devils. So objectionable was their conduct that U.S. Army general Zachary Taylor ordered that no more troops from Texas be sent to Mexico, and the Rangers' experience in the Cortina War a decade later only hardened their animosity toward Mexicans. Moreover, unlike the Mounties, the Rangers relied less frequently upon people of mixed race to serve as guides and interpreters (with notable exceptions), and there is little evidence to suggest that they established romantic liaisons with Mexican women. In Canada, both types of relationships—despite the obvious inequality between the parties—likely softened the impact of the police presence; such was not the case in Texas.

Two Ranger engagements with Mexicans in 1875 illustrate the schism between their tactics and those of the Mounties, and prove George Durham's point about McNelly's strategy. In the first of these, McNelly's squad encountered a party of Mexicans on the Palo Alto Prairie—about ten miles north of the Rio Grande—commanding a large herd of cattle, allegedly stolen from white ranchers. The Rangers attacked them without warning, with McNelly later explaining to the adjutant general: "Not one [of the Mexicans] escaped out of the twelve that were driving the cattle. They were *all* killed." Their bodies—along with those of three other Mexicans dispatched earlier in the skirmish—were collected and displayed in the plaza at Brownsville as a warning to other would-be rustlers.[99] The Rangers recovered 216 head of cattle, many bearing Texas brands, and returned them to their owners.[100] For their part, Mexicans in the valley were incensed by the slaughter, particularly the attention lavished by Brownsville's white residents on L. B. "Berry" Smith, the one Ranger who had died in the engagement. Margarito Vetencourt, a friend of one of the dead Mexicans, insisted that the group "had been unjustly killed and fouly [*sic*] murdered . . . by the State troops."[101]

Five months later, McNelly learned that Mexicans had crossed approximately 250 cattle to the south bank of the Rio Grande—again, all of them supposedly stolen from Texas ranchers. Against the advice of Major D. R. Clendenin, the senior U.S. Army official at nearby Ringgold Barracks, Mc-

Nelly traversed the river with a squad of thirty men on the night of 18 November.[102] Acting on a tip, at dawn the following day the Rangers attacked the Las Cachuttas ranch, cutting down at least five men inside the compound.[103] It was only after the skirmish that McNelly learned he had charged the wrong stockade; his intended target, the Cuevas ranch, was a half mile farther along the trail.[104] Rounding up his men, McNelly quickly made his way to Las Cuevas, but the Rangers had lost the element of surprise, and a party of 250 Mexican ranch hands chased the Texans for several miles to the bank of the river. There, instead of crossing back into the United States, McNelly ordered his men to dig in and prepare to fight the Mexicans—who outnumbered them nearly ten to one—on their own soil. Surveying the situation from the north side of the Rio Grande and fearing that the Rangers would be wiped out, a U.S. Army detachment crossed over to cover the Rangers with a Gatling gun, enraging officials on both sides of the river.[105] Incredibly, McNelly was able to bluff the Mexicans into returning sixty-five head of cattle, which he delivered personally to Richard King.[106]

Such escapades served well the Anglo ranchers of the Nueces Strip, none more than King, who along with several prominent South Texans outfitted McNelly's squad and lavished them with gifts and supplies. For instance, several weeks before the June fight at Palo Alto, McNelly wrote the adjutant general from King's massive Santa Gertrudis ranch, explaining that he could not yet move against the Mexican raiders as he was "waiting for some horses kindly furnished by the stock men of this section."[107] Before the November invasion of Mexico, members of the Special Force stayed as guests at the ranch, and when they returned driving cattle marked with the King brand, the grateful owner wrote McNelly a $1,500 check, from which the captain distributed $50 to each man.[108] King then threw a banquet for the squad and had his daughters bake them a cake with the following decoration: "Compliments of the two Miss Kings to the McNelly Rangers." As a final gesture of appreciation—and one certain to reap future rewards—King presented the company a few weeks later with "thirty spanking new 44–40 Winchester repeater carbines and several thousand rounds of shells."[109]

Armed engagements with alleged Mexican thieves were not the only means employed by the Special Force to tame the Nueces Strip and safeguard cattle for Anglos. The Rangers directed their efforts against the larger Mexican community, becoming, in effect, an occupation force in post–Civil War South Texas, aiming to crush Mexican resistance to white hegemony.

12. Ranger camp on the grounds of the King Ranch near Alice, Texas, ca. 1890s. Courtesy of the Texas Ranger Hall of Fame and Museum, Waco TX.

Facilitating this duty was their reflexive view of Mexicans as criminals. As Webb once explained to a colleague at the University of Texas, "to a Ranger [in this period], anyone with an olive skin, black eyes, black hair and a hint of a Mexican accent must be guilty of something illegal, presumably murder, robbery, cattle-rustling, or invasion."[110] Such beliefs led to practices like Captain Warren Wallace's system of mandatory registration in Nueces and Duval counties, which even he conceded was illegal. Hoping to "fix the habitation" of all Mexicans in the region in order to monitor the movements of suspected cattle thieves, Wallace and a small detachment of Rangers visited every ranch in the area in the summer of 1874, recording the names of all Mexican residents. Mexicans, however, lodged so many complaints of "unlawful and outrageous conduct" against Wallace and his men that officials in Austin soon disbanded the company.[111]

Still more effective perhaps in lessening the Mexican hold on South Texas cattle were the organized campaigns of intimidation launched by the police. As Ranger N. A. Jennings explained, members of the force in the 1870s would visit border towns in order "to carry out a set policy of terrorizing the residents at every opportunity," believing that "the more we were feared, the easier would be our work of subduing the Mexican raiders." Jennings noted: "If we could find a *fandango*, or Mexican dance, going on, we would enter the dancing-hall and break up the festivities by shooting out the lights. This would naturally result in much confusion and, added to the reports of our revolvers, would be the shrill screaming of women and the cursing of angry

Mexicans." These operations had the desired effect, for "in a few weeks we were feared as men were never before feared on that border."[112]

Ranger abuses not only turned the Mexican community against them but also drew the attention and reprobation of federal observers. One congressional inquiry of the late 1870s into the troubles along the Texas frontier determined that the Rangers regularly used torture in gathering intelligence or coercing confessions from suspected Mexican brigands. As one military officer stationed in South Texas explained, "The State troops . . . resorted to means of extorting information, which, if it had been adopted by the United States troops, would have led them into serious troubles, probably a trial before the courts."[113] The deponent may well have been referring to the practice of Jesús Sandoval (called "Casuse" by the Rangers), one of McNelly's men, who would sometimes slip a noose around the throat of a mounted suspect to facilitate interrogation. When he was finished with the "bandit," Sandoval would slap the horse so that it jumped away, breaking the suspect's neck instantly. As to why Sandoval would participate in the torture and assassination of his own countrymen, Ranger William Callicott explained that Sandoval had once killed four men from the south side of the river who were attempting to steal his cattle, thus earning the enmity of Mexicans.[114] He found an eager employer in McNelly, who enlisted Sandoval as a Ranger private in 1875 and thereafter relied upon his knowledge of the land and people of the Rio Grande Valley.[115]

In the final analysis, the Special Force was highly successful in meeting its objective: namely, the eradication of livestock theft by Mexicans and the defense of expanding Anglo cattle interests in South Texas.[116] One historian of the Rio Grande Valley has argued that "probably the most effective single factor [in ending the cattle raids] was the appearance on the frontier of the Texas Rangers under Captain L. H. McNelly in the summer of 1875."[117] Statistics from the period lend credence to this claim. Whereas ranchers in the trans-Nueces claimed losses of an estimated 900,000 head of livestock between 1869 and 1874, the Texas adjutant general—who reported such figures assiduously in order to increase appropriations for the Rangers—listed only 1,160 cows stolen between September 1873 and 1875 and a negligible number thereafter.[118] While men like Richard King benefited from this Ranger assistance, South Texas Mexicans paid a heavy price. Looking back on his service under McNelly, George Durham wrote: "I'd come to Texas to get me a piece of ground, maybe a few head of stock, build me a house. But what I'd really done was to hire out at thirty-three dollars a month to kill people. That's all I'd done. Kill people."[119]

South Texas was not the only section of the state to experience a conflict over resources between Anglos and Mexicans in the period after the Civil War. More than a thousand miles upriver from Brownsville, near the point where Texas, New Mexico, and the Mexican state of Chihuahua all intersect, conditions in and around the town of El Paso bore a striking resemblance to those of the Lower Rio Grande Valley. Only about 80 Anglos lived in the area, amid a Mexican population of nearly 12,000 divided by the river. As explained by one observer, the Mexicans on the U.S. side of the Rio Grande were "bound to those of the other by more than the ordinary obligations of race and hospitality," including generations of intermarriage and a shared Catholic faith.[120] As in South Texas, a handful of whites had assumed control of the area's commercial operations, while the Mexicans earned their living primarily by farming, and on occasion by bartering salt in Mexico that they had collected from a group of saline lakes about a hundred miles northeast of El Paso.

Mexicans had enjoyed communal use of the Guadalupe Salt Lakes for years, a principle first established by Spain in 1656 and later upheld by the Mexican government in 1824. Following the Mexican-American War, however, area residents were unable to secure continued public access to the deposits, in part because of the disappearance of the titles from the archives in Paso del Norte (the Mexican town just across the river) during the 1846–47 military expedition of Colonel A. W. Doniphan.[121] The consequences of this Mexican legal impotence emerged with the 1863 completion of a road to the lakes, when Anglos quickly sought to acquire the territory as private property. One of them, the legendary San Antonio cattleman Sam Maverick, managed to secure a section of the lakes just three years later, although Mexicans continued to use the unclaimed area without much trouble until the summer of 1877.[122]

The El Paso "Salt War" began that summer when Charles Howard, a Missouri lawyer who had lived in the region for five years, acquired title to the remainder of the lakes and announced that anyone wishing to use them would have to pay a fee.[123] Incensed by this assault on their common rights, a group of Mexicans—spurred by Louis Cardis and Antonio Borajo, a state legislator and parish priest, respectively—vowed to defy him. When two Mexican men declared their intentions a few weeks later to visit the lakes and haul away cartloads of salt, Howard had them brought before the county judge at San Elizario, a small town thirty miles downriver from El Paso. This led a group of perhaps 400 Mexicans to apprehend Howard and three other whites, forcing the would-be entrepreneur to sign a bond of $12,000, by which he promised to relinquish his claim to the lakes and leave the county for good. Upon his release Howard fled to Mesilla, New Mexico, but he returned to El Paso shortly thereafter in the company of twenty U.S. soldiers, and on 10 October he shot and killed Cardis in a local store.[124]

It was at this point that Austin intervened, and Major John B. Jones of the Rangers arrived in El Paso on 6 November, warned by the local sheriff to be wary, as "these greasers are very treacherous."[125] Once in West Texas, Jones made a series of decisions that in the eyes of area Mexicans placed the Rangers squarely on the side of Howard and his supporters. In the first place, Jones resisted the requests of local leaders to include Mexicans in the makeshift Ranger detachment he assembled. As the major explained afterward to one reporter, "I determined not to enlist Mexicans, as I could not trust them."[126] Instead, he turned to John B. Tays, the brother of the local Episcopal priest, commissioning him as a second lieutenant and sending off to Austin for ten Winchester rifles, twelve pistols, and cartridges for both.[127] More importantly, the major—who had promised outraged citizens that he would arrest Howard for murder—instead took him before the justice of the peace, who released Howard on $4,000 bail and ordered him to stand trial the next spring.[128] Believing that all was under control, Jones returned to Austin, and Howard left once again for Mesilla.

The inequity of the situation rankled area Mexicans, who grew even more upset in early December when Howard returned once again to San Elizario—accompanied by a squad of Rangers—to challenge a caravan that had started for the salt lakes with sixteen carts. This proved to be the tipping point for the aggrieved Mexicans, and on 12 December a group of more than 500 (from both sides of the river) killed Charles Ellis, a local merchant and Howard associate, and then surrounded the barracks where Howard and the Rangers had taken shelter. Thus began a siege that lasted until 17 December, when the police surrendered (becoming the only Ranger squad ever to do so) to the Mexicans, who were led by a man named Chico Barela. Despite Barela's repeated assurances that no one would be harmed, the angry crowd nevertheless executed Howard and two others—local merchant John Atkinson and Ranger sergeant John McBride—by firing squad, and then mutilated their corpses.

With the arrival of U.S. troops between 20 and 25 December, the insurrection came to an end, but not before most of those involved had crossed the river into Chihuahua to escape arrest and prosecution.[129] Meanwhile, the Rangers, who had been joined by thirty white volunteers from Silver City, New Mexico, fanned out to patrol El Paso and the surrounding area. This motley squad, roundly condemned in most histories of the force, then perpetrated a number of abuses against Mexicans in the region. In the first instance, two Mexicans who had been pressed into service to bury the dead whites were themselves shot and left in the road near the town of Ysleta. Another suspected member of the crowd was killed at his home in Socorro, allegedly while resisting arrest. Such actions earned the condemnation of U.S. Army colonel Edward Hatch, who blamed the state troops and "denounced this inhumanity in no measured terms." Still, this did not put an immediate end to "the rapes, homicides, and other crimes of which the people justly complained," which continued for several weeks.[130]

If the men who committed these excesses were Rangers in name only— and not the equals of "McNelly's boys," as some have argued—their tactics and the net effects of their involvement in the conflict mirrored those of their counterparts in the Nueces Strip. While no doubt motivated by a desire to avenge the murders of Ellis, Howard, Atkinson, and McBride, Ranger abuses against Mexicans in El Paso served also to frighten Mexicans into accepting Anglo hegemony in the region, defined in this case by the privatization of a formerly communal resource. This, of course, is to say nothing of their work—as well as that of Major Jones—in protecting Howard's economic interests even after Howard had murdered the unarmed and unsuspecting Cardis. Just as Anglos tightened their grip on the cattle of South Texas, so, too, did El Paso area whites succeed in breaking the Mexican hold on the salt deposits of West Texas: George Zimpleman, Howard's father-in-law, secured the claim after the end of the Salt War. Thereafter, Zimpleman charged a fee for the salt, which the Mexicans paid without protest to his agent, former Ranger sergeant J. D. Ford.[131]

There are striking similarities between the mixed-race groups of Texas and the Canadian West and the dilemmas that each faced in the late nineteenth century. For one thing, Mexicans and Métis were both, in a very real sense, "peoples in between," neither white nor native. Unlike the Indians of the Great Plains, peoples of mixed ancestry established settled communities, just as they were separated from their white countrymen by race and religion and especially their communal and traditional use of resources. Attempts by Mexicans and Métis to defend these assets led each to challenge growing white encroachment. Even the early conflicts between mixed-race peoples and white outsiders bear a powerful resemblance to one another, as young, charismatic leaders (Louis Riel and Juan Cortina) organized groups of confederates in defense of their "sacred" rights to land, liberty, and self-preservation.

The outcome of these contests marked a clear transition from inclusion to exclusion for peoples of mixed race at either end of the Plains. Before the mid-nineteenth century, Mexicans and Métis alike had enjoyed some measure of acceptance in the frontier societies of Texas and the Canadian West, as intermarriage and trade had created spaces (admittedly, near the bottom) for peoples of mixed ancestry in the social hierarchies of these colonial outposts. The Anglo successors to the Spanish and French regimes in North America made no accommodation for the remnants of earlier European empires, who spoke different languages and practiced other religions, and most importantly, pursued less commercially oriented economies. Ultimately, there was no room for them in the ascendant Anglo societies on the Plains, and they were thus denied de facto equal citizenship in Texas and the North-West.

The consequences of their exclusion yielded similar results, for Mexicans and Métis alike experienced a rapid process of proletarianization, conjuring up images of seventeenth- and eighteenth-century Great Britain, when the enclosure of large estates by the English gentry forced smallholders to leave their lands and seek wage work. Driven from their property and deprived of their cattle, many Mexicans became laborers, taking jobs in mining, farming, and railroad construction. Others found work as line riders on white ranches in South Texas, including the King and Kenedy spreads; this marks a bitter irony, given that some Mexican hands probably herded steers and patrolled lands that had once belonged to their families. The choices facing the Métis were no less difficult; those who did not attempt to move beyond the reach of federal authority migrated to the cities of the North-West, such as Winnipeg, Edmonton, and Calgary, where they lived on the fringes of white society. Many of them became wage earners in jobs that—no less than for the Mexicans in Texas—signaled the complete reversal of their social and economic fortunes. In laying track, for instance, the

Métis facilitated the extension of the very machine that had opened their lands to white settlers while rendering obsolete the freighting services they had performed for generations.

Such parallels, however, should not obscure the significant divergences between Mexican and Métis circumstances and the relationships of each group to the expanding state entities that sought to control them. On the most fundamental level, basic historical circumstances had created very different social climates in Texas and the North-West, which in turn shaped the intervention of the police. In Texas, an intense Anglo hatred of Mexicans—born of Southern origins and raised on the struggles of 1836 and 1848—helped to justify Tejano dispossession. The Rangers of the 1870s, many of whom came from states of the former Confederacy, imbibed such racial prejudice, which—when combined with the bitter legacy of the constabulary's involvement in the Mexican and Cortina wars, among other conflicts—created conditions ripe for violence. A similarly corrosive mixture of racial animosity and conflict had fueled the constabulary's effort to exterminate the state's Indian population. Both of these Ranger campaigns against the state's nonwhite groups were characterized by the dehumanization of the enemy through language (Indians thus became "savages" and "red devils," while Mexicans were referred to as "greasers" or "bandits") and the application of astonishing levels of violence.

In the Canadian North-West, on the other hand, there existed no history of racial antagonism comparable to that in Texas, since the fur trade had produced relatively peaceful relations between Europeans and the First Nations peoples with whom they interacted, up to and including intermarriage. To be sure, the advent of the Mounties no doubt complicated matters for indigenous groups, since the police symbolized the newly confederated nation's intent to absorb the region. Furthermore, like their counterparts in Texas, members of the constabulary imported their own prejudices to the region. These beliefs, however, were usually of a more class-based (as opposed to racial) variety.[132] Infused with a chauvinistic perspective based on the tenets of Victorian paternalism, the NWMP approached the Métis much as they had the Blackfoot and the Cree, armed less with abhorrence and suspicion than with a pervasive condescension. This attitude, however, did not prevent a number of Mounties from developing romantic relationships with Métis women, and in some cases taking wives from Métis communities in the North-West. These unions, unequal though they may have been, likely mitigated some of the tensions between the NWMP and peoples of mixed ancestry in the Canadian North-West. There was no such buffer in Texas.

Demographics also conditioned the vastly different responses of the police. The Métis dispersal throughout the North-West during the 1870s and 1880s had diluted their numbers, so that their tiny collectives in present-day Saskatchewan and Alberta were in constant danger of being overrun by white migrants, a concern they brought repeatedly—if unsuccessfully—before the federal government.[133] These thinly spread communities posed an insignificant threat to Eurocanadian settlers; not surprisingly, perhaps, the rare instances of friction between Ottawa and the Métis occurred when peoples of mixed race attempted to establish semiautonomous settlements, first at Red River in 1870 and then in the area around Batoche in 1875 and after. As for violence directly involving the NWMP and the Métis, the only such episode erupted when a Mountie squad tried to enter the embattled settlement at Batoche by force of arms in 1885.

In South Texas, by contrast, Mexicans—though beset on all sides by an aggressively expansionist Anglo minority—retained demographic (if not necessarily political) control well into the twentieth century. The trans-Nueces and especially the area along the Rio Grande thus served as something of a Tejano homeland, albeit one under siege, where a distinctive Mexican culture survived the emergence of a white elite.[134] The relative stability of this region as a Mexican redoubt helps in part to explain the much higher levels of violence associated with the Rangers when compared to the NWMP. Considering that Tejanos far outnumbered Anglos in South Texas, whites turned to the constabulary for assistance in strengthening their tenuous grip on the land and resources of the area. In this context, intimidation became an especially attractive and useful tool for the police: by torturing suspected "bandits" and raking otherwise peaceful assemblies with gunfire, a small force of well-armed men, backed by the power of law, could frighten a more numerous but doubly disadvantaged foe.

Basic geographic considerations no doubt heightened Anglo concern about their control of South Texas and likewise influenced Ranger tactics to subjugate Tejanos. The sheer proximity of Mexico posed a dilemma of enormous significance to whites, for many believed that the social and political loyalties of Mexicans living above the Rio Grande were oriented toward the south, rather than the north. This was a reasonable fear, considering that the Lone Star State was only a few decades removed from Mexican control. Moreover, many Mexicans considered the Rio Grande a thoroughly arbitrary border, for they maintained close ties with family and friends who lived on the other side of the boundary. The problems for whites inherent in this scenario emerged during events such as the El Paso Salt War, when Mexicans from above and below the Rio Grande joined forces to challenge Anglo rule, and then retreated to the south bank in order to escape the reach of U.S. law enforcement.

The nearness of the United States gave authorities in Ottawa cause for their own concerns as they confronted Métis resistance in the North-West, but such anxieties were of a different nature than those prevailing in Austin. To be sure, Canadian officials worried that disgruntled Métis might look to recruit from mixed-race communities in Montana and the Dakota Territory for help in challenging Dominion power on the Plains, just as Mexicans sometimes joined Tejano insurrections like the Cortina War.[135] And such qualms were not far-fetched, considering that Louis Riel and a number of other Métis had taken refuge in mixed-race settlements south of the 49th parallel (which was even more permeable as an international border than the Rio Grande). Of greater concern to Canadian authorities than the prospect of a trans-national Métis resistance, however, was the ever-present threat of U.S. annexation. Unrest among indigenous peoples along the boundary, they feared, could provide Washington with a ready excuse to move into the region and assert its control.[136]

Political calculations of this sort comprised still another level of difference distinguishing the interactions between Mounties and Métis from those involving Rangers and Mexicans. As a federal force, the NWMP carried with it onto the prairies a host of Ottawa's conflicting anxieties and directives, which consequently mediated the behavior of the police. With fresh memories of the 1869–70 insurgency, national authorities clearly hoped to avoid compounding Métis antagonism toward the government, and at any rate did not want to generate negative international publicity attendant to their handling of Canada's indigenous peoples. And yet Ottawa was no less resolved to open the North-West to white settlement, as the events of 1885 made clear. These goals were difficult—if not impossible—to reconcile, and the Mounties were caught squarely between the competition of these aspirations. In the end, they aimed to preserve the status quo, namely, peaceful and unopposed Eurocanadian migration.

The Rangers, on the other hand, enjoyed far more leeway as a state force. For one thing, Austin received considerably less assistance from Washington than it had in opposing Indian incursions into Texas. Federal authorities, it seems, considered Kiowas and Comanches part of a larger native "problem" afflicting much of the U.S. West and responded in kind with military force. Mexicans of South and West Texas, meanwhile, appeared to pose more of a local concern. Even had Washington decided to intervene, however, the fact that many Mexicans in Texas were residents of the state imposed severe jurisdictional limitations on the army. This meant, in effect, that the Rangers answered to Austin alone, which was highly responsive to the needs of its Anglo citizens. And because the greatest concern facing South Texas whites in the mid-1870s was not westward migration but rather the defense of their cattle, the Rangers likely saw the need to adopt more aggressive tactics suited to the protection of a movable, and thus more vulnerable, resource.

Such differences continued to shape the interactions between the constabularies and the mixed-race groups they policed as the nineteenth century waned. In Canada, despite the violence of 1885 and the attendant Eurocanadian suspicions it generated, the central postwar duty of the NWMP with respect to the Métis was essentially a benevolent one: the distribution of rations to destitute communities. The Métis economy, already threatened by the expansion of the railroad and the influx of new settlers, had been severely disrupted by the conflict. As one NWMP officer in Saskatchewan noted in a typical report from 1888, thirty Métis men had approached him that winter stating "that they were all more or less in a semi-starving condition" and adding that "never in the history of the place has there been so little freighting done." Another Mountie explained in an 1890 letter that accompanied by a priest he had visited various Métis families near Batoche to assess their circumstances. At one home shared by several families, he discovered three or four severely malnutritioned little girls, and explained that "at the sight of the provisions, which I gave them, the two oldest started crying."[137]

Although some police, including Comptroller Fred White, evinced an unmistakable sympathy for the plight of the Métis, there was also a quietly coercive dimension to the relief issued by the Mounties. In order to obtain supplies of beef, coffee, and flour, among other staples, the police required supplicant Métis to perform work around the barracks. For example, in the case of Caroline Peltier, a Métis widow with eight children, Superintendent R. B. Deane instructed a subordinate to "enquire as to the woman's character, and endeavour to get work for her eldest boy and any other able to work."[138] Deane's implication that Peltier's character was untrustworthy is characteristic of a typical gender bias associated by some historians with white racism.[139] Other Métis men seeking assistance were charged with such tasks as cleaning camp buildings and chopping or hauling firewood, menial work that subordinated them to their employers.[140] The intent behind these efforts was to force the Métis, whom many of the police considered lazy and improvident, to adapt to the new economic ethos on the prairies that emphasized thrift and self-sufficiency and above all else the sanctity of private property.

For the Rangers, by contrast, benevolence toward Mexicans was out of the question. Instead, they sustained their anti-Tejano vigilance, especially in South Texas, which remained highly volatile throughout the rest of the nineteenth century and well into the twentieth. In 1891, for instance, they were called into service during another cross-border uprising, this one led by newspaper editor Catarino Garza. Although his revolt differed from the Cortina War—indeed, Garza's Texas-based insurrection had as its goals the overthrow of Mexican president Porfirio Diaz and the restoration of Mexico's 1857 liberal constitution—it nevertheless attracted Mexican followers exasperated by the state's oppressive Anglo regime.[141] While the U.S. Army assumed chief responsibility for securing the border, Austin dispatched a Ranger company to maintain law and order in South Texas, an assignment they likely relished given Garza's harsh editorial treatment several years earlier of one of their own, customs inspector and former Ranger Victor Sebree.[142] The Rangers enjoyed limited success in their pursuit of the Garzistas, though Garza himself fared much worse, aborting all three of his invasions of northern Mexico and suffering a number of casualties before he perished during a military filibuster in present-day Panama.

The Rangers also continued to defend with brute force the interests of Anglo cattlemen, a strategy that embroiled the constabulary in a 1902 episode that became something of a cause célèbre among Mexican residents of South Texas. In May of that year, Ranger sergeant A. Y. Baker and two other policemen were scouting for thieves on the outskirts of the King Ranch when Baker discovered Ramón de la Cerda—an opponent of King Ranch expansion—illegally branding a steer. Both men fired at the same time, and de la Cerda was killed. Given that Baker escaped unharmed (although de la Cerda's bullet felled his horse), the event exacerbated simmering racial tensions in the area. Complicating the situation was the fact that members of the King family and several other leading Anglos pledged their support for Baker, while the results of another (unofficial) inquest into the killing suggested that de la Cerda had been bound and dragged before his death.

Such circumstances nourished Mexican resentment throughout the summer, and on 9 September Ranger Emmet Roebuck was killed when he, Baker, and a King Ranch employee were waylaid on their way to Brownsville. Baker was wounded in the leg, but survived. Ramón de la Cerda's nineteen-year-old brother, Alfredo, who had threatened to kill Baker while the Ranger was released on bond, was among the five primary suspects in the ambush. Less than a month later, Baker killed Alfredo de la Cerda in a Brownsville store, claiming self-defense (although it was never determined whether or not de la Cerda was armed).[143] In what seems to have been an act of quiet protest, someone sent a copy of the younger de la Cerda's formal death notice to Governor Joseph D. Sayers.[144] Nevertheless, to the outrage of valley Mexicans, a Brownsville court released Baker on bond and then acquitted him of murder the following year, evidently satisfied by his account of the shooting.[145]

Notwithstanding the significant differences that shaped the course of their dispossessions, the mixed-race groups at either end of the Great Plains confronted comparable realities at the dawn of the twentieth century, a notion underscored by their similarly strained relations with the constabularies that supervised them. In Canada, while some Métis came eventually to accept Ottawa's hegemony on the Plains, others adopted a less conciliatory posture toward the government and withdrew to remote portions of the North-West. The Mounties were never far behind though, sent by Ottawa to enforce game laws but more importantly to remind nontreaty natives and their Métis allies that, in the words of one officer, "the law of the land is all powerful even in way out places."[146] Such lessons did not sit well with the Métis, as suggested by a police report from Saskatchewan in 1900, which explained that a group of Métis had cheered when they heard a rumor that the Boers had killed 500 Englishmen in a skirmish in the South African War (1899–1902). An Indian in the same district announced that were he to serve in the conflict "he would fight for the Boers," as he had been told that they were struggling "for their land and liberty, and that their cause was similar to that of the Indians and Half Breeds."[147]

Given the racism that the Boers (who were white) displayed toward the native Africans they themselves had displaced in the 1830s and 1840s, this seems a curious comparison. And yet the struggles of the two groups had much in common, which may explain the appeal of this conflict for native and Métis peoples in the Canadian West.[148] Like the Métis, the Boers were farmers who resisted the attempts of the British Empire (or its descendants) to appropriate their lands for settlement. Both groups, moreover, faced off against the Mounties; the NWMP contributed most of the men who made up the First Battalion, Canadian Mounted Rifles, and the unit known as Lord Strathcona's Horse.[149] Just as the Métis succumbed in 1885, the Boers surrendered to the British in 1902. Their legacies, however, diverged sharply in the twentieth century: while the Boers quickly achieved political pre-eminence in the British Commonwealth of South Africa and introduced the system of apartheid, the dispossessed Métis continued to press Ottawa for a land base, waiting, in the words of one historian, "for a day that never comes."[150]

Tejanos could no doubt identify with such despair, which only deepened for them during the early years of the twentieth century. One measure of their resentment emerged in the *corrido*, a style of narrative folk song or ballad unique to the Rio Grande border that developed in the years after the Mexican-American War. Given the inequities in South Texas and the role of the Rangers in their perpetuation, it is no surprise that the *rinches* (a derogatory slang term for members of the force) were often the subject of such tunes. In numerous songs Mexicans trumpeted the heroism of otherwise peaceful men driven to violence by an unjust and racist system, while jeering at the police lackeys of an expanding capitalist state. Consider the final stanza from "The Ballad of Gregorio Cortez," which celebrates the title character's epic 1901 flight from Anglo law enforcement officers:

> Then said Gregorio Cortez,
> With his pistol in his hand,
> "Ah, so many mounted Rangers
> Just to take one Mexican!"[151]

The nadir for Tejanos came during the decade of the Mexican Revolution, when the Rangers helped to crush the irredentist Plan de San Diego insurrection, which erupted in South Texas in 1915. This rebellion called for the creation of an independent republic from the lands taken from Mexico

13. Members of Ranger Company D at Ysleta, Texas, with a shackled Mexican prisoner, 1894. Courtesy of Western History Collections, University of Oklahoma Libraries.

by the United States after 1848 and the killing of all white males over the age of sixteen.[152] Aided in their work by armed vigilance committees, the Rangers killed hundreds—perhaps thousands—of Mexicans, the overwhelming majority of whom had no connection to the uprising. Only then did officials in Austin yield to Mexican demands for an investigation of Ranger tactics in South Texas. The findings of the commission—headed by J. T. Canales, a descendant of Juan Cortina—would not have surprised Mexicans living in El Paso or below the Nueces, with its reports of pistol whippings, torture, extrajudicial murder, and other abuses of power.[153] But by that point the transition in Texas from Mexican to Anglo rule was complete, epitomized by the size of the King Ranch, which would eventually grow to more than 825,000 acres.

That they may have suffered little of the indiscriminate violence visited upon the Mexicans would probably have been of cold comfort to the Métis. Just as surely as the mixed-race peoples of Texas, those in the Canadian West witnessed a process of dispossession in the last decades of the nineteenth century, one aided considerably by the efforts of rural police. Pushed from their lands and denied access to other resources on which their communally oriented economies had depended, Mexicans and Métis alike were excluded from the hegemonic Anglo societies of the northern and southern Plains. As the nineteenth century gave way to the twentieth, these peoples of mixed ancestry found themselves increasingly absorbed into the new and much larger community of global capitalism, built in part from assets that had once belonged to them.

4 Defending the Cattleman's Empire

In March 1886 an Alberta newspaper reprinted an article that had run earlier in a U.S. ranching journal describing the state of the cattle industry in Texas. Explaining that just a few years earlier Texas had been "the Mecca of emigrants, the centre of attraction for capital and the home of prosperity," the American editorialist noted that avarice had compromised this Lone Star Eden. Specifically, the writer pointed to the sins of the "cowboy-cattle-king-lobbyist" who had pushed for the passage of legislation that would allow him to buy up vast amounts of land on which to run his herds. By acceding to the large stockman's wishes, the columnist insisted, Austin had overseen the destruction of the industry, caused by "a net-work of wire fences strung on the north side with dead cattle, broken stockmen, tottering stock companies and the development of the western part of the state indefinitely postponed."[1] He claimed, in effect, that private ownership and enclosure had benefited the very few at the expense of the many in Texas.

By publishing this item in his own paper, the editor of the *Macleod Gazette* clearly hoped that it would serve as a cautionary tale for federal officials and Canadian stock growers alike by precluding the rise of livestock monopolies on the prairies of Alberta. By the time the column appeared, however, Ottawa had established a land policy with respect to its western ranchers that bore some fundamental similarities to the system devised by Austin and decried by the editorialist. Although Canadian ranchers could not purchase all the territory they desired (unlike their Texan counterparts), Ottawa's lease system allowed each individual or company to secure at low cost up to 100,000 acres of land for the raising of livestock. Moreover, federal policy permitted leaseholders to exclude others from settling on their lands, a feature that rendered much of the Canadian cattle country closed to the farmer or small stockman, like the ranch lands of central and West Texas.

The decisions by authorities at both ends of the Great Plains to cede control of their peripheries to ranching syndicates grew from a handful of common factors, especially the cattleman's pioneering settlement along the frontier as well as his ability to wring profit from undeveloped lands. Not everyone shared this enthusiasm for the large stockman, however, as indicated by the editorial reprinted in the *Macleod Gazette*. Most skeptical were the farmers and middling ranchers expected to reap the greatest benefit from the trailblazing efforts of the cattlemen. Instead, these settlers experienced great difficulty in establishing themselves and their families, since the cattle kings maintained tight control of the best ranch land. For their part, big ranchers resented the challenge of the "nesters" and sought to exclude them. In Texas, ranchers stretched thousands of miles of barbed wire across the fertile lands of the state, enclosing tracts that belonged to them as well as many acres that did not. Meanwhile, Canadian cattlemen pursued eviction proceedings against individuals who attempted to settle on their leaseholds.

Incensed by these tactics, disgruntled homesteaders and small ranchers resisted their exclusion by cutting fences in Texas and squatting on sequestered lands in Canada. In response, officials in Austin and Ottawa turned to their rural constabularies, just as they had done when faced with the challenges posed by Indians and peoples of mixed ancestry. While it was clearly uncomfortable to set the police against the homesteader—who, after all, embodied the ideals of agrarian independence and virtue—state and federal authorities believed that they had little choice, given the profits and capital investment generated by the industry, as well as the ranchers' extensive political influence. Placing the examples of Alberta and Texas side by side reveals that farmers and small ranchers at both ends of the Great Plains faced similarly bleak circumstances on the cattleman's frontier, as Austin and Ottawa supported "bonanza ranching" by sending in the police to protect a closed but embattled range.[2]

The Origins of Ranching in Texas and the Canadian North-West

Cattle ranching in Texas began in the mid-eighteenth century, introduced by the Spanish as a means of providing food for their Franciscan missions clustered along the San Antonio River. Although frequent attacks by Native Americans and the outmigration of both animals and herders caused this initial venture to decline by the 1780s, a growing trade network between Texas and its neighboring colony of Louisiana helped to establish a flourishing ranching center further east, near the present-day boundary dividing the two states. It was here, on either side of the Sabine River, that Anglo-Texan ranching was born in the early nineteenth century, as whites moving westward from the lower South, especially the Carolinas, learned the Hispanic herding skills that would later define ranching in the greater American West.[3]

The Texas coastal prairie, with its lush grasses and plentiful water, offered an ideal environment for the longhorns, which roamed canebrakes and salt marshes unsupervised by their owners, a combination of circumstances that allowed the herds to reproduce rapidly. In the 1840s alone, the number of cattle in the state multiplied by a factor of seven, from approximately 125,000 animals to more than 900,000. This growth created staggering ratios of cows to people, which in some places ran as high as 40:1. Given the negligible costs of raising cattle on free grass and water as well as the rapid rate of their natural increase, many Texas whites were lured by the possibilities of profit and thus abandoned farming, turning their attention exclusively to livestock. In twice-yearly hunting expeditions, Anglo-Texans would gather up their herds—augmented by the cattle of Mexican residents forced from the area—for counting, marking, and branding, before trailing the animals to markets in California and New Orleans or, to a lesser extent, the states of the lower Midwest. These modest drives, each probably numbering only a few hundred animals, marked the beginnings of the range cattle trade.[4]

The outbreak of the Civil War in 1861 disrupted Anglo ranching in Texas. Thousands of men left the state for service in the Confederate army, and the Union blockade of the South and occupation of New Orleans beginning in 1862 prevented those who remained behind from driving or shipping their cows eastward to markets. Veterans returning to Texas in the spring and summer of 1865 thus found an estimated five million longhorns, many of them feral, roaming the grasslands of the eastern and central parts of the state. Fanning out across their pastures in "cow hunts" (forerunners of the roundup), ranchers gathered as many animals as possible, marking them and then turning them loose once again on the range to feed. The next year saw the first large-scale movement of Texas cattle northward to markets in

Kansas, Missouri, and Iowa, with an estimated 260,000 animals making the trip. Over the following two decades, more than five million head of Texas livestock would be driven north, representing "the largest short-term geographical shift of domestic herd animals in the history of the world."[5]

Many future Rangers served as cowboys on these trail drives of the late 1860s and early 1870s, since cattle herding was one of the few economic opportunities available to young Texan men who owned little or no property. Such was the case with John Banister, who would eventually enlist in Ranger Company D in 1877. Banister had left his home state of Missouri at the age of thirteen in order to search for his father, a Confederate army veteran who had abandoned his family and taken up with a woman in Texas following the Civil War. Upon locating him, however, the younger Banister found life on his father's small farm to be dull and unpromising, and thus he opted instead to work on a ranch in Coleman County, in North Texas, where he made regular cattle deliveries for his boss to legendary rancher John Chisum. Banister first went up the trail to Kansas in the spring of 1874 and made another drive in 1876 before joining the Rangers in the autumn of the following year.[6]

While working in North Texas Banister befriended the sixteen-year-old James B. Gillett, who served as a cowhand on a neighboring ranch. The two met in the summer of 1873 on the banks of the Concho River, where their bosses—along with men from another outfit—were delivering herds of cattle to John Chisum. Like Banister, the Texas-born Gillett came from a poor Missouri family, and he also found it difficult to resist the temptation of more adventure and better pay working as a cowboy. Gillett herded cattle in north-central Texas for several ranches until the summer of 1875, when—perhaps frustrated by the underemployment characteristic of the cattle business—he responded to a Ranger recruitment drive in Menard County aimed at expanding and strengthening the force for the increased Indian combat of the mid-1870s.[7]

Before they became Texas Rangers, however, Banister, Gillett, and a great number of their fellow police earned a living from the postwar cattle boom, which was made possible by the confluence of several events. In the first place, demand for beef in the industrial North mushroomed after 1865, fueled by growing urban populations and the depletion of the region's own cattle resources by the Union army, as well as the federal government's need to provision Indian reservations with beef rations. Another factor was the emergence of a major meatpacking industry in Chicago, where Texas live-stock—weakened by the long northward journey—could fatten up in the corn belt region of the Midwest before being led to the slaughterhouse. Most important, however, was the extension of railroads, which allowed for the transportation of cattle to a vast network of markets. Towns such as Abilene, Kansas—established in 1867 by Joseph G. McCoy along the route of the Union Pacific—became major shipping points, where Texas cattle trails like the Shawnee and Chisholm intersected the iron roads.

No less important to the growth of the livestock industry was the influx of investment capital, some of it from the northern United States but even more from Great Britain. Given its early prominence in the cattle trade, Texas attracted much of this financial support, with English monies back-ing ventures such as the Matador Land and Cattle Company and the Pan-handle's Rocking Chair Ranche, both founded in 1882.[8] These followed by one year the formation of the massive Texas Land and Cattle Company, a London-based corporation valued at more than $3 million. Many of these early operations were located in West Texas, where vast tracts of land were available for purchase or lease at low cost. Estimated annual profits of be-tween 30 and 40 percent during the boom years of the late 1870s drew local ranchers as well to the sparsely settled Llano Estacado, the so-called Staked Plains that border New Mexico. Few were more successful than Charles Goodnight, who along with his wealthy English partner, John G. Adair, ac-cumulated 100,000 head of cattle, which they grazed on the 700,000 acres of the JA Ranch located in the Panhandle's Palo Duro Canyon.[9]

§

The first range cattle introduced onto the prairies of southern Alberta were part of the great northward diffusion of the Texas herds. In 1874 Method-ist missionary John McDougall and his brother David drove a small group of animals from Fort Benton, Montana, to the mission at Morley, about thirty miles west of Calgary in the foothills of the Rocky Mountains. The next year, the McDougalls were joined at their site along the Bow River by John Shaw and some 450 cattle he had trailed east from neighboring British Columbia, where the end of the gold rush led some ranchers to fan out in search of new markets. Some ranchers were attracted to the region by its rivers and the moderating effects of the Chinook, a warm, dry wind that made winter feed more abundant. By 1881 there were an estimated 9,000 head of stock on the range lands of southern Alberta and nearly 200 individuals pursuing cattle ranching between the international boundary and the Bow River Valley.[10]

If the Rangers are forever linked in both historical and popular memory with the Texas longhorn, the North-West Mounted Police deserve even more recognition for their contributions to the livestock interests of southern Alberta. Whereas the Rangers worked with South Texas ranchers in the mid-1870s to smooth the transition of an extant enterprise from Mexican to Anglo control, the Mounties arrived in the West with their own herd of 235 cattle shortly after the McDougall brothers, and thus contributed a sizable portion of the region's foundation stock. As important, perhaps, as the security offered by the NWMP to intending ranchers was their constitution of a proximate and viable market for beef. After John Shaw tried unsuccessfully to sell his herd to the Hudson's Bay Company trader at Morley, he secured a contract to provide beef rations to the NWMP post at Fort Calgary.[11]

The Mounties, though, were more than mere defenders and customers of Alberta's early cattlemen. In fact, the police themselves were among the region's first and most successful ranchers, since many of those who had arrived in 1874 went into the livestock industry at the conclusion of their three-year enlistment contracts. In the words of one English visitor to Fort Macleod, south of Calgary: "Nearly all the men about here are in [the ranching] business in a small way and a funny thing, nearly all have been in the Police. Yet it is quite natural as when a man is in the police round here he sees the country and goes in for ranching as soon as he comes out." Ex-policemen founded some of the first ranches in the district and also claimed the two initial brands recorded in Canada: "71," which was secured by partners Percy Neale and Samuel Steele in January 1880, and William Winder's "double crank," granted two months later.[12]

Coupled with their broad experience in the North-West, the Mounties' social status gave them access to wealthy entrepreneurs in eastern Canada, which was home to many of the officers. On return visits to the East in the late 1870s, members of the force extolled southern Alberta's potential as a livestock district, firing the imagination of investors—particularly those from the ranching areas of Quebec's Eastern Townships—who were eager to benefit from the well-publicized cattle boom. Such was the case with Mountie William Winder, whose 1879 trip to his native Compton County piqued the interest of Senator Matthew Cochrane, Winder's neighbor and a successful livestock breeder. Cochrane quickly developed plans to start a $500,000 venture in the North-West on which he planned to run 8,000 head of cattle. No less intrigued by the opportunities in Alberta was Inspector Winder's brother-in-law, Frederic Stimson, who sought assistance from a wealthy Montreal shipping family in order to raise the $150,000 necessary to found the North-West Cattle Company (or Bar U) in 1882.[13]

The contributions of the Mounted Police to Canadian ranching did not end once the industry was up and running. Rather, Ottawa directed the force to nourish the venture in order to enhance its long-term prospects. The most fundamental measure of police support for ranchers was the NWMP's sheer accessibility to stockmen. The Mounties quickly established permanent stations within a few miles of each of the so-called Big Four ranches—the Cochrane, Bar U, Oxley, and Walrond—the largest spreads in the area. Moreover, by the end of the decade, the Mounties had developed a "vast surveillance network" of "flying patrols" that thoroughly covered the settlements and trails of southwestern Alberta, allowing the police to check in on ranchers and to respond decisively to the concerns of the ranching population.[14]

Stockmen, of course, were also free to drop in at police outposts to socialize or discuss business, as suggested by the diary of ranch manager William F. Cochrane, the senator's son. In just two months during the spring of 1885, the younger Cochrane ate dinner or spent the night at least four different times at various NWMP camps in the Fort Macleod area, indicating the ranchman's unfettered access to the police.[15] Some police—especially from the officer corps—developed close relationships with ranchers, leading the NWMP to play an integral role in the development of southern Alberta's genteel ranching society, hosting sporting and social events at which cattlemen and the Mounties mingled freely. In return, the police were welcomed into the upper echelons of frontier society, such as Calgary's Ranchmen's Club, which customarily extended honorary membership to the commanding officer of E Division, stationed at a fort on the outskirts of the city.[16]

Alberta cattlemen relied upon their good relations with the police as a means of addressing their grievances. One of their more common complaints concerned the killing of their animals by local Indians. This, to be sure, was precisely the issue that inspired many of Billie Cochrane's visits to NWMP posts.[17] Although the Blackfoot (like most native peoples) had been confined to reserves by the early to mid-1880s, some bands had retained limited hunting privileges in the region, while others sought merely to augment their meager government rations by poaching from area herds. For their part, many police seem to have regarded such losses as inevitable given the proliferation of ranches and the resulting temptations placed before starving natives. Indeed, Superintendent Sam Steele explained to a superior that "it is not to be wondered at, if [the Indians] occasionally take advantage of a dark night to steal across and slaughter a calf or two."[18] Such incidents, however, drove stockmen nearly to distraction, causing the NWMP to pursue native cattle thieves with zeal. In one 1881 case, the force responded to the killing of several cows near Pincher Creek by dispatching a party of twenty men to track the poachers. The detachment returned after its six-day expedition—covering 250 miles—with two Indians, who were tried and sentenced to prison terms that included hard labor.[19]

Far more vexing to ranchers (and thus the police) was the problem of keeping U.S. cattle off the Canadian range, a dilemma with multiple causes that persisted throughout the late nineteenth century. American animals often drifted north into Alberta in search of water and forage, a trend that increased with the deterioration of the Montana range country due to overstocking. In other cases, U.S. ranchers simply lost track of the boundary (marked only by piles of stones placed at two-mile intervals) or ignored it altogether, taking advantage of lax border enforcement in order to feed their animals on "free" grass. Adding to the confusion was the fact that some ranching companies owned land on both sides of the line but did little to distinguish their Canadian and U.S. herds from one another. The additional animals—in groups sometimes numbering 6,000 or more cattle—pressured the already strained resources of southwestern Canada, while introducing dangerous bovine diseases carried by some American livestock.[20]

Besieged by complaints from Alberta stock growers, Ottawa turned to the Mounted Police and charged the force with regulating cattle traffic along the border and collecting customs duties. In the hopes of checking the spread of blackleg, anthrax, and bovine tuberculosis, among other ailments, the Mounties attempted to enforce a strict ninety-day quarantine, during which time animals entering Canada from the United States were supposed to be subjected to rigorous inspection and treatment by NWMP veterinarians.[21] While the police showed little affection for this task—their enthusiasm muted by irate American stock owners as well as competing directives from different federal agencies—still more distasteful to the Mounties were their orders to herd strayed American cattle back across the line into Montana. Expressing the frustration of his border detachments, who were serving in effect as cowboys and line riders, NWMP commissioner A. B. Perry explained that "it is useless driving [the cattle] back, as they return at once."[22] Superintendent R. B. Deane put it more bluntly: "We are riding our horses off their legs on what is not legitimate police work."[23] So intractable was the problem that Comptroller Fred White exhorted the minister of the interior to consider fencing the boundary at its most porous spots in order to obviate any unpleasant "International complications."[24]

Though they enjoyed inverse class-based relationships with the nascent cattle-ranching frontiers of Texas and Alberta—with many Rangers working first as cowboys, while some Mounties were among western Canada's first stockmen—one nevertheless discerns clear parallels between the constabularies' early service to the industry. Both police forces smoothed the development of cattle-raising operations by confining or expelling indigenous peoples, which allowed for domesticated livestock to occupy the physical and ecological space created by the disappearance of the bison. And just as the Rangers attempted to prevent incursions into Texas by Mexicans seeking to steal or reclaim disputed cattle, the NWMP worked to secure the Canadian boundary against American interlopers. A comparison of police roles in defending the big cattlemen's frontiers that emerged at either end of the Plains in the late 1870s and early 1880s enriches this understanding of their functional similarities. At the same time, such an examination also highlights key contrasts between the government policies and social conditions that shaped the ranching societies of Texas and Alberta.

The Big Cattleman's Frontier

At the time that Charles Goodnight and his partner founded the JA Ranch, such a large and sophisticated enterprise was the exception in Texas rather than the rule. Unlike the JA, most of the state's cattle ranches were small operations without access to external sources of capital. Moreover, the industry of the early to mid-1870s was typified by a fluid sense of human ownership and control over livestock, a reflection of conditions on the state's open ranges. In 1875, for instance, an estimated nine-tenths of the state's cattle lived off the free water and grass of the public domain.[25] Under such a system, herds might drift from one county to another during inclement weather, with the owners meeting later to settle up and divide their animals each from the other. Such practices, however, changed abruptly with the introduction of barbed wire in Texas.

Successfully patented in 1874 by an Illinois farmer named Joseph Glidden, barbed wire revolutionized settlement on the Great Plains by providing homesteaders with a means of staking out their claims and protecting their crops from wandering livestock. Among its many virtues as a fencing material were its resistance to snow drifts, relative affordability, and consumption of considerably less space and building material than either a stone wall or the common zigzagging "worm" fence. Most important to settlers on the relatively treeless Plains, though, was the fact that such an enclosure required little wood for its erection. Annual sales from the 1870s offer an indication of barbed wire's growing popularity: in 1875, 600,000 pounds of the material were bought and sold in the United States; five years later, that number had climbed to more than 80 million.[26]

Despite its obvious attractions to settlers, cattlemen were the first to use barbed wire in Texas. Purchases in the state began slowly but picked up after an impressive 1876 demonstration in San Antonio's Military Plaza by salesman John "Bet-a-Million" Gates.[27] Among the clients he attracted were South Texas ranchers, who—having experimented with fencing for some time—admired the product for its potential to deter trespassers while also allowing for the isolation of breeding stock. Cattlemen in agricultural East Texas, meanwhile, used the wire to comply with laws requiring the enclosure of their animals, a reflection of English herding statutes that shifted responsibility to the livestock owner.[28] Settlers who migrated westward from these districts were thus well acquainted with the uses of barbed wire, and they turned to it now to safeguard their homes and crops on the open ranges of central and western Texas, which by 1880 had become the core of the state's cattle industry.

Ranchers in such areas looked upon the arrival of these "nesters"—so named because the rudimentary enclosures for their gardens that they fashioned from brush and tree branches looked like a bird's nest—with a mixture of trepidation and contempt.[29] Cattlemen worried that the fences of the newcomers would hinder the access of their cattle to water and grass. In contrast to their counterparts in the eastern half of the state, central and West Texas cattlemen—like most ranchers throughout the U.S. West—enjoyed free and unimpeded use of the area's natural resources, because officials believed that the region's aridity made it suitable only for the raising of livestock. Indeed, this was precisely the position taken by the Stockmen's Association of Nolan and Fisher counties in 1883, which unsuccessfully petitioned the state legislature to prohibit fencing—and thus homesteading—in its district on the grounds that farming was impossible west of the 100th meridian. Likewise, the commissioner's court in nearby San Saba County failed in its bid to keep settlers at bay when Austin rejected the claim that barbed wire posed an excessive danger to livestock.[30]

For some ranchers, such legislative defeats suggested that the free-grass era in Texas was coming to a close and that rapid settlement was all but inevitable. In an effort to protect grazing lands and water holes from incoming farmers, many stockmen in the state's central and western regions secured title to vast sections of the prairie, especially those containing rivers or streams. Several factors facilitated this rapid transformation from public use to private ownership. One of these was Texas land law. Unlike other territories in the West that would later become states, Texas entered the Union in 1845 in full possession of its unclaimed lands, which totaled 216 million acres.[31] When conservative Democrats returned to power in Texas after the bitter Reconstruction era, they implemented a policy of divestiture with respect to the public domain that reflected their deep suspicion of government.[32]

Of course, simple budgetary concerns also drove the fire sale of the state's public lands. The economic disruptions of the Civil War and its aftermath, coupled with the growing population of Texas, had created an urgent need for basic internal improvements such as roads, wells, and irrigation canals. Even closer to home for state officials was the need for a new capitol building in Austin, since the existing structure had burned down in 1881. The state commission charged with overseeing the project settled upon a novel idea, endorsed by the legislature, which involved the offering of public lands in exchange for the construction of a new edifice. In the end, a Chicago ranching syndicate accepted three million acres of West Texas prairie as compensation for the job, and thus was born the XIT Ranch.[33]

Perhaps most important in the push for privatization in Texas, however, was a strong official belief that individual or corporate ownership of the land was essential if the state's natural resources were to be fully developed. Such a perspective led the Texas legislature to pass mineral and timber laws in 1876 and 1881, respectively, that ceded control of those resources to the owners of the lands on which they were located.[34] While this decision cost the state an estimated $1 billion in lost revenue over the ensuing five

14. The Texas State Capitol shortly after its completion, marked "Souvenir, May 1888." Courtesy of Texas State Library and Archives Commission.

decades, it nevertheless ensured the widespread use of Texas's forests and lodes for commercial purposes. These legislative initiatives thus mirrored in time and scope what one historian has termed the "industrial versions of the Homestead Act"—the Pacific Railways Act (1862), the General Mining Law (1872), and the Timber and Stone Act (1878), among others—federal measures aimed at developing the resources of the greater U.S. West.[35]

Austin's decision to sell vast quantities of land to Texas stockmen fit squarely within this ascendant political economy, as exemplified by the perspective of W. H. King, the state's adjutant general and the former owner of a sugar plantation in Central America. After a visit to West Texas in 1883, King returned to Austin convinced of the ranching industry's importance to the economic future of the state. The adjutant general endorsed the large cattlemen's view that the westward migration of stockmen had pushed back the Indian frontier of Texas, making settlement safe for others who would follow in their wake, and driving up land values in the process. "This," King wrote, was "the immediate and direct result of the lawful permission to own and fence up, so as to be able to control, large, solid blocks of land upon which to graze stock."[36] The adjutant general's was clearly not a lone voice in the capital, since the state customized its land policy to suit the conditions of the Llano Estacado and sold large tracts that were ideal for grazing cattle. With public lands offered in unlimited quantities at only fifty cents per acre, ranchers came to possess much of the western half of Texas during the late 1870s and early 1880s.[37]

§

Though a big man's frontier also developed in Alberta during the late nineteenth century, it followed a different trajectory than in Texas. For one thing, the growth of an entrenched landholding ranch society in the Lone Star State took place over the better part of a decade and was largely the result of conditions on the ground, especially the land grab motivated by the westward migration of settlers. In western Canada, on the other hand, prospective stockmen such as Matthew Cochrane urged the government to create favorable conditions for their ventures before the arrival of settlers, prompting Ottawa to establish a grazing lease policy in 1881 that turned southern Alberta into a large stockman's preserve practically overnight.[38] These agreements allowed individuals or corporations to secure twenty-one-year leases for up to 100,000 acres of land, at a per annum rate of one cent per acre (or ten dollars for every 1,000 acres). The leaseholder had the right to purchase as much as 5 percent of the tract at a cost of two dollars per acre and enjoyed the privilege of importing his foundation stock duty-free from the United States. Additionally, areas under lease were excluded from homestead entry without the explicit consent of the lessee.[39]

Ottawa's decision to rent—rather than to sell—its western lands marked a critical departure from the model in Texas, where state officials were all too eager to transfer outright land ownership to ranchers and syndicates and thus largely forfeited their jurisdiction over such tracts. The Canadian policy of leasing territory, however, allowed the government to maintain a much greater degree of control over its ranching interests, reflected in the fine print of the lease agreements, which permitted Ottawa to reclaim and dispose of the leaseholds after only two years as officials saw fit. Furthermore, the matter of scale deserves mention: whereas the maximum amount of leased land in Alberta was no more than five million acres, the XIT Ranch alone made up three-fifths of that total.

Some of Ottawa's motivations for establishing a big man's frontier in the first place differed from Austin's, too. Though Texas cattlemen clearly wielded influence in the state capital, partisan politics played a more decisive role in establishing ranching in western Canada. For instance, Senator Cochrane relied upon his Conservative Party connections to appeal for assistance to fellow Tory Sir John A. Macdonald, prime minister of Canada, whose government had returned to power in 1878. Thus began a strong relationship between the Conservatives and the ranchers of southern Alberta, who became one of the party's core constituencies and helped keep the Tories in power until the Liberals triumphed in 1896.

Moreover, the imperatives of the National Policy were critical in shaping federal support for the ranching interests of southern Alberta, since Ottawa desperately hoped to occupy the North-West before the United States could expand into the vacuum of the unoccupied prairies. Of course, in certain symbolic ways the Americans were already there: the main supply routes to the Canadian West originated in Montana; U.S. stamps were used at Fort Macleod; and—at least initially—members of the NWMP were paid with money from Montana.[40] Still, the establishment of a ranching industry in Alberta addressed some of these concerns by populating the region (however sparsely) with Canadians loyal to the government who controlled large blocs of real estate from which they were permitted to exclude outsiders, whether they were Canadian or American.[41]

Notwithstanding these divergences, the pivotal factor in Ottawa's sponsorship of big ranchers resembled Austin's priorities in a fundamental way: like their Texas counterparts, Canadian officials recognized the significance of the cattle trade to the industrial growth of the new nation. Conjuring the sentiments of Texas adjutant general W. H. King, Canada's interior minister wrote in 1880, "It is hardly necessary to say how important it is to the future of [the North-West], how intimately connected with the development of its best interests, that this and kindred schemes should be successful."[42] Stockmen put marginal land to profitable use, and the export of their animals allowed the Dominion to profit from an expanding global economy: thousands of cattle traveled across the Atlantic to Great Britain, returning huge profits and—more importantly—spurring investment in the Canadian West from England, Ireland, and Scotland.[43] This mirrored to a great extent the hopes of Texas officials, who believed that the establishment of ranching in the Panhandle and on the Llano Estacado would generate commercial development and bind those regions into the economy and geography of the state.

Settler Resistance

Having acquired title to vast amounts of formerly public land (lest homesteaders buy and enclose small but crucial plots of their own), Texas ranchers experienced a predictable shift in their attitudes toward barbed wire: they embraced the very invention that they had but recently opposed. In the Panhandle, for instance, 1881 saw the erection of a 175-mile drift fence and the total enclosure of the Shoe Bar Ranch. The following year, foremen at the Frying Pan Ranch, inventor Joseph Glidden's spread in northwest Texas, acquired enough barbed wire to fence 250,000 acres of pasture.[44] Significant as these ventures were, neither compared to the undertaking at the nearby XIT, which by the middle of the decade had enclosed all but 35,000 of its more than three million acres, with one section of the fence stretching out for 150 miles without making a single turn.[45]

The Panhandle was not the only portion of the state to witness the rapid construction of barbed wire fences. In the late 1870s a belt of counties running through the geographic center of the state, from the Red River to the Rio Grande, experienced its own furious transformation, as stockmen from the west attempted to halt the migration of settlers advancing from the east. For instance, Bee County, southeast of San Antonio, had only twenty-five miles of fence in 1879; four years later, the entire county was under wire. Two hundred miles to the northwest, one rancher alone fenced up one-fourth of Coleman County, where Ranger-to-be John Banister had herded cattle on the open range. Fencing became so popular in central Texas that some counties held "fencing bees," community-wide efforts that corresponded to log-rolling competitions or cornhusker festivals. In light of such developments, even stockmen opposed to enclosure gave in and fenced up. As rancher E. P. Earhart remembered years later, "I believed [fencing] would ruin us, but there was no other way out," and thus he enclosed 5,000 acres in Jack County, building the first fence in the area.[46] According to one historian, "By 1883 the fencing of the whole state was almost an accomplished fact."[47]

Though a helpful development to some Texans, enclosure caused vexation for many others. Barbed wire suited large ranchers who hoped to protect their lands or to control the breeding of their cattle, but it was beyond the reach of the homesteader or even the small stockman, who ran no more than a few hundred animals and relied on the free-grass system. Even had he (or she) managed to acquire title to a section or two, the middling rancher could not possibly afford to fence enough pasture to feed his or her livestock. In 1884 barbed wire in West Texas cost three dollars per hundred pounds, and mesquite posts ran between ten and fifteen cents apiece.

With added expenses for freight and labor, fencing cost at least $175 per mile (some estimates are twice that amount), making no allowance for the necessary upkeep of the enclosure, which included the replacement of rotted wood and felled strands.[48] Given such expenditures, barbed wire fencing was simply out of the question for the homesteader or small stockman, while an outfit like the XIT—backed by ample British capital—could spend an estimated $181,000 on fence construction alone.

The farmer or small rancher had countless other reasons to resent barbed wire, beyond the simple fact that he could not afford it. For one thing, its spikes could puncture the skin of animals rubbing against it, crippling them from the injury or a subsequent infection from screwworm. Such losses were perhaps insignificant to a syndicate with a big herd, but devastating to a poorer individual with few animals to spare. More vexing was the large cattleman's habit of enclosing lands that did not belong to him as well as those that did. Sometimes this was accidental, as in a case from 1892 involving the Mitchell County ranch of barbed wire manufacturer I. L. Elwood. When informed by his manager of a homesteader's grievance, Elwood instructed his employee to conduct an investigation and to compensate the farmer in the event that the ranch was in error. Such acts of restitution, however, would probably not have swayed skeptics like "Pie-Biter" (a cowboy so named because of his buckteeth), who insisted to rancher E. P. Earhart that "barbed wire is going to ruin Texas."[49]

Other stockmen took a more deliberate approach to seizing lands they did not rent or own. As recalled by one cowboy who worked for the Red River Cattle Company during the 1880s, his bosses "got too greedy" and fenced up lands they only leased as well as several tracts belonging to settlers, an act that provoked the farmers to organize in their defense.[50] Some individuals or corporations went so far as to acquire only the alternate sections in a given swath of public land, but then to enclose the neighboring government-owned tract as well. And on at least one occasion, a group of Panhandle ranchers ran off prospective settlers by enclosing a public pasture and letting the cows "graze it off bare" in order to ruin the land for farming.[51]

Some small Texas cowmen opposed the use of fences altogether (legal or otherwise) on moral grounds, insisting that such practices stood in violation of their traditional rights to free grass and water. In this way, their complaints echoed the objections of eighteenth- and nineteenth-century

English farmers who protested against the enclosure by the gentry of the peasants' strips of land and the common pastures where they held grazing privileges. Antagonism to Parliament's Enclosure Acts turned on a handful of concerns, the most significant being the enrichment of the few at the expense of the many and the evaporation of independence enjoyed by the small farmer and his family. Opponents of the measures insisted that even the gentry would suffer from this transformation of public land into private property, since landlordism—coupled with growing wealth—would inevitably breed indolence, apathy, and isolation among the rich.[52]

Texas farmers expressed strikingly similar concerns about fencing, as captured by W. H. King, the state's adjutant general. In his annual report for 1883, King explained that during a recent tour of West Texas he had been inundated with objections to the widespread use of barbed wire in that part of the state. Characterizing the nature of their complaints, King wrote that the anti-fence men believed that enclosure contradicted "the true spirit of our government," adding that

> this system serves to produce the two undesirable extremes of social and political life—a small number of rich and a large number of very poor people, with a constant increase of class and class distinctions between them; ease, luxury, idleness, indifference and haughty disdain on the part of the wealthy few, and ignorance, poverty, and practical enslavement and loss of self-respect on the part of the great body of poor people, accompanied by a cringing spirit of obsequious humility.

With great concern, King noted that the frustration of farmers and small ranchers needed only a little encouragement and a cause—either real or perceived—to lead them to seek their own redress.[53]

The drought of 1883 provided just such a catalyst. With many parts of central and West Texas receiving scant rain throughout the spring and summer, streams and creeks dried up and grasses shriveled. While virtually all Texas cattlemen were affected by the weather conditions, the small stockman suffered the most, since he found that pastures and water holes once available to his animals had been fenced up by wealthier individuals and corporations. Thousands of acres of unclaimed land and miles of public road had also been fenced, thus cutting off access to schools and churches. Residents of one county complained that they could not even reach the county seat because of the thicket of fences strangling their district.[54] Furious at this assault on what he believed were his common rights, the homesteader or small cowman—joined by other opponents of barbed wire—took matters into his own hands by cutting down the enclosures.

Working in small, close-knit groups, armed men—calling themselves by such names as "The Land League, The Owls, The Javelinas and The Blue Devils"—began snipping offending enclosures with wire cutters, destroying the fences and liberating the animals held within.[55] In order to avoid detection, the cutters worked mainly at night, and they used passwords to prevent infiltration by outsiders or law enforcement officials. On occasion, fence cutting outfits would also drag the posts from the ground and set fire to them, aiming in the process to scorch thousands of acres of sequestered pasturage. Other nippers left behind menacing notes, such as this one discovered near a razed fence in Tom Green County, from which an imported bull had been driven off: "If your bull you hunt for, call at the first ranch this side of Hell, and brand him when you get him."[56]

Some historians have pointed to such threats and the fact that fence cutters counted cattle rustlers and hide peelers among their number as evidence that the nippers were little more than petty criminals.[57] While there is no doubt that many fence cutters helped themselves to the cattle of pasture men whose enclosures they destroyed, to dismiss them as mere thieves is to ignore the source of their grievances, as captured in an impassioned letter to Governor John Ireland in September 1883. Describing conditions in Jack County, James Keiffer explained that in his twenty-nine years as a state resident he had never witnessed the sort of oppression visited upon the small stockman by his larger counterpart, alleging that nine-tenths of area ranchers did not hold title to half the lands they fenced. Moreover, he added that "no sooner does [the farmer or small stock grower] raise his hand [to object] than the stockman will raise his sword." In closing, Keiffer sounded an ominous note, saying that the aggressors would be met "on the battlefield."[58]

While the cutters' strenuous efforts to keep their identities secret make it hard to generalize about them as a group, stories like the one told by cattleman E. P. Earhart suggest that many were, in fact, facing the bleak economic circumstances described by James Keiffer. Exasperated by the repeated cutting of his three-wire fence, Earhart tried several strategies to catch the nippers, including sitting in his pasture one night and holding the middle wire between his teeth in order to detect any snipping along the length of the fence line. Eventually, Earhart and a neighbor caught a lucky break, trailing one of the cutters by following the tracks of the man's horse, identified by a break in the hoof. Upon apprehending the cutter, Earhart proved more compassionate than most of his fellow ranchers: "I went to the house and told the man that I didn't want to send them all to the 'pen' and would give them time to get out of the country. In just about a year every one of them had moved out. The old man we got was the leader of the cutters. All four were poor men and had families."[59]

Notes posted by the cutters in towns and pastures captured the frustration of such men and attest to a consciousness shaped more by ideological conviction than criminal deviance. Consider this message found on a street in Coleman, south of Abilene:

> Down with monopolies, they can't exist in Texas . . . away with your foreign capitalists; the range and soil of Texas belong to the heroes of the South; no monopolies and don't tax us to school the nigger; Give us homes as God intended, and not gates to churches and towns and schools and above all give us water for our stock.[60]

By this telling, outsiders—whether they were foreign investors or officials at the Freedman's Bureau—had crushed the aspirations of common (white) folk in Texas with their greed and tyranny (although it overlooked the important role played by the state's own General Land Office). Other fence cutters cast the struggle in historical terms, as indicated by this note from Hopkins County: "This pasture business is getting to a nice pass now that a man can't buy himself a little home. We dont care to be made serfs of yet like poor Ireland and the majority of England."[61] Letters such as these suggest that the cutters were motivated less by blind opposition to fencing than by the perception that avaricious individuals and companies prevented the social and economic advancement of the poor. The cutters loosed their anger on the barbed wire fences that caused their animals to perish and their families to go hungry.

That more than half of all counties in Texas reported downed wires in 1883, at the height of the troubles, is further evidence that such activity was not merely "petty crime." Predictably, fence cutting was most widespread along the fault line between ranchers and farmers in the center of the state. B. R. Cannon of Frio County (west of San Antonio) sought help from Austin after cutters had hacked three miles of his fence between every second

$100

REWARD.

I will pay the above Reward for information which will lead to the conviction and incarceration in the Penitentiary of the felon who maliciously cut the "Hamilton Pasture" fence on the Bandera road, last night.

W. G. HUGHES.

Boerne, August 6, 1889.

15. An 1889 wanted notice for fence cutting in Boerne, Texas. Courtesy of Texas State Library and Archives Commission.

post.[62] Several hundred miles to the north, in Shackleford County, J. M. Lee wrote Governor Ireland in July to state that a "communistic organization" had destroyed two and a half miles of his fence and turned his cattle loose onto the range.[63] From neighboring Callahan County, rancher C. W. Powell contacted Ireland to complain that fourteen miles of fence "constructed at great expense" had been ruined. Seething, Powell noted that the present troubles had caused him more anxiety and inconvenience than either Indians or horse thieves.[64] By the end of autumn, damage estimates in Texas approached $20 million, with at least $7 million in beleaguered Brown County alone.

With settlers and investors avoiding portions of the state altogether and newspapers as far away as Chicago bearing headlines such as "Hell Breaks Loose in Texas!" Governor Ireland called a special session of the state legislature. Addressing the body in January 1884, Ireland argued that the advocates of "free" water and grass should submit to the realities of private ownership so as to avoid "disruptions" to the civil order. Unsurprising considering his reputation as an advocate of strict—even harsh—law enforcement, Ireland urged Texas lawmakers to declare fence cutting a felony punishable by a prison term in the state penitentiary.[65] The legislature did not disappoint, passing a bill less than a month later that prescribed one to five years' confinement for those who "wilfully cut, injure or destroy any fence, or part of a fence" and—in an unusual move—appropriating $50,000 for use in combating the cutters.[66] Although the act also prohibited unlawful enclosure and required fence builders to provide a gate for every three miles of wire, failure to comply with these guidelines constituted only a misdemeanor, marking a significant victory for the big ranchers.

§

In contrast to Texas, where private individuals and companies had restricted the access of farmers and small stockmen to the range, in Canada it was the federal government that had effectively closed southern Alberta to the settler of modest means, though it was not necessarily by design. The middling stockman had access to neither the capital nor the political benefactors in Ottawa enjoyed by men such as Matthew Cochrane, conditions that made obtaining a grazing lease between the international boundary and the Bow River Valley practically impossible. Furthermore, the no-settlement clause meant that securing a homestead entry—the only viable alternative for establishing a foothold in the region—was nearly impossible, since Ottawa rarely considered withdrawing leased lands for settlement purposes.[67]

Still, such obstacles did not stop prospective settlers from seeking entry into the area stretching south from Calgary to the 49th parallel. For example, in the mid-1880s Charles Ora Card—a Mormon who had fled Utah to avoid facing charges of polygamy—arrived in southern Alberta in search of a homestead. Though he eventually founded an eponymous community in the region, ranchers and government officials repeatedly rebuffed Card's initial attempts at renting or purchasing land.[68] Meanwhile, the "big man's frontier"—backed by waves of foreign investment capital—quickly took shape, with 60 percent of the area's total leased acreage held in blocs of 75,000 acres (or more) by 1882, less than a year after the introduction of the policy. Inspired by this transformation of Alberta's range country, the Marquis of Lorne remarked during his 1881 visit to the West, "If I were not Governor General of Canada, I would be a cattle rancher in Alberta."[69]

As in Texas, the perceived inequality between large cattlemen on the one

16. Settler's buildings and cattle on the Bow River Horse Ranche, ca. 1890s.
Courtesy of Glenbow Archives, NA-2084-40.

hand and farmers and smaller stockmen on the other generated mounting friction between the groups, and opposition to Ottawa's grazing lease policy emerged less than a year after its December 1881 enactment. Most upset by the terms of the legislation were would-be settlers. In 1882 alone, Ottawa authorized 75 applications from a pool of 154, sequestering more than four million acres of prime grassland.[70] There were, to be certain, a handful of area residents who were allowed to remain on their lands, provided that they had obtained title prior to the passage of the lease law. They were limited, however, to a maximum of 320 acres: their initial homestead entry plus a quarter-section preemption. Newcomers like Charles Card were not so fortunate, finding that large cattle companies—worried lest settlers compromise their access to the open range—vigorously exercised the leaseholder's right to exclude squatters from any portion of reserved grazing lands.

Taking up the cause of the small farmer was the *Macleod Gazette*, founded in 1882 by C. E. D. Wood, a rancher and ex-Mounted Policeman who served as the paper's editor. While acknowledging that southern Alberta had the finest stock ranges in the world, Wood argued that the region should be

17. Office of the *Macleod Gazette*, with editor C. E. D. Wood at left, ca. 1890s.
Courtesy of Glenbow Archives, NA-1171-10.

able to support both rancher and farmer, and he blasted the government for its no-settlement clause, which he claimed retarded immigration to the area.[71] Wood was hardly less critical of the 20.5 percent import duty levied on livestock entering the country, from which leaseholders stocking their ranges were exempt (so long as they kept the cattle in Canada for at least two years). Small farmers and ranchers, on the other hand—who, like their Texas counterparts, hoped to run a few hundred head of cattle to augment their agricultural ventures—could not meet such costs. This financial obstacle effectively prevented them from competing with large cattle operations like the Cochrane or Oxley ranches. In a thinly veiled jab at the British origins of many ranchers and much of the investment capital in Alberta, the *Gazette* likened such disparities in the North-West to the English colonial policy in Ireland, to which fence cutters in Hopkins County had also alluded.[72]

Wood's insult, if overheated, was nevertheless well supported by an informed reading of events taking place across the Atlantic. England's lengthy colonization of Ireland was well known, as was the English gentry's record of oppressive absentee landlordism with regard to its Irish country estates. In an extension of the English process of enclosure during the late 1870s, however, the struggling Irish farmer had suffered another setback. Several years of bad harvests led to a spate of evictions by property owners who were eager to maximize agricultural efficiency and punish the defaulters. Some indication of the plight facing the Irish peasantry in the mid-1870s emerges from an official analysis of landholdings in Ireland: fewer than 2,000 landlords owned nearly 70 percent of the country, while more than three million tenants and laborers possessed virtually no property at all.[73] To Wood and the settlers of southern Alberta, the Irish example—with its stark division between the landed elite and the small farmer—spoke volumes about the state of affairs along the Canadian ranching frontier.

Francis Girard, a doctor on the Blood Indian reserve, captured the growing frustrations of settlers in an 1884 letter to the minister of public works, in language bearing an arresting resemblance to Texas adjutant general W. H. King's report from West Texas the year before. Explaining that the population of Alberta was divided into "two well distinct clans"—stock raisers and farmers—Girard noted that the large cattlemen had developed a "monopoly of the lands in this part of the country," forcing the farmer to submit to his will. To illustrate, Dr. Girard sketched the following scenario: Upon his arrival, the newcomer—lured to the region by government promotion—located a section of land on which to settle, only to be told that the parcel was already claimed and that he should inquire with the land office at Macleod. No such agency existed, however, and when the settler returned and began plowing fields and erecting structures, he was promptly sued by the leaseholder. In the likely event of the cattleman's vindication, the squatter, having lost time and money in mounting a losing defense, was "condemned to pay costs—always onerous—and expelled without mercy." In driving home his point, Girard added that "what has recently happened to some of them, will, no doubt, happen to the great number for some time to come."[74]

Ottawa, for the most part, was unsympathetic to the squatters. In the first place, government officials insisted that "the main stream of immigration" had not yet reached the area, but when it did, lease contracts contained a safety valve to alleviate such pressures on the land: namely, a clause providing for the opening of select sections with demonstrated agricultural value.[75] That the two-year waiting period, as well as the costs of filing and pursuing such an application, made this impractical to settlers seems not to have mattered. Another source of federal indifference to the farmer's cause was official suspicion that newcomers were not "bona fide" settlers, but rather speculators hoping to acquire title and then sell out at a profit. This practice seems to have been particularly widespread in the "boom" period immediately following the passage of the lease legislation, although it was in retreat by 1883.[76]

Notwithstanding these concerns, it appears that the decisive factor in shaping federal disregard of settler resentment was Ottawa's strong commitment to the ranching interests of southern Alberta, frankly stated by Secretary of the Interior A. M. Burgess in an 1883 letter to Wood. In words bearing a powerful resemblance to those of the Texas adjutant general (which were published in exactly the same year), Burgess extolled the courage of the risk-taking stockman, taking pains to emphasize to the editor the rationale behind Ottawa's support for the industry. Burgess wrote that "the grazing leaseholders are fulfilling a vitally important function in the North-West, and the true interests of the Government the settlers and the country generally are intimately connected with their success."[77]

Emboldened by such clear support from the capital, Alberta cattlemen stepped up their eviction campaign in order to keep pace with the rising tide of settlement. Their aggression prompted one exasperated editorialist from Pincher Creek to reflect on the government's numerous concessions to the ranchers. He noted scornfully that, "in spite of these advantages, and others too numerous to mention, the cry [from the cattlemen] is still for more."[78] The conflict reached a crisis point in the spring of 1885 when a handful of aggrieved homesteaders met south of Calgary to form the Alberta Settlers' Rights Association. Among the most frustrated of its members was Sam Livingston, an area farmer who had been unable to obtain patent to his lands despite the fact that he had occupied his current homestead more than five years before the lease legislation went into effect. Livingston now vowed to resist any further attempts by leaseholders to dislodge him, promising to defend his claim with a Winchester rifle.[79] Furthermore, in a move calculated to grab Ottawa's attention, the association linked its goals to those of another group seeking federal redress on complex land issues: the assembly passed a resolution urging the Dominion to recognize Métis claims in the North-West.

Alarmed by the settlers' complaints, federal officials sought to resolve

18. Sam Livingston, ca. 1890s. Courtesy of Glenbow Archives, NA-152-1.

the impasse between squatters and cattlemen. As important in stirring Ottawa to action was Prime Minister Macdonald's unhappiness with his leaseholding friends, many of whom had exploited their close relationships with the Conservative Party by failing to make rent payments and especially by flouting the minimum stocking guidelines. A Cochrane relative, for instance, was alleged to have only six horses on his 57,000-acre lease, despite requirements of at least one animal for every 10 acres.[80] In order to appease those clamoring for lands, Ottawa instituted sweeping changes to its land policy in southern Alberta. Officials canceled unstocked leases and announced that all new agreements would contain provisions for entry via homestead and preemption application. But the government went even further, doubling the rent for leased lands and encouraging ranchers bound by the old agreements to make some of their lands available to settlers.[81]

This response diverged sharply from the path chosen by Texas legislators, whose anti–fence cutting bill of 1884 appeared to favor the interests of big cattlemen at the expense of farmers and smaller cowmen. Several factors may explain Canada's more measured approach. First, by virtue of the lease agreements, Ottawa had maintained tight control over the country's range and could thus retool its policies as needed (or when politically expedient); no such option existed in the Lone Star State, where divestiture had created entrenched landholders largely inoculated against governmental intervention. Moreover, the absence of criminal activity (such as fence cutting) on the part of the aggrieved likely made compromise a much easier sell in Parliament; Texas officials, on the other hand, reacted predictably to the property destruction by seeking to curb lawlessness and to preserve order in the countryside.

Still, these alterations to the lease policy did not have a serious impact on Alberta's big ranchers. In order to appease the cattlemen—who were, after all, one of the core constituencies of the ruling Conservative Party—and also to guarantee the continued success of the industry, in 1886 Ottawa approved the permanent establishment of certain lands as stock-watering reserves. By this legislation, such parcels that bordered on or contained a body of running water were made inaccessible for lease, purchase, or enclosure, in order to guarantee livestock unimpeded access to fresh water, especially during the cold winter months when standing pools froze over. In theory, anyone owning cattle—from a few head to several thousand—stood to benefit from the government's new policy, since the reserves supposedly prevented the monopolization of essential resources. In practice, however, the set-asides allowed just that to occur, as large ranchers maintained control of the water—and thus the lands—of southern Alberta.

William Pearce, the superintendent of mines for the Department of the Interior, had proposed the idea of the reserve system the year before. Pearce was an impassioned advocate for the livestock interests of southern Alberta, in part because of his sincere belief that the region was unsuitable for farming, at least until the advent of improved irrigation technology. During the early 1880s, he had noted with alarm the practice of many Alberta settlers of homesteading on springs and rivers in order to cultivate the nutrient-rich bottomlands. This was problematic for a number of reasons, Pearce explained to the minister of the interior, not the least of which was the tendency of settlers to fence their plots so as to keep cattle from trampling their crops. In so doing, however, the farmers obstructed livestock from reaching the water. To prove his point, Pearce noted in his annual report for 1885 that a mere eighteen settlers had—through the construction of fences—rendered inaccessible twenty-five miles of the Belly River south of Fort Macleod. "For the purpose of settling 3 per cent. of the country [with farmers]," he asked rhetorically, "is it advisable to render 97 per cent. comparatively valueless [to ranchers]?"[82]

To be sure, Pearce was convinced that the reserve system would benefit the small farmer as well as the large cattleman, a perspective informed by his belief that all settlers in the region were in fact aspiring stockmen whose animals, too, would one day need access to springs and creeks. While many farmers would certainly have welcomed the chance to become big ranchers, and the isolation and aridity of southern Alberta no doubt complicated their plans to grow grain and vegetables, most had few alternatives to farming, given the prohibitive costs of leasing land and importing foundation stock. Moreover, as Pearce learned, homesteaders insisted that Ottawa had encouraged them to migrate to the region in the first place, and that with even a little support from the government they could manage to cultivate crops on precisely the lands that the superintendent and others hoped to deny them.

Most compromising to the notion that the set-asides were meant to assist all Albertans was the fact that Pearce closely coordinated his recommendations for reserve lands with the largest and most powerful ranchers in the area, soliciting their opinions on the matter. Even before the passage of the legislation establishing the stock-watering reserves, Pearce delivered a note to Stanley Pinhorne, the manager of the Oxley Ranch, urging him to contact the Department of the Interior with specific suggestions for reserve lands at present contained in the company's lease. That way, Pearce explained, even if Ottawa opened select townships in the Oxley territory, "the public should forthwith understand that . . . settlement or fencing would not be allowed on certain lands"—namely, those containing water and, in some cases, hay needed as livestock feed. Moreover, Pearce provided the manager with a complete list of townships embraced in part or whole by the Oxley lease and suggested a strategy for appealing to the secretary of the interior in order to secure them from homesteading.[83]

Pearce's dogged efforts smoothed the expansion of the reserve system during the second half of the 1880s. This extension gave the cattlemen even more control over southern Alberta than they had previously enjoyed under the closed lease policy.[84] Although the total amount of sequestered land was negligible considering the vastness of the region, the reserves effectively prevented homesteading on attractive river-bottom sites, prolonging the big ranchers' hegemony. While this was cause enough for farmers' concern, their passions were further inflamed by Ottawa's decision to reduce stocking requirements, which prescribed only one animal for every twenty acres (instead of every ten), a shift that had obvious and profound implications for the control of Alberta lands.

As before, some settlers squatted on lands to which they did not possess title, hoping that Ottawa—having decided that new leases were to be open and therefore applicable for homestead entry—might recognize their claims. Instead, Pearce worked closely with cattlemen to prevent squatters from gaining a foothold in the region, supporting ejection proceedings initiated by irritated leaseholders and even issuing warning letters to individuals who had staked claims to unsurveyed land. For instance, Pearce drafted a form letter in 1889 that he intended to mail to persons settling ahead of survey, urging them to move out.[85] Tensions between settlers and leaseholders thus remained high into the 1890s, as confirmed by a Mounted Police report from October 1891. Returning from a visit to several of the largest ranches in the area, scout Cecil Denny reported "a very irritated feeling existing on all sides," with settlers insisting that there were no lands open to them.[86]

Rangers and Mounties

With the passage of the 1884 fence cutting legislation, Austin had demonstrated its resolve to protect private property and to defend an industry of unquestioned economic value to the state. Officials now charged the Texas Rangers with eradicating fence destruction, which became the primary mission of the force in the spring of 1884. This was not, however, the first time the Rangers had been considered for such a job. Two years before, King had proposed to use the force—albeit in a relatively nonconfrontational way—to mediate range conflicts before they reached the boiling point.[87] If such a plan was put into effect by King before the 1883 troubles, though, it did little good in bringing about tranquillity between large and small ranchers on the cattleman's frontier: Rangers were investigating fence cutting cases less than six months after the adjutant general had filed his report.

There are at least two reasons why King and Ireland enlisted the Rangers to suppress fence cutting. First, the police had already proven their usefulness to the cattle industry by driving Native Americans from the state and dispossessing South Texas Mexicans of their livestock. More importantly, Austin had little faith in local law enforcement officials, many of whom reportedly backed the cutters. Governor Ireland, in fact, had said as much in his 1884 address to the state legislature, recommending that—in addition to the prosecution of wire cutters—the lawmakers levy a hefty penalty against any sheriff, deputy, or constable failing to investigate allegations of fence destruction.[88] His concerns were not unfounded, since Rangers and worried citizens alike wrote frequent letters complaining that local officials were in sympathy with the cutters and that juries would not convict men charged with such an offense.[89]

The state police, however, did not serve alone in their campaign against the wire cutters. Recognizing the difficulties inherent in apprehending the nippers, Ireland sought help from two detective agencies, Pinkerton's and Farrell's.[90] With the $50,000 appropriated to him by the legislature, the governor lured operatives from Chicago and New Orleans, who upon their arrival in Texas were sworn in as Rangers and issued police credentials.[91] Once established, the detectives disappeared into the countryside, hoping to infiltrate wire-cutting gangs by posing as disgruntled cowmen. Having ingratiated themselves with suspected perpetrators, the agents set about collecting names and evidence to be used at trial before calling in the Rangers to make arrests. Although this procedure worked well in one case from May 1884, resulting in the apprehension of eight Runnels County nippers caught in the act, King tired of this complex and largely unsuccessful approach by early spring. Explaining that he had little confidence in the detectives and preferred the Rangers' more immediate and direct efforts, the adjutant general canceled undercover operations by the end of June.[92]

Fueling King's frustrations, no doubt, was the fact that—given the support of local communities for men charged with fence cutting—convictions were hard to come by even in the face of overwhelming evidence. One detective reported with disgust on court proceedings in Erath County, where a grand jury had refused to indict alleged cutters for the offense despite the presence of excellent witnesses. As the operative explained to the adjutant general, he learned only afterward that a leading anti-fence man had served on the jury, along with several others of like mind.[93] For his part, Ranger captain G. W. Baylor—a strapping Confederate army veteran placed in charge of the Frontier Battalion with the express purpose of ending the cutting—was no less exasperated. Noting the difficulty of winning convictions against alleged fence cutters, Baylor suggested that better results might be obtained by moving the trials to particularly embattled locales such as San Antonio, Waco, Austin, and Fort Worth. Repeated failures to secure jail time for the offenders were dispiriting, Baylor said, and he urged that the punishment of even a few men would bring about a more desirable end.[94]

By the middle of 1884, Ranger squads were taking more aggressive action to halt the cutting, as suggested by a case from Edwards County, seventy-five miles northwest of San Antonio. The previous October, rancher G. B. Greer of Green Lake had suffered a downed fence, and in July 1884 he contacted Governor Ireland to express his concern that the rebuilt enclosure had been targeted once again for destruction.[95] Greer requested a Ranger detachment for protection, but before the arrival of the police, cutters had snipped the wire in order to water their cattle at a small lake surrounded by the fence. Upon reaching Greer's spread two days later, the four-man Ranger unit hid a short distance from the water, where they later witnessed several men attempting to undo the rancher's repeated patch work. Emerging from their position, the police advanced on the cutters, who—according to the Rangers—ignored squad leader P. F. Baird's order to surrender, shouting instead for the Rangers to "come on & take us in you damned sons of bitches." After what Baird described as "quite a hot but short battle" of ten minutes, one cutter lay dead with two gunshot wounds to the chest and one to the head.[96]

Though no doubt satisfying to Greer and the Rangers alike, this success—along with the arrest of thirty-six cutters between 1 December 1883 and 30 November 1884 alone—did not put an end to fence destruction.[97] Most vexing, perhaps, was the assassination in February 1885 of Ben Warren—the prosecution's star witness in the Runnels County case from the previous spring—which allowed a band of particularly active cutters to escape conviction. Such setbacks led one frustrated rancher to claim that the statute passed by the legislature was useless, and that stockmen in his part of north-central Texas had begun to despair of ever breeding fine-blooded cattle in separate pastures.[98] Stung by the criticism, King decided on a new approach in 1886, reviving undercover operations but with Rangers—and not private detectives—now serving as the infiltrators. Additionally, King resolved to focus police efforts on Brown County, the district with perhaps the most intractable fence cutting epidemic, and whose troubles reveal a wealth of information about the competing pastoral interests in central Texas in the mid-1880s as well as rare details about the cutters and their discontent.

Located near the geographical center of the state, Brown County developed rapidly as cattle country after its 1856 founding, with the number of animals rising from just under 4,000 to nearly 50,000 two decades later.[99] Most of the longhorns were owned by a handful of prominent cattlemen, who were among the first residents in the county. Like their counterparts throughout the state, these men responded to the arrival of settlers by fencing up their pastures, enclosing their own property as well as many of the county's 64,000 acres of appropriated school lands, a practice that infuriated farmers and small cowmen. Fence cutting thus began in the spring of 1883, and that fall a group of cutters razed two miles of a barbed-wire enclosure belonging to L. P. Baugh, one of the largest landowners in the county. They left behind a note that read: "Mr. Baugh, take down this fence; if you don't, we will cut it and if we cut it and a drop of the cutters' blood is spilled, your life will pay the forfeit."[100]

Baugh—who was legendary in Brown County for having nearly decapitated an Indian scout in the 1860s with a blast from his .8-gauge shotgun—did not take the threat lightly, and answered the message with one of his own: "You cowardly cur, this is my fence, and you let it alone."[101] When his fence was cut again one month later, Baugh approached Sheriff W. N. Adams and with his assistance organized a posse of twenty-six cattlemen, who visited the homes of suspected cutters and sternly warned them against any further fence destruction. This act so angered the small cowmen that 200 of them marched on Brownwood, the county seat, where they held a "Fence Cutters Convention" in the courthouse. Although Sheriff Adams managed eventually to disperse the men—and even wrangled a promise from their leaders to cease the cutting—tensions escalated once again in March 1885 when a grand jury indicted ten men for fence cutting on evidence supplied by Baugh. After two continuances, however, the charges were dismissed, lending credence to Ranger G. W. Baylor's complaint that the courts would not convict (or in this case, even try) alleged cutters.

It was at this point that the Baughs appealed directly to Adjutant General King, who dispatched Ira Aten, a young Ranger whom King had personally recruited earlier in the year for special duty in a fence cutting case in Lampasas County. The twenty-four-year-old Aten had been inspired to join the force (over his parents' objection) by an episode he witnessed as a young boy: the death of the outlaw Sam Bass, killed by a Ranger squad in the town of Round Rock after a botched bank heist.[102] On his new assignment in Brown County, Aten quickly insinuated himself with the cutters (mostly young men who lived near the Baughs) and learned that they planned to cut a fence belonging to the family on the night of November 9, 1886. King promptly sent four Rangers from Company F to Brownwood, where they set an ambush in conjunction with the Baughs and some of their hired hands. What happened after the cutters arrived on the scene was a matter of some dispute, with Aten maintaining that the cutters fired first, even though one local history insists that the police cut down the perpetrators in the act of escape.[103] Whatever the case, two men—Amos Roberts and twenty-four-year-old Jim Lovell—were killed. Ironically, they were buried in a remote corner of the Baugh property.

In the end, a grand jury indicted seven cutters in February 1887, but the cases were transferred that fall to Bell County, more than one hundred miles away. This, according to the judge, was because "a fair and impartial trial cannot be had in Brown County because of the existing combination and influence on the part of influential persons in favor of the accused and against the State of Texas."[104] Such circumstances indicate broad support for the cutters in their struggle against the large cattlemen, as does the reminiscence of a Baugh relative, offered nearly seventy years after the gunfight on his family's property. As George Baugh explained to a local historian: "We have been criticized for the course the Rangers took, but the wirecutters were no angels, and something had to be done to make a man's life and property safe."[105] For his part, Aten said at the time that the deaths had "done more to suppress fence-cutting than any other thing" in Brown County, although his colleague Captain Scott believed that prospects for a "Gay Christmas" depended on another killing before the holiday.[106]

A closer look at Ira Aten's career as a detective sheds additional light on fence cutting in Texas, including the shift in Ranger tactics during the late 1880s and the mounting dilemmas faced by opponents of enclosure.[107]

Following his 1886 success in Brown County, Aten traveled throughout the state on assignment, usually working alone. By the early autumn of 1888, however, he was ordered back to central Texas by Governor L. S. "Sul" Ross (himself a former Ranger), who commanded Aten to put an end to rampant fence cutting in Navarro County.[108] This time Aten took along fellow Ranger "Fiddling" Jim King, whose musical expertise they hoped to use to gain the cutters' confidence. Posing as newcomers to the region, the men were aided by the breakdown of their wagon outside of town, which wound up providing them with ample pretext to remain in the area indefinitely.[109]

Hoping to deflect any suspicion and also to meet some of the anti-fence men, the Rangers looked for work but found few opportunities, since the cotton crop that year was so poor that many people had simply abandoned the area. In the end, King and Aten secured positions baling and picking cotton, respectively, but at reduced pay. While waiting for the cotton season to begin, they busied themselves building a rock furnace around the gin, an activity that afforded them the opportunity to meet some of the cutters. The cover and access provided by these choices of employment are illuminating, for they suggest that some anti-fence men were forced by economic insecurity to move back and forth between positions as owner-operators and wage laborers. William Scott had made precisely this point about the Brown County gang in February 1887. He described the homestead of that region's average cutter as consisting of "from one to two Hip Shot Crosseyed Bandy Shanked sore backed good for nothing ponies, and a poor woman for a wife with two to five poor little half starved and necked [sic] little children."[110] The heads of such families likely turned to wire cutting when it appeared to them that should the fences stay put, they would inevitably become permanent wage workers.

Aten explained that the fence cutters in his region were generally "cowboys or small cow men" who owned somewhere between 15 and 200 cattle, with perhaps a hundred acres of land under cultivation. Although they targeted primarily the fences of area ranchers, they resented "grangers"—small farmers who often fenced up their lands—just as much, for many of the cutters nursed a fierce opposition to the very notion of enclosure, regardless of its purpose. In secret meetings of more than a hundred sympathizers, the anti-fence men vented their indignation about the pasture men and their supporters, on one occasion vowing to storm the local jail and rescue a handful of compatriots caught in the act. While Aten dismissed such threats as mere bravado, he did confess to a friend that he wished fellow Ranger detective John Hughes were with him in Navarro County, for "it is awful risky business as these villains are hard men."[111]

One month into his Navarro County investigation, however, Aten had soured on his mission. For one thing, he thought it impossible to gain the confidence of the wire cutters, because the anti-fence men did not appear to need any help, and at any rate they were wary of taking in anyone whom they did not know well. Without inside information, Aten knew that the execution of a successful Ranger ambush was unlikely. More troubling to him, though, was the clandestine nature of the work. As he explained in one letter, "We have had to tell ten thousand lies already & I know we wont get away with-out telling a million."[112] In addition, he loathed the prospect of actually destroying fences—essential if he and King were to establish any credibility—and found it "disgusting" to encourage the "good men" of the county to keep putting up their fences just so they could be cut down once again.[113] Still, he remained convinced that "nothing will do any good here but a first class killing & I am the little boy that will give it to them if they dont let the fence alone."[114]

This mixture of frustration and resolve led Aten to create what he called a "dynamite boom," an explosive device constructed from a shotgun packed with dynamite, gunpowder, and a blasting cap. Concealed underground, the contraption was designed to detonate when a cutter snipped the strand of barbed wire to which the "boom" was attached, triggering the cap and scattering "small pieces of that gun . . . all over Navarro County."[115] However, after Aten had set charges on all of the fences that had been cut in the previous year, Governor Ross learned of the plan and summoned him to Austin to explain. Aten later recalled that "while I was telling [Ross] of my experiences . . . that bald head of his got redder and redder, and when I had finished my story it was on fire." Ross did not order him to be court-martialed and shot, though, as Aten feared. Instead, the governor insisted that Aten return to Navarro County and remove the bombs, which the Ranger did by exploding them and thus terrifying the residents (cutters and noncutters alike) into believing that all the area fences were mined.[116] That ended fence destruction in the region, and Aten, who had sworn from the beginning of the operation that this would be his last mission, sold his belongings and left the area in mid-October.[117]

§

The frustration of settlers in western Canada reached a full boil in the early 1890s when Ottawa undertook a massive extension of the stock-watering reserve system, driven in large part by the demands of area ranchers. According to one historian, the government's action was the fulfillment of an "unwritten promise" between cattlemen and federal authorities which held that in exchange for accepting the complete cancellation of all closed leases by 1896, stockmen would receive expanded reserves.[118] Such an agreement exposes the conundrum faced by the Conservatives at the time. On the one hand, the party relied heavily on support from Alberta's ranching community and thus had to make large concessions to it, yet some members of the government recognized that waves of migration would be difficult to repress for much longer. As Deputy Minister of the Interior A. M. Burgess put it in 1887: "There can be no doubt that when an actual settler desires the land for the purpose of making his home upon it, it would be impossible, even if it were expedient, to keep him out."[119] The expanded reserves were Ottawa's attempt to seem responsive to farmer grievances while simultaneously advancing the big rancher's interests. Settlers, however, saw the plan as merely another handout to the cattlemen.

Beyond cementing their control of the region's scarce water supply, the extension of sequestered lands provided ranchers with a new weapon to use against the nesters: the NWMP. Until the expansion of the stock-watering reserve system in the 1890s, most squatting had taken place on leaseholds—lands privately held by individuals or companies, who were thus responsible for taking action against the interlopers. Therefore, eviction proceedings tended to go through the court system and usually resulted in an order for the squatter to desist. While the Mounted Police may have occasionally enforced such mandates, evidence supporting these assertions is spare. Rather, it seems that most squatters recognized the futility of their cause and simply abandoned the contested ground. With the extension of the reserve system, however, growing numbers of settlers now found themselves on public lands claimed by the government for the cattlemen, a circumstance that gave the NWMP (as a federal agency) unquestioned jurisdiction in the matter. While it seems unlikely that this feature was instrumental in the expansion of the reserves, it was clearly a perquisite for Alberta ranchers.

Pearce, for one, was determined to involve the Mounted Police in the new eviction proceedings because he believed it was imperative to send a strong and symbolic message that such practices would not be tolerated in cattle country. As he explained in an 1894 letter to the secretary of the Department of the Interior, "If this course [ejection by the NWMP] were taken in one or two cases it would undoubtedly effectually stop such attempts in the future."[120] Ranchers were no less interested in such a development, with the High River Stock Association urging the minister of the interior "that power be given the N.W.M. Police under the authority from the Superintendent of Mines, Calgary, to prevent & remove settlers attempting to take up land" near creeks or springs.[121] Such entreaties led the Department of the Interior in the spring of 1894 to retain police services in posting warning notices and even removing squatters from sequestered lands when necessary.[122]

For their part, police officials expressed skepticism about participating in the eviction campaign. Upon receiving a request from Secretary of the Interior John Hall to send a police detachment to destroy a collection of squatters' buildings near Calgary, NWMP comptroller Fred White wrote the deputy minister of justice to be certain "of the legality of [the squad's] action." White was subsequently informed by Hall that "there can be no doubt whatever both as to our having the power to do what is requisite and the propriety of exercising that power." Despite these assurances, White appears to have delayed issuing any orders to his force, since Pearce sent an angry letter to Hall several weeks later explaining that no action had been taken by the NWMP post at Calgary. The superintendent of mines added that "weakening on the part of the Department . . . would be fatal to the welfare of the stock interests."[123]

Police circumspection was not limited merely to concerns about the authority of the force to remove offenders. Mountie reluctance may have stemmed also from the sheer unpopularity of evictions among the wider public, a sentiment confirmed by letters and petitions sent to Ottawa in support of several squatters.[124] Moreover, the actual process of eviction could be highly unpleasant, as in the case of Felix Thiboutott, a farmer who had spent an estimated $250 in establishing himself and his family on lands deemed too close to a spring. When on 21 January 1895 a deputy sheriff from the town of Macleod—supported by a Mountie constable—began to empty the furniture from Thiboutott's house in preparation for pulling it down, the man's wife "declared herself ill and I believe went to bed," temporarily interrupting the proceedings. In the end, the family received permission to remove their shack to a distant corner of the Alberta Ranche

Company leasehold, far from the water source in question. Pearce, however, was irritated by the compromise, insisting that "the easiest way of dealing with such cases is to eject squatters when they first attempt to settle on reservations."[125]

Perhaps the most intriguing source of police distaste for eviction may have been the fact that, on occasion, members of the force who hoped to get a preretirement jump on ranching careers became squatters themselves, as suggested by one case from 1893.[126] That summer the manager of the New Oxley Ranch applied to the government for the purchase of some lands contained within the company's leasehold, between the forks of the Belly and Kootenay rivers. Upon making his investigation of the site, Pearce discovered that NWMP staff sergeant Chris Hilliard illegally occupied the territory. The policeman defended his actions by expressing his intent to leave the force and become "a bona fide settler." The case caused considerable discomfort at NWMP headquarters, where top officials were forced to acknowledge that some officers in the field looked the other way when men under their command acquired property while serving in the force. Worried that allowing Hilliard to persist would send the wrong message and appear to give license to the police to flout the very rules they had been ordered to enforce, Mountie brass supported Ottawa's command for Hilliard to desist (though allowing him first to remove his buildings and fences).

Hilliard's case suggests several important differences between the circumstances and aspirations of men who served in the Mounted Police and those who were Rangers. First, Hilliard (and other Mountie squatters) must have had personal wealth or access to capital that would have financed the improvements he made to the land he hoped to acquire. Moreover, Hilliard's plan to become a rancher immediately after his discharge from the NWMP contrasts sharply with the prospects awaiting former Rangers, many of whom entered the employ of a rancher or syndicate after leaving the force. Instead of raising their own cattle, these ex-Rangers were far more likely to find themselves riding fences or stringing wire for a big outfit, just as many of them had done before their enlistment. Finally, the more itinerant nature of the Ranger force provided the Texas police with limited opportunities to scout prospective homesteading locations on which to eventually settle. Mountie detachments, on the other hand, often spent extended periods posted at permanent forts, allowing men like Chris Hilliard to identify and even prepare nearby areas for residence.

At any rate, notwithstanding their misgivings the Mounted Police assisted in a number of squatter evictions between 1894 and 1896, complying with Ottawa's firm demands that they take such action. Although officials at the Department of the Interior noted that legal proceedings offered a viable means of effecting the squatters' removal from reserves, the minister of the interior had decided "that it would be in the public interest that the second of the methods"—eviction—be adopted.[127] While such a procedure no doubt had the symbolic value desired by Pearce, one historian has argued that it served also to "avert the attendant publicity of lengthy court battles," no small consideration given the unpopularity of the practice among many Albertans.[128] Tearing down offending structures proved to be more efficient and expedient.

Police involvement usually began with a request from Pearce (spurred by a rancher's complaint) to investigate the erection of a building or fence along a spring earmarked for stock-watering purposes. Provided that the Mountie detachment found that the squatter was indeed in violation of the law, the police were authorized to seize the ground "on behalf of Her Majesty" and raze or remove the illegal structures. Superintendent Sam Steele described the process matter-of-factly in his report for 1895: "Several evictions of settlers charged with illegally squatting have been conducted at the request of the Department of Interior. All parties had been previously warned that certain lands had been set aside by the department as 'stock watering reserves,' and the risks they ran by squatting without first obtaining proper authority had been explained to them."[129] Although on occasion members of the force showed some of their previous reluctance for the task—in one instance granting a squatter three weeks to harvest his crops before returning to evict him—they nevertheless faithfully executed their orders.[130]

In the end, the efforts of the Rangers and the Mounties to defend the cattleman's empire at the edges of the Great Plains produced different results. In Texas, fence cutting declined sharply throughout the remainder of the 1880s, with arrests plummeting from a high of thirty-six in 1884 to an average of only four per year for 1886 and 1887.[131] (Given the clandestine nature of the offense and the difficulty in apprehending cutters in the act, however, these figures must be read with caution.) Although Rangers and pro-fence men alike maintained that the occasional killing of a wire cutter was the most effective means of ending the destruction, it seems rather that Adjutant General King's new tactics deserve most of the credit. By using small Ranger squads to eradicate the offense in the handful of the most troubled counties—including Lampasas, Navarro, and especially Brown—King demonstrated both the resolve and the ability of the police to protect the ranchers' private property. Fear of Aten's "dynamite boom" was also significant, particularly its role in deterring would-be cutters in the area south of Dallas.

The dramatic decline in fence cutting led W. H. King to declare in 1888 that the epidemic had come to an end, and he gave credit to the police under his command, noting that "the efforts of the Rangers have had an immense and seemingly lasting effect."[132] To be sure, sporadic reports of fence destruction persisted into the following decade, as suggested by an impassioned letter from 1893 written by county judge (and future governor) John N. Garner, who asked for "three good Rangers" to wipe out the practice in his South Texas district.[133] Most other complaints at this time came from West Texas and especially the Panhandle, which in the 1890s experienced the ripples of westward migration that had produced such conflict in the central portion of the state. Yet most settlers arriving in those parts had witnessed the Ranger-assisted triumph of barbed wire further east and simply accepted the victory of enclosure as inevitable, leaving the large cattleman to breed and graze his stock unencumbered by the protestations and anonymous violence of the small Texas cowman.

Events took a dramatically different turn in Canada, where the forced removal of squatters by the NWMP came to an abrupt end with the victory of Wilfrid Laurier's Liberal Party in the 1896 parliamentary elections. Out of sheer political necessity, the Liberals had come to champion the rights of settlers who opposed Alberta cattlemen, almost all of whom backed the ruling Conservative Party, which had been in power since 1878. Ranchers expressed considerable anxiety over the change in leadership, exacerbated by Laurier's appointment of a new minister of the interior, Clifford Sifton, who—while not hostile to ranching interests per se—believed fervently in promoting farm settlement.[134] Sifton received staunch support from Frank Oliver, a Liberal M.P. from Edmonton (and later Sifton's successor at the Department of the Interior), who inundated him with memos opposing evictions and decrying the biased nature of the reserve system.

The reserves did not simply evaporate, since the Liberal government recognized the importance of the cattle industry to the financial health of the Dominion. Still, the Department of the Interior developed new policies with respect to the creation of reserves. In the first place, no longer could the mere recommendations of cattlemen or their associations serve as grounds for the alienation of a given tract. Prior to the establishment of any new reserves, officials were now required to conduct a thorough inspection of the lands in question in order to ascertain the possible existence of any private rights. Such inquiries led to decisions such as the one contained in a July 1897 letter from an interior official to Pearce (soon to be demoted to inspector of surveys), denying a request by the powerful Bar U Ranch for the government to evict a settler from prospective reserve land.[135] The upholding of the rights of squatters was "a complete reversal of earlier government policy."[136]

The tactics of the police in ejecting squatters from established stock-watering reserves experienced a seismic shift as well, a change initiated even before the end of 1896. As the deputy minister of justice explained in a November letter to his counterpart at the Department of the Interior describing appropriate police actions in the case of eviction, if "the squatter does not peaceably give up possession of the premises . . . it would not be proper to use force to remove him."[137] Indeed, the NWMP reverted to the pre-1894 practice of taking such matters before the court for reasons outlined by Comptroller Fred White in a 1905 letter to the secretary of the interior. White noted that "on one occasion, when it was thought that the Police were using their uniform, prestige and official position to frighten settlers . . . newspaper articles immediately appeared charging the Police Force with eviction similar to those in Ireland, and warning people against coming to Canada."[138] Negative publicity of this kind was anathema to the immigration policy of the new government.

The divergent outcomes for farmers and small ranchers in Texas and Alberta suggest a host of other key differences between the policies of government officials in Austin and Ottawa and their enforcement by the two constabularies. On the most fundamental level, the contrasting systems of land tenure in Texas and Canada distinguished their respective ranching empires. Although federal officials strongly desired to populate the North-West with whites loyal to the government, they were no less resolved to maintain tight control over those lands, and thus chose to lease rather than sell off vast portions of southern Alberta. This system permitted Ottawa to make changes to its land policy as circumstances required, such as the amending of lease laws and the opening of select townships for settlement in the mid-1880s. Although such moves did little to redress the basic imbalance between big syndicates and smaller ranchers and farmers, initiatives like these nevertheless allowed the federal government to seem responsive to the demands of settlers.

In Texas, by comparison, Reconstruction-era distrust of government and the powerful impetus of resource development fueled the state to divest itself of its public lands. In the wake of this liquidation, Austin retained little direct control over vast swaths of now private real estate, and could thus institute few proactive measures to reduce the tensions between big and small ranchers. In marked contrast to the Canadian example, Texas lawmakers only inserted themselves into the debate after the eruption of violence in 1883, and even then produced a decree—the anti–fence cutting legislation of 1884—that clearly favored one interest at the expense of the other. Furthermore, the privatization of the state's public domain imbued Texas cattlemen with a powerful sense of entitlement, leading them to defend their claims with thickets of barbed wire (as was their right), even as the enclosure of the range created a sense of desperation among small cowmen and poorer homesteaders.

While the inequity of the Canadian lease system clearly irritated individuals of more modest means, both the fine print of the agreements (permitting cancellation) and the rhetoric of the government (promoting settlement) indicated a level of official flexibility totally absent in Texas. The Canadian elections of 1896 clearly demonstrate the importance of this political latitude. Because Alberta's land base remained under federal control, once the Liberals were in charge they could modify the government's positions on land use to suit their own constituency, attacking the entrenchment of the cattlemen by curtailing the stock-watering reserves. This was an impossible scenario with an alienated land base, as in Texas, where—even had the Populist moment occurred ten years earlier, in the mid-1880s—undoing the transfer of title in fee simple would have been a very tall order indeed, given the sanctity of private property.[139]

The timing and conditions of settlement played significant roles in determining the course of events in Texas and Alberta. At the southern end of the Plains, tensions between big and small ranchers erupted at the moment and in the zone of the abrupt transition from one pastoral system (the open range) to another (enclosure). People who had formerly relied upon a common resource now found themselves bitterly divided over its use, and in many cases (as in Brown County) the new order pitted neighbors against one another in an intensely personal conflict. Complicating matters was the fact that some cattlemen acted illegally, appropriating lands that did not belong to them along with the sections to which they were entitled by purchase, actions that fueled the irritation of the farmer and small cowman. Because the state government had largely divested itself from the contested lands, those who opposed enclosure directed their anger at the big ranchers, loosing their frustration on the barbed wire they blamed for their suffering.

In Alberta, on the other hand, Ottawa planted a large cattleman's empire well ahead of the tide of Eurocanadian settlement. By the time sizable numbers of white migrants arrived in the far reaches of the North-West, the dominance of the big rancher was an established (if resented) fact. Moreover, while they may have acted aggressively in pursuing the eviction of squatters, Canada's ranching elite rarely broke the laws set by Ottawa (save for the flouting of stocking guidelines and such), and they did not build structures to prevent trespass. (In this way, the "closure" of the Canadian range was actually the very act of keeping it open by preventing farmers from fencing up water or feed, which provides a neat inversion of the situation in Texas.) Thus it was that squatters in Alberta—unlike fence cutters in the Lone Star State—generally aimed their disappointment at the officials responsible for the land policy in the West and had few hallmarks of syndicate hegemony (such as a fence) on which to visit their rage.

These factors help to explain the higher levels of violence in Texas—where at least three people were killed—than in Canada, where there is little evidence of any gunplay (and certainly no fatal confrontations) between squatters and cattlemen. Aggravated by local conflict and despairing of any assistance from the state, disgruntled farmers and small cowmen in Texas took up the wire cutters in order to halt fencing. Part of their plan, no doubt, was to dissuade ranchers from enclosing land through the dissemination of fear and threats of violence, hence the nighttime raids, the menacing notes, and the brandishing of firearms. The ranchers, on the other hand, responded to the threats against life and property by resorting to force and, when that failed, calling upon the state to send in the Rangers, who entered a highly combustible situation after 1884. Armed with a mandate to eradicate the offense and—as explained by Ira Aten—a healthy fear of the fence cutters' hostility, the Rangers seem to have adopted a "kill or be killed" perspective in their dealings with the perpetrators.

None of these conditions obtained in western Canada. First, given the ranchers' roots in southern Alberta and their broad political influence, the best that the squatters could hope for was to establish a toehold in the region; directly challenging the power of the big cattlemen—as the fence cutters in Texas sought to do—was out of the question. Second, while it is hard to determine the extent of squatting on leaseholds or reserves, census figures suggest implicitly that the practice was much less widespread (and thus less troublesome to authorities) than fence destruction in Texas. While in 1881 there were an estimated 56,000 residents of the entire North-West Territories (which comprised the present-day provinces of Alberta, Saskatchewan, and Yukon), Brown County alone had more than one-seventh that number.[140] Finally, the court system in Canada worked well enough to adjudicate many squatting cases; in Texas, the perceived inability of the state to win convictions against alleged cutters incited vigilantism and, in some instances, convinced the Rangers that shotguns were a more useful deterrent than the threat of legal action.

These observations alone, however, do not necessarily explain why the Rangers worked so diligently to suppress fence cutting. To a man, they appear to have hated the assignment, especially the secrecy and patience it required, not to mention the necessary deception of cutters and pro-fence men alike. Some members of the force even expressed the belief that just picking up a pair of nippers—no matter how essential to their disguise—made them as guilty as the cutters themselves. Additionally, the average Ranger likely had more in common socially and economically with the small cowmen and farmers who did most of the cutting than they did with those Texans who could afford spools of barbed wire. Aten, for instance, while on assignment in Navarro County, expressed his desire upon his retirement from the force to move to the Panhandle, where he would "settle down on a little farm [and] get to nesting."[141] Enclosing a few thousand acres and running a herd of fine-blooded stock, on the other hand, was probably beyond his monthly salary of fifty dollars.

One possible explanation for the loyalty of the police to the pro-fence men turns on the clandestine nature of the cutters' operations. As much as the Rangers disliked their own secrecy, they reserved a special scorn for the wire cutter who anonymously destroyed the property of others. Still more

19. A posed photo of Ranger Ira Aten taken during the height of the fence cutting epidemic in Texas during the mid-1880s. Courtesy of Western History Collections, University of Oklahoma Libraries.

damning in the eyes of the police was the association of the anti-fence men with petty criminals. Rangers, for the most part, saw little justification behind the cutting and, in the words of Captain G. W. Baylor, attributed the destruction to horse, cow, and hog thieves who took advantage of the confusion in order to enrich themselves.[142] That large sections of the population, including some local law enforcement officers, backed the cutters was of little consequence; the nippers, according to Captain William Scott, were "of the lowest order originating from a cross between the Hiena and the Javiline Hog," raising their children to become thieves and murderers.[143]

There were also clear economic advantages for Rangers who defended pasture men. Just as George Durham took a position at the King Ranch after his tour of duty in McNelly's unit, so, too, did Rangers working in North and West Texas find employment with some of the very cattlemen they had protected. In De Witt County east of San Antonio, the owners of a large ranch convinced three Rangers to quit the force and accept positions guarding their pasture, which had been targeted by fence cutters.[144] Aten, meanwhile, did retire and move to the Panhandle. He never became a nester, as he had hoped, but instead served as the sheriff of Castro County until he tired of law enforcement work altogether. Despite his wife's protestations, Aten then accepted an offer from the XIT Ranch, where he—along with former Rangers Ed Connell and Wood Saunders—tracked cattle rustlers and kept watch over the Capitol Syndicate's 6,000 miles of fence.[145]

The support of Alberta ranchers by the Mounted Police is much less difficult to fathom, given that former Mounties were among the region's first cattlemen and that many more hoped to enter the business upon their retirement from the force. It stood to reason that they would protect an industry that they had helped to found and promote and which held the promise of future economic advancement. Much more than the Rangers, the Mounted Police—especially its officer corps—stood on relatively equal footing with members of the ranching community they served, and they developed strong social ties to area stockmen through both work and leisure. The occasional empathy they showed toward the squatters must be read in the context of their class prejudices, and thus appears more as a streak of paternalism than deep-seated ambivalence about the nature of their duties or the authority of the state to impose its will.

Despite these critical differences, the ranching empires that developed at opposite ends of the Great Plains in the 1870s and 1880s bore striking similarities to one another and thus illuminate the process of incorporation that transformed Texas and the Canadian North-West at the end of the nineteenth century. On the most fundamental level, each government decided to turn over vast amounts of public land to bonanza ranchers at virtually the same moment, and for nearly identical reasons. Politics played a role in both cases, since the ruling Conservative Party in Ottawa sought to reward one of its core constituencies, while in Texas an ideology of divestiture partly inspired the liquidation of the state's land base. More important in the capitals, however, were the prospective financial gains—such as the influx of foreign investment—of such an enterprise and especially the big rancher's strategic significance in establishing a beachhead for white occupation in areas previously beyond the control of Austin and Ottawa.

The land policies that facilitated these developments heavily favored wealthy individuals and corporations and placed smaller ranchers and homesteaders at both ends of the Plains in a similar predicament. In Texas, Austin's rapid (even aggressive) sale of the public domain left those who had depended on the free-grass system watching with dismay as rich syndicates erected miles of barbed wire fence around formerly communal pastures and water holes. Those who fenced up lands that did not belong to them further aggravated a tense situation, made still more desperate by the vagaries of the Texas climate. Farmers and small cowmen in Alberta fared little better, as the leaseholders took control of the best lands of southwestern Canada almost overnight and rigidly expelled outsiders. Like his Texas counterpart, the Canadian farmer became increasingly frustrated with his exclusion from the most attractive range, staked off by Ottawa as stock-watering reserves.

The perspectives and responses of the farmers and small cowmen in Texas and Alberta invite clear comparisons to the protests against enclosure in eighteenth- and nineteenth-century England. At the southern end of the Plains, farmers and small ranchers complained that a handful of wealthy individuals backed by foreign investors had seized more than their share of the public domain, by means both fair and foul. The rural poor objected less to the privatization of property than to the fact that a few people or corporations could control a disproportionate amount of real estate, barring the economic and social advancement of others. Likewise, Alberta farmers—or, more precisely, their advocates—attacked the perceived injustices of Ottawa's lease policy through explicit reference to English colonial policy in Ireland. Such an analogy carried weight, since the provinces of Canada had only joined together in Confederation in 1867, and the ties to the British Empire and the Old World were still very strong. By likening the situation on the Canadian ranching frontier to the Irish experience of the eighteenth and nineteenth centuries, observers conjured images of landlords, tenants, and evictees—actors in a historical drama characterized by wealth for the few and destitution for the many.

When fence cutters and squatters challenged the control of the range by large cattlemen, Austin and Ottawa turned to their rural constabularies to enforce regulations favoring the "big man's frontier." Texas officials passed legislation that made fence cutting a felony (a statute still in force today), and charged the Rangers with eradicating the offense, initially backing their efforts with a $50,000 appropriation. Ottawa, on the other hand, sought more symbolic assistance from the Mounties. While the NWMP did, on occasion, forcibly remove squatters and tear down their improvements, the vigilance of the police in attending evictions and barn razings executed by local law enforcement officials demonstrated the unwavering support of the distant federal government for large cattlemen. That they performed essentially the same task as the Rangers, however, is quite clear: in the words of one historian, the Mounties were called upon "to man the final line of defense against the homesteaders' advance."[146]

If, in the end, the Liberal triumph of 1896 marked a victory for farmers and small ranchers in Alberta, they would suffer once more with their Texas counterparts in the second and third decades of the twentieth century. This time, however, big cattlemen and government policies were not to blame; after all, a precipitous decline in beef prices and the brutal winter of 1906–7 had crippled the Canadian ranching industry, smoothing the path of the farmers' ascent.[147] Rather, the new political calculus in Ottawa—coupled with several years of abundant precipitation and the aggressive promotion of the West by boosters—convinced hundreds of thousands of settlers to head for the region straddling the provincial boundary between Alberta and Saskatchewan.[148] Although they had prevailed in their struggle for the lands of the former North-West, when the rainfall reverted to its normal patterns, farmers in the Canadian West learned that William Pearce (though arrogant and sanctimonious) had been right all along about the unsuitability of the lands for intensive cultivation. It was a lesson that nesters in the Texas Panhandle might also have understood. Having defied the odds to take up homesteads among their cattle-ranching neighbors, they could only watch as the dust storms of the 1930s swallowed their farms and their dreams.[149]

5 Policing the Industrial Frontier

One day in 1889 Ranger private John L. Sullivan witnessed an argument at a drugstore in Thurber, Texas, between Colonel Robert D. Hunter, president of the Texas and Pacific Coal Company (T&PCC), and Thomas Lawson, a saloon keeper and ex-company official. Tensions between the former associates had simmered for some time, since the Colonel—who effectively ruled the town—had tried repeatedly to run Lawson out of business, insisting that the bar owner had encouraged disgruntled miners to quit work at the company.[1] On the day in question, Hunter had a chance encounter with Lawson, and the two men began to curse loudly at one another. Hearing the commotion, Sullivan rushed into the store "just in time to see Hunter burst the bottom of a spittoon out over Tom Lawson's head." Sullivan quickly intervened in the fight, and for his troubles he received a severe pummeling at the hands of Lawson's 230-pound bartender, who caught the Ranger by the neck and "commenced beating my head, nose and eyes until my face looked like jelly."[2]

Sullivan's role in the melee was neither as a mere bystander nor as a law enforcement officer; rather, he intervened on Hunter's behalf as a company employee, having taken a leave of absence from the force in order to serve the Colonel during a labor disturbance at the T&PCC. Hunter had asked specifically for Sullivan, and the company paid him $100 per month for his services, double the rate normally earned by Ranger privates at the time. The Colonel also picked up some of Sullivan's expenses, including a fine of $12 charged to the Ranger for his involvement in the altercation, which cost the other participants $200 apiece. Although the intimacy of this particular arrangement was atypical, the close relationship between the constabulary and company management was not, since T&PCC officials relied on the

20. Ranger W. J. L. Sullivan, 1896. Courtesy of Texas State
Library and Archives Commission.

Rangers to keep the peace at Thurber during a series of unionization drives at the mines between 1888 and 1903 that the company opposed.

At the opposite end of the Great Plains, federal and territorial officials called on the NWMP to intervene at Lethbridge, Alberta, in a similar dispute at the Alberta Railway and Coal Company (AR&CC) that flared up time and again from 1894 to 1906. Although no Mounties took the liberties enjoyed by Sullivan at the T&PCC, in many respects the circumstances at Lethbridge were nearly identical to those in the North Texas mines. As with the works at Thurber, the AR&CC was the largest and most important colliery in its region, delivering much of its output to railroad companies. Miners at Lethbridge faced the same abject living and working conditions as their Texas counterparts, and sought unionization as a means of improving their lot. And just as T&PCC officials vigorously contested the organizational efforts of their workers, so too did AR&CC management resist the insinuation of labor activists among their employees.

An examination of the T&PCC, the AR&CC, and the bitter strikes against them suggests the extent of industrial development and conflict that had emerged at the edges of the grasslands as early as the 1880s. This picture revises the usual perceptions of late nineteenth-century Texas and Alberta as exclusively rural domains, home only to cattle ranches and wheat fields. Moreover, in focusing on the antistrike roles played by the Mounties and Rangers, such a study says much about the importance of state intervention on management's behalf. By delaying or preventing unionization among miners, rural police assisted the smooth functioning of fledgling collieries, which sped overall industrial development on the prairies. In this way, government use of the two constabularies was less a regrettable excess than an essential feature of nascent industrialization on the late nineteenth-century Great Plains.

Coal Mining in Texas and Western Canada

Though lagging behind the wealthier and more populous eastern sections of the country, the Canadian Plains had begun to develop an industrial base by the end of the nineteenth century. In Alberta, for instance, the late 1880s and early 1890s witnessed the relative decline of local craft enterprise and its replacement by more significant manufacturing operations. While most of these ventures were small, with each establishment averaging only about twenty employees, they were backed by more than $5 million of capital investment from eastern Canada and Great Britain. According to one political economist, by the time Alberta obtained provincial status in 1905, "Large-scale capitalist manufacturing was becoming evident in brewing, electric power generation, lumber milling, flour milling, meat packing, and some textile production."[3]

More impressive as a measure of industrial development on the prairies was the torrid pace of railroad construction there, epitomized by the completion of the transcontinental Canadian Pacific Railway (CPR), which connected Montreal to Port Moody, British Columbia.[4] With the securing of the last spike at Craigellachie in 1885, the CPR—along with numerous smaller branch railways—made possible the development of the vast natural resources of the North-West. Though rich in timber reserves and mineral deposits, the region also boasted an expanse of fertile prairie, seen by the government as the basis for an agricultural empire that would feed the towns and cities of eastern Canada.

Resource development, however, was not the only factor behind the push to extend Canada's railways. In the 1870s and 1880s there was a deep and growing anxiety in Ottawa that the rapid trans-Mississippi growth of the United States posed a significant threat to Canada's own national aspirations. Most significant was the Canadian fear that American belief in the Manifest Destiny of the United States to occupy the entire continent might lead its settlers to claim lands north of the international boundary. These concerns contributed to the implementation of Canada's National Policy, a general development plan based on protective tariffs, state-sponsored immigration, and—most importantly—western expansion.[5] The CPR was the linchpin of the government's strategy, a lifeline that would bind the eastern and western sections of the nation and make clear that the Canadian frontier belonged exclusively to the Dominion.

Given the central importance of a dependable energy supply to this urgent railroad expansion, coal production likewise became a national imperative in Canada during the late nineteenth century, particularly in the West, where the existence of large coal deposits had been known as early as the 1830s. With the construction of the CPR and other rail networks, the limited mining ventures on the prairies grew at an impressive rate.[6] For example, between 1884 and 1906 annual output from mines in Alberta, Saskatchewan, and the Crow's Nest Pass area of British Columbia jumped from a mere 3,000 tons to more than 2,075,000 tons. Given the railroads' bottom-less demand for fuel—coupled with the heating needs of settlers during the frigid winter months on the Canadian Plains—industry titans such as James Dunsmuir and Sir Alexander Galt turned carbon into cash. For instance, the estimated value of the coal produced in the Galt mines of southern Alberta rose from just $11,000 in 1884 to $677,000 twenty years later.[7]

This wealth did not necessarily trickle down to the men and boys who actually dug the coal and hauled it to the surface. Although some Canadian miners could earn upwards of three dollars daily—decent wages for the time—their unskilled coworkers toiling aboveground took home less, sometimes as little as twenty-four cents per hour for the grueling jobs of cutting timber or dumping tailings, the unwanted rocks mixed in with chunks of coal.[8] Moreover, employment conditions in the Canadian West were dangerous, exacerbated by the incentives for swift work, which led some miners to cut corners in an attempt to increase productivity. One historian has shown that death rates in the coal mines of western Canada in the early twentieth century were more than twice those in Nova Scotia, the nation's other major coal-producing region.[9]

That the majority of the miners were immigrants placed them at a still greater disadvantage in the economy of western Canada. Their low status—born in large part of their ethnicity—invited exploitation, first from the *padrones* who lured them to Canada, and then from their employers, who received an assist from the federal government.[10] One scholar has explained that, before World War I, "the Dominion's immigration policy emphasized the recruitment of 'stalwart peasants' from Europe who could both push back the frontier of settlement and provide the labour needed on a casual or seasonal basis in the country." In this way, the Canadian government's loftier goal of promoting immigration by Finns, Czechs, Italians, Hungarians, and Poles as a means of settling the West was quickly displaced by a policy aimed more at "importing an industrial proletariat." Of the three million immigrants who entered the Dominion between 1900 and 1914, more than half of them settled in the West.[11]

These new arrivals discovered that living conditions in the prairie mining communities befitted management's—not to mention Ottawa's—perception of them as little more than "surrogate brutes."[12] As described by one historian: "The mining camps displayed all the worst features of company towns. Operators owned everything. Workers were obliged to trade at company stores where, miners charged, prices were outrageously high. The men and their families lived in company houses. Few of the cabins had sanitary facilities, because companies refused to permit municipal incorporation."[13] This last feature—poor sanitation—created conditions so inhospitable that men in one Alberta community recalled finding bedbugs in their pancakes, while workers at another mine in the same province considered "a typhoid epidemic . . . to be an annual event."[14]

In spite of the physical hazards they faced at the mines and in their ramshackle houses, probably the greatest concern to the men who worked the coalfields of the Canadian prairies—which stretched eastward into Saskatchewan from the border between British Columbia and Alberta—was their perpetual job insecurity. Because of the seasonal nature of the Canadian coal market, businesses such as Alexander Galt's AR&CC, easily the dominant mining operation on the prairies at the end of the nineteenth century, would regularly lay off half their workforces during the slower summer months. With few employment opportunities available in the community, discharged miners often left town in search of agricultural labor. Those chosen by management to retain their positions worked fewer hours at reduced wages.[15]

During the coal industry's early years, miners in the Canadian West could not count on much assistance in challenging the conditions of their employment, since unions had made marginal inroads into the prairie labor scene by the late nineteenth century. The slow pace of organization was due in part to the strident efforts of employers to crush unionism before it took root, as bluntly expressed by a coal magnate from British Columbia in a 1903 interview with a royal commission investigating labor practices. When asked by the board if he fired men suspected of belonging to a union, the mine owner replied simply: "Every time."[16] Moreover, the polyglot nature of the mining camps severely limited the attempts of the primarily English-speaking activists to attract workers to unions, already a difficult task given the challenges in uniting laborers across ethnic lines.[17] The relative weakness of organized labor in the West, however, did not stop miners from agitating for better living and working conditions.

§

Late nineteenth-century industrial development in Texas mirrored the slow and steady transformations taking place on the Canadian prairies. Although

Texas was not on a par with industrial giants of the eastern United States such as Pennsylvania and New York, by 1890 the state—much like southern Alberta—had developed a growing manufacturing base. With capital investments of $46 million and gross production values of more than $70 million (figures roughly comparable to those of Virginia), Texas ranked second only to California in industrial development among all western states.[18] Lured by jobs in textiles, lumber, and clay, roughly 35,000 Texans (representing nearly 2 percent of the state's population) sought work in more than 5,000 factories in 1890, numbers that rose sharply throughout the decade.[19]

As in the Canadian West, the expansion of the Lone Star State's rail network offers a still more dramatic indication of its accelerating industrial growth. At the completion of the nation's first transcontinental line in 1869, Texas contained fewer than 500 miles of track. Just two decades later, however, more than 8,500 miles crisscrossed the state, with only Illinois and Kansas boasting more mileage.[20] This hurried construction—the work of companies such as the Missouri Pacific, the Gulf, Colorado and Santa Fe, and the Southern Pacific—spread out in all directions from Houston, connecting the state's resource-rich hinterlands to its largest port and railroad depot, which served as the gateway to domestic and international markets. By 1890 rail lines had reached all the state's major cities—from San Antonio to El Paso, Dallas to Laredo—facilitating rapid settlement. The state's population nearly doubled between 1870 and 1880 and grew by at least 28 percent during each of the next three decades, so that by 1910 the population of Texas hovered at around four million.[21]

The massive construction of railroads during the late nineteenth century gave rise to the other major industrial development at this time in Texas: coal mining. The presence of large coal deposits in the state was known as early as the 1830s, when a geologist reported the discovery of lumps and outcroppings of lignite along the banks of the Trinity River in the north-central part of the state. Although federal explorations in the two decades that followed turned up additional lodes close to the Rio Grande, near Laredo and Eagle Pass, none of the beds received much consideration as the source of a fuel industry until the 1880s. By that time, the expansion of the state's rail network had created a demand for additional fossil fuels needed to drive locomotives as well as the smelters involved in steel production. Indeed, as one historian has noted, "In every respect, railroads became the prelude to the opening and extension of the coal industries in . . . Texas."[22]

In light of these developments, mining boomed in the southern part of the state. Northern Texas, however, soon emerged as the heart of the industry, with the discovery in the mid-1880s of a "pencil" vein of bituminous coal running through Erath and Palo Pinto counties, an arid and desolate region located seventy-five miles west of Fort Worth. How and by whom the lode was found remains unclear; the most enduring story involves a chance meeting between a local farmer and William Whipple Johnson, an entrepreneur who had arrived in Texas in the late 1870s, perhaps to escape bankruptcy proceedings in his native Michigan. According to the story, Johnson—who had contracted to procure cross ties for the Texas and Pacific Railway (T&PR)—was searching for timber one afternoon when he stopped in at a farmhouse to ask for a drink of water. The farmer who offered Johnson refreshment told the young entrepreneur about a thin layer of black rock he had encountered while digging a well. This piqued Johnson's interest, and—guessing that the black rock was probably coal—he offered to buy the property.[23]

Whatever the circumstances of the deposit's discovery, Johnson and his younger brother Harvey sank their first shaft in North Texas in late 1886, striking a twenty-six-inch vein of coal. They quickly incorporated, naming their venture simply the Johnson Coal Mining Company, and agreed to provide fuel to Jay Gould's T&PR, which in turn planned to build a spur line directly to the mines in order to facilitate extraction and delivery. The area's industry dominance was cemented two years later when the U.S. Geological Survey issued a highly favorable report concerning the potential for commercial production of the North Texas coal beds, boosting investor confidence. By 1889 Erath County mines produced 75,000 tons of coal per annum, representing nearly 60 percent of the state's total.[24]

In addition to bankers and railroad officials, the Johnson operation drew the attention of experienced miners, some of whom had come from as far away as Pennsylvania to work a nearby vein at Coalville, in Palo Pinto County. That venture, first developed in 1880, had closed down by 1886, owing in large part to ongoing labor strife.[25] Also looking for employment were former ranch hands, put out of work by the enclosure of the Texas range and the obsolescence of the trail drive. European immigrants constituted a third group of workers at the Johnson mines, although it is difficult to determine their numbers and countries of origin. The census of 1890 indicated 351 foreign-born residents living in Erath County, and it seems safe to assume that many (if not most) of them worked at the mines.[26]

As in Canada and elsewhere throughout North America, employment conditions in the Texas coal mines were poor, although circumstances in the Johnson shafts were made harder still by the thinness of the coal seam, so that excavation required twice as much labor. Working on their sides or their knees in "rooms" thirty feet wide but usually less than a yard high, Erath County miners dug and blasted their way through the earth, sending tons of coal and rock to the surface for separation and weighing. Such work, of course, took a grave toll on the men of the "subterranean community," as described by one historian:

> Certain physical signs identified workers as coal miners. They often looked pale because of limited exposure to the sun. They walked with a stooped back caused by years of working under low mine roofs, and streaks of coal dust had invaded their skin through scratches and cuts. . . . "Second knees," large calluses caused by constant pressure on the kneecaps, and strained necks from lying on the side and stretching to undercut, shoot, and pull down coal, further distinguished the low-coal miner from other workers.

These ailments probably seemed minor, however, when compared to the suffering inflicted by cave-ins, unpredictable explosive equipment, and out-of-control mining cars, to name but a few of the more lethal occupational hazards lying below ground.[27]

Conditions back on the surface did little to alleviate the miners' physical miseries. Given the workers' dependence on other employees, the myriad delays involved in such a complex and labor-intensive industry cost the miners between 20 and 30 percent of their potential earnings as valuable work time was consumed in waiting for empty mine cars or passenger elevators to return. Moreover, the short working season characteristic of North American coal production meant that miners in Erath County experienced vexing slack periods, averaging more than seventy days per annum, which had the effect of driving down their wages. For example, in 1890 miners earned about $400 per year, while tracklayers—whose work required less skill and kept them above ground—were paid approximately $480.[28]

In an attempt to win better employment conditions, workers at the Johnson mines—like many of their counterparts, from Pennsylvania to Idaho—sought assistance from unions. In sharp contrast to the labor situation on the Canadian Plains in the 1880s, the influence of such organizations in Texas was on the rise at this time. Indeed, unions called almost as many strikes (64) in 1886 alone as they had during the first half of the decade (74), with many actions aimed at railroad companies operating within the state.[29] Directing many of these strikes was the Knights of Labor (KOL), which had largely controlled the labor scene in Texas since the advent of the state's first local assembly in 1882, and which by the mid-1880s counted an estimated 30,000 members statewide, including many of the workers at Coalville.

Described by one historian as "the quintessential expression of the labor movement in the Gilded Age," the KOL began in 1869 as a secret society of Philadelphia artisans.[30] Accepting both skilled and unskilled workers, the Knights pressed for a variety of political and workplace reforms, including an eight-hour day, the abolition of child labor, and a graduated income tax. Membership grew slowly at first, but the union received a boost in the wake of the Great Strike of 1877, and by the mid-1880s an estimated 750,000 workers in the United States belonged to the KOL (with tens of thousands more in Canada).[31] While Knights leadership tended to favor less confrontational tactics (such as mediation and boycotts) in struggles against employers, the KOL called strikes when it seemed absolutely necessary.

Circumstances in Erath County appeared to represent just such a case, since the Johnson brothers offered their new recruits a rate of only $1.50 per ton, a reduction of 25 cents from the wage they had received previously in the Coalville mines. Backed by the Knights—whose chapter the miners had resuscitated at the Johnson operation—the workers called a strike that lasted for two months and culminated in a clear victory for the miners. In addition to defeating the proposed pay cut, the miners won a grievance procedure, whereby KOL representatives would meet with management officials in the event of unresolved work disputes.[32]

Labor Strife at the AR&CC and the T&PCC

In 1884, two years before the Johnson brothers sank their first shaft in Erath County, Sir Alexander Tilloch Galt incorporated the AR&CC near the town of Lethbridge, about 135 miles southeast of Calgary. Born in London in 1817, at age eleven Galt had moved with his family to Canada, where his father—a businessman and land promoter—was sent to debtor's prison in the wake of a failed development scheme. Alexander Galt began his own career in 1835, working as a junior clerk with the British American Land Company, located in Quebec. The younger Galt was endowed with a sharper business sense than his father, and made profitable forays into real estate and insurance before solidifying his position in Canada's entrepreneurial elite by marrying the daughter of a prominent Montreal banker and shipping magnate. Galt's successes smoothed his entry into local and then national politics, where he became a close friend of Prime Minister Sir John A. Macdonald and served as the newly confederated nation's first minister of finance.[33]

Although he spent the majority of his professional life in eastern Canada, by the late 1860s and early 1870s Galt had become increasingly interested in "civilizing" the resource-rich hinterlands of his adopted country through rapid industrial development, including the extension of rail lines and the tapping of mineral reserves. With help from his eldest son, Elliott, Galt's mining operations at the AR&CC grew quickly, so that by 1891—only seven years after its inception—annual coal production at the company had jumped from 3,000 tons to 165,000 tons, with an estimated value of $413,000. These figures gave Galt a position of industry dominance, since he enjoyed at least a 50 percent share of both the quantity and the value produced by Plains collieries into the mid-1890s. Much of the coal output went to the CPR, which in 1893 secured the future of the AR&CC by contracting for the delivery of 200 tons per day.[34]

The portly and balding Sir Alexander was deeply suspicious of organized labor and thus evinced little sympathy for the working conditions that faced the men in his employ, many of whom were of Hungarian or Slavic descent. Galt's apparent noninterest was likely exacerbated by the fact that he was an absentee director, leaving most of the operational responsibilities to his Lethbridge-based son while he remained in eastern Canada. Notably, the AR&CC had led the successful fight to repeal Regina's territorial mandate of an eight-hour workday in the mines. In stating the company's position on the matter, mine superintendent P. L. Naismith complained that "the enforcement of this law imposes a grievous burden on the capitalist who has for years been endeavouring to build up an industry in a new country."[35] One historian has argued that the Galt family's entrepreneurial philosophy eroded the relationship between management and laborers by reducing the worker to a means for maximizing profits.

This severe capitalist ethos was brought home by the periodic spring layoffs that accompanied the reduced demand for coal. Though an established

21. Alberta Railway and Coal Company locomotive and shop staff at Lethbridge, Alberta, 1894. Courtesy of Glenbow Archives, NA-1167-3.

practice in the mines of western Canada, the seasonal dismissal of employees created a perpetually uneasy climate between labor and management, one that came to a full boil at the AR&CC in the early months of 1894. The cutbacks that year were even worse than usual, as indicated by the complete shutdown of the Anaconda works across the border in Montana. Responding to the sharp drop in earnings, Elliott Galt—who had assumed full control of the company after his father's death the previous year—dismissed all 580 of his employees. He announced that he would rehire only 130 of them who matched the following profile: married men with "interests in the town" (probably meaning property ownership) who were willing to accept a 17 percent wage cut.[36]

Although about 150 of the "more transient" workers left immediately, the remaining 430 prepared for a struggle with the company, faced as they were with a dearth of jobs in the area and the prohibitive cost of transportation back to eastern Canada. Because the coal season was still in full swing, the miners were hopeful they could get better terms from Galt if the entire labor force, even those selected for reinstatement, refused to work.[37] For his part, Galt clearly felt that the very survival of his company depended on

22. View of Lethbridge, Alberta, with coal cars and North-West Mounted Police barracks, 1890. Courtesy of Glenbow Archives, NA-3267-2.

the reduction in workers and wages, what with the example of the closure of the Anaconda mines. He thus resolved to shut the works on 15 February, giving the miners one week to accept the company's new terms. Galt also requested assistance from Superintendent Richard Burton Deane of the NWMP, who dispatched a four-man detachment from the post at Lethbridge. Although company officials sent them away, declaring that the police were not needed, by the end of the month conditions led Deane to station a total of ten Mounties at the mine shafts and in town.[38]

§

In the wake of the workers' victory at the Johnson mines in 1887, labor troubles in the North Texas coalfields had abated. However, frictions between management and employees surfaced once again in the autumn of 1888, when financial difficulties overtook William Johnson, who had assumed sole control of the company following the death in January of his brother Harvey. In mid-September, Johnson announced that he could not meet the August payroll, due for distribution on the 20th of the month. Miners met and agreed to a five-day grace period during which time they continued to work, but when Johnson failed to meet their deadline they struck, demanding their unpaid wages. Eager to rid himself of the mines, Johnson sold his venture to the T&PCC, owned by Colonel Robert D. Hunter.[39]

Like Sir Alexander Galt, as a boy Hunter had immigrated to North America from the United Kingdom (though Scotland, and not England, was Hunter's home) and was of modest economic means at the time of his arrival. At the age of twenty-six Hunter had abandoned farming in the Midwest and headed to the Rocky Mountains, hoping to strike it rich in the Colorado gold rush of 1859. After meeting with only mixed success as a prospector and speculator, Hunter moved first to Missouri and then to Texas, where he became involved in the range cattle trade and in 1873 established an enormously successful livestock commission house headquartered in Kansas City. With the decline of the cattle industry in the late 1880s, Hunter sold out to his partner and began to look for new investment opportunities in the Fort Worth area. The Johnson mines caught his eye.

Upon taking possession of the mines in November 1888, "the Colonel" (as he was often called) sought to reinvigorate the company—using cash provided in part by his friend H. K. Thurber, a wealthy New York grocer for whom Hunter named the settlement—and to get the miners back to work.[40] This he sought to do by posting notices "that any employee of the old company would be given work on personal application to the superintendent at one dollar and forty cents for coal-mining, and one dollar and fifteen cents for clay-mining." He received no inquiries, however, since his enthusiasm for resuming coal production was not matched by the miners, who refused to call off their strike simply because the establishment had changed hands. They were also not about to accept a 20 percent reduction from the wages paid by the Johnsons per ton of coal mined.[41]

Hunter further alienated the former Johnson miners by attempting to reshape living conditions in Thurber as well, and within a few months management had remade the settlement into an archetypal company town which developed a notorious reputation among labor organizers nationwide. Hunter ordered all miners who had built homes on company property either to tear down the structures or to sell them to him at prices set by management. Even more onerous to the men and women of Thurber was Hunter's insistence that all household items be purchased at his grocery, drug, and dry goods stores. Strict punishment awaited those men whose wives dared to buy meat and vegetables from peddlers who managed to enter the compound, which was surrounded by a four-wire barbed fence.[42]

Most troublesome to the miners, though, was Hunter's intransigence concerning unionization at the shafts of the T&PCC. As explained years later by Gomer Gower, who with his father and four brothers-in-law had worked for the Johnsons, "The Colonel was not of the type to tolerate interference by a union and forthwith discharged all the employees who were members of a union," adding their names to a widely circulated blacklist. In meetings held shortly after Hunter assumed control of the company, the Colonel reiterated his antiunion position, dismissing out of hand all propositions from former Johnson employees that provided for worker organization. Before sending the group of miners away, he promised that before he was through with them, "*he would make a dollar look as big to each one of us as a wagon wheel.*" Looking back after a long career as a miner and labor organizer, Gower recalled that "to his credit, or discredit, [Hunter] signally succeeded in carrying out his statement."[43]

Although Hunter's antiunion stance no doubt derived from a wish to exercise total control of his company, basic economic considerations informed the Colonel's position as well. Coal mining in Texas, as in the rest of the West, was risky business in the late nineteenth century, given the relative scarcity of capital and the high costs associated with such a venture. For instance, for the year ending 31 December 1889, the T&PCC reported total expenses of more than $200,000, with net earnings of just $22,003, a figure that promised to shrink if workers should unionize and demand better pay. Having witnessed the financial troubles experienced by the Johnsons, which the Colonel attributed to "refugees from Justice and Mollie Mac-Guires," Hunter believed that the very future of his coal company depended on keeping fixed costs to a minimum, which he aimed to accomplish by squeezing his employees.[44]

The workers were unwilling to consent to such conditions, particularly Hunter's flat refusal to recognize their affiliation with the KOL, and in response more than 300 of them (representing about 85 percent of the workforce) refused to resume work at the shafts. Unable to remain in their former homes—which were located on land now owned by the T&PCC—many of the workers and their families retreated to a nearby ten-acre tract belonging to the Knights, on which the union chapter had built a two-story community house. Given the geographical isolation of the mines and the consequent difficulties in attracting labor from the surrounding communities, the miners hoped to bring Hunter to terms by shutting down production, believing that lost money, if not humanitarian appeals, might force the Colonel to reconsider his position.[45]

The success of the miners' strategy, of course, depended on the total closure of the T&PCC shafts; to that end, groups of strikers made regular visits to the company compound, where they hoped to coerce those few workers who had accepted Hunter's stipulations. For his part, the Colonel tried to keep the dissidents away, a tactic that led to an open confrontation just one month after Hunter took control of the mines. In a letter to the editor of a local newspaper, Hunter explained that on 12 December 1888, strikers had assaulted a T&PCC employee outside the worker's home and later that evening had fired "several hundred rounds" into the camp, with the intent of "driving away our employees." Enlisting the aid of Erath County judge J. J. Humphries, Hunter appealed the next day to Governor L. S. Ross, with Humphries writing on the Colonel's behalf that "the Sheriff of Erath Co is unable to suppress said Riot and he calls for military aid . . . to assist in keeping the peace & protecting life & property." Just over a week later, Captain S. A. McMurry and nine members of Ranger Company B arrived in Thurber from their headquarters at Quanah.[46]

Contexts for State Intervention at Lethbridge and Thurber

A handful of factors prompted Superintendent Deane to intervene in the dispute at the AR&CC.[47] On the most basic level, the police were on hand to preserve law and order, which in practical terms meant protecting private property and those individuals who wished to continue working in the mines. Moreover, the large number of immigrants figured prominently in management's plea for Deane and in his decision to send in a police squad. As one historian has explained, prejudice against the "foreign element" ran high in southern Alberta (and elsewhere in Canada) before the turn of the century. The local newspaper captured these anxieties a short time later, in response to a much smaller disturbance at the AR&CC: "It is to be hoped that the present trouble will be the means of clearing out the Hungarian and Slav element from the mines. As citizens they have never been valuable or desirable as a class."[48]

There was more behind the intervention of the Mounties at Lethbridge, however, than mere concern about the presence of the Slavic and Hungarian miners. By 1894 the Canadian government had established a record of strong support for corporate interests, seen most famously in its considerable aid to the owners and investors of the CPR. Federal subsidies to the CPR in the 1870s and 1880s included a grant of 25 million acres of land, the cession of 700 miles of government-owned railway, and a monopoly clause that prohibited the construction of any competitive lines between the CPR's tracks and the U.S. border.[49] Although Ottawa's largesse provoked an outcry from some observers who considered the deal scandalous, the strong personal and professional ties between many Canadian bankers, politicians, and entrepreneurs made federal generosity toward the railroad practically a foregone conclusion.

Ottawa's commitment to the CPR went beyond financial assistance, though, since federal officials deployed the NWMP to ensure the steady progress of railroad construction across the prairies and through the Rocky Mountains. The Mounties regularly patrolled work camps, enforcing a ban on alcohol sales within twenty miles of the rails, while also supervising the efforts of track and grading crews, making sure the "navvies" stayed on task. On other occasions, the police arrested men who had deserted their workstations, returning some to the job while others were fined and punished for breach of contract.[50] The most important service rendered by the police to railway interests came during strikes and work stoppages. One historian has noted that during construction on the main line of the CPR "the Mounted Police allowed nothing to interfere with construction," arresting suspected agitators and in one famous 1883 incident operating engines abandoned by striking workers who were protesting a wage cut.[51]

Although such intervention by Ottawa in the affairs of a private corporation was unusual, the activist role of the Canadian state during the 1880s must be understood as a product of the intense demands of the National Policy.[52] Given the depth of official concern about the continental ambitions of the United States, it stood to reason that completing the CPR and pulling the prairies into Ottawa's orbit was an objective of the highest political and economic importance. The same calculus applied to the development of Alberta's coal reserves, which were vital to the operation of rail lines and manufacturing establishments and facilitated settlement by providing fuel for residents of the North-West.

Of course it is worth asking why Ottawa chose to rely on the Mounties to keep the peace at Lethbridge instead of sending in the militia, which was called out thirty-three times between 1876 and 1914 to intervene in labor disturbances.[53] There are several answers. First, the lockout at the AR&CC—although involving 580 men—probably seemed too small an event to requisition the militia, which was an expensive and complex process that the government usually sought to avoid. Federal officials thought it more appropriate for local, provincial, or territorial authorities to handle such problems when they arose, and the presence of an NWMP detachment right in town made the Mounties an obvious choice for managing the conflict at the AR&CC. Moreover, there was growing concern at the end of the century that many militiamen themselves belonged to labor organizations and were thus overly sympathetic to strikers. Members of the NWMP, on the other hand, had no such entanglements, and many of its policemen—especially those in the officer corps—were drawn from Canada's social elite, thus obviating any conflicting loyalties.[54]

§

A similar—though not identical—set of circumstances informed the decision of Texas Adjutant General W. H. King to send Captain McMurry's Ranger squad to Thurber. Like authorities in Canada, King was obligated to preserve law and order in areas under his jurisdiction. He thus used the Rangers in much the same way that officials employed municipal police to contain civil unrest in urban areas of the Northeast and Midwest during the labor troubles of the late nineteenth century.[55] As with the larger conflicts of the day, such action usually involved the protection of replacement workers and tight control of striker protests. Although the police stood on solid lawful ground in such situations, the issue, as one scholar has explained, "involved more than legal rights," since police vigilance denied workers even a peaceful means of improving the conditions of their employment.[56]

Moreover, just as Ottawa had demonstrated its clear support for corporate interests deemed vital to national development, King had served, in effect, as a one-man chamber of commerce since his appointment in 1881, promoting the state's economic growth as nothing short of a political imperative. As he wrote in an annual report for 1882:

> In view of the fact that Texas has upon her borders an immense territory of broken, mountainous country, with marked evidences of rich deposits of gold, silver, lead, copper, quicksilver and coal, it would be well for the Legislature to adopt and authorize by law some plan by which a certain

23. Members of Ranger Company C on duty at Fort Worth during the Southwest Strike, 1886. Courtesy of Western History Collections, University of Oklahoma Libraries.

interest would be given for a term of years to all minerals found upon public lands. . . . Mining centers would soon be established throughout the border, and capital and population would soon flow in; the busy hum of human industry and the noble and beautiful results arising therefrom would fill the lonely valleys, the endless hills and towering mountains of this far off portion of our State with happy homes, bustling towns and growing cities.[57]

As surely as the National Policy would draw the Canadian West into Ottawa's administrative and economic orbit while securing it from American designs, King saw resource exploitation along the frontiers of Texas as a way to expand the state's coffers while safeguarding its borders against incursions by Indians and Mexicans.

In contrast to the disturbance at the AR&CC, however, the presence of a "foreign element" in Thurber seemed to be of less concern to King and other state officials than the specter of labor activism in Texas and the United States more generally. This made sense, considering that the incidence of strikes and lockouts was on the rise nationwide during the last quarter of the nineteenth century, with an estimated 10,000 work stoppages occurring in the 1880s alone.[58] King had seen powerful evidence of this trend in the

Lone Star State, most significantly in the massive Southwest Strike of 1886, called by the KOL to protest wage cuts and layoffs on Jay Gould's Missouri-Pacific (or MoPac) network. Three Ranger companies as well as 277 members of the Texas National Guard were dispatched to Fort Worth, where they broke the strike by getting trains up and running once again.[59]

Though defeated, the KOL action against the Gould network inflamed King's suspicions of organized labor—just as the Great Strike of 1877 had marked a turning point in the antilabor thinking of eastern law enforcement officials—and likely influenced his decision to send the Rangers to Thurber two years later. Reflecting on the events of 1886, King blamed "the mad and murderous teachings of Communists and Socialists" for all the troubles, excoriating workers' groups for "pursuing plans and uttering sentiments dangerous and destructive to any and all free government." In a stark indication of his newfound resolve to resist these "oath bound organizations," King vowed to "meet force with force at every point when it is lawful and necessary."[60]

Particularly vexing to King was the impediment to capitalist development posed by the strike at the T&PCC, and he considered the workers' actions at Thurber to be an indefensible challenge to the future well-being of Texas and its law-abiding citizens. With supreme indignation, he noted in his annual report for 1889–90 that

> the opening of abundant beds of coal in this section, of a quality to burn and to coke well; the necessary employment of hundreds of hands; the upbuilding and success of many local enterprises; the influx of population and the creation of a home market for many local products—all these desirable things might be expected to begin and grow with the development of coal here, if the company was allowed to proceed peaceably in its enterprises, but to this the so-called strikers objected.[61]

Adding that the struggle between the T&PCC and its workers was no less a moral battle than a material one, King made it clear that the state would crush "with the mailed hand" those who threatened industrial progress in Texas.

King enlisted the Rangers for this duty for many of the same reasons that Canadian officials relied on the NWMP to police labor disputes on their western frontier. As at Lethbridge, the disturbance at Thurber seemed small enough that the services of the militia were not needed, and even had the troubles reached such a point, there would have been little official enthusi-asm for such a move.[62] Although the Texas National Guard had effectively ended the Southwest Strike just two years earlier, state authorities placed very little faith in the militia, which was perpetually underfunded and com-posed mostly of poorly trained volunteers.[63] King viewed the Rangers, on the other hand, as "the advanced guards, so to speak, of the in-rolling tide of civilization," adding that the police represented the surest means of offer-ing protection to people and property in the new industrial communities of the state.[64]

Mounties and Rangers at Lethbridge and Thurber, 1889–1894

At first glance, Superintendent Deane seemed to adopt the company's hos-tile position toward the workers, in part because of his own anti-immigrant bias, which emerges in his annual report for 1894. At one point in describ-ing the locked-out miners, Deane noted that "the Hungarians and Slavs are not a very desirable element, a great number were compelled to seek 'fresh fields and pastures new,' and they are not much loss. Some of them have great aptitude at collecting and hoarding shekels." Moreover, consid-ering that Elliott Galt had requested Deane's assistance at the AR&CC and later presented him with a threatening and anonymous letter addressed to a company official, it seems reasonable to assume that Deane's initial reading of the situation was shaped largely by the AR&CC and its representatives.[65]

And yet a closer look at Deane's correspondence from the mines suggests that the superintendent had grave misgivings about management's strategy. As he wrote to the NWMP commissioner: "The Company lay to their souls the very flattering unction that they have managed this 'Lock-Out,' very well, but the 'proof of the pudding is the eating.' For myself, I question the expediency of throwing a large number of men out of employment without warning." Moreover, Deane seems to have given considerable thought to the grievances of the miners—with whom he spoke frequently—writing to his superiors that the workers attributed their misfortunes to management's poor operation of the business, a sentiment with which Deane evidently concurred. As he noted in his monthly report for February 1894: "It goes without saying that there is something wrong somewhere. Other mines can be run at a profit, why not these?"[66]

Several factors may explain the superintendent's equanimity, especially when compared with more aggressive police tactics south of the 49th parallel. In the first place, labor disputes were more common in the United States than in Canada at this time. For instance, in one five-year period at the turn of the century, work stoppages directly involved nearly three million Americans, which represented almost 4 percent of the U.S. population. By contrast, during the same period only 123,000 Canadians (slightly over 2 percent of the national total) were locked out or went on strike.[67] Aside from being more frequent, industrial disputes in the United States were also more violent, resulting in more than 300 deaths between 1890 and 1910, a figure sixty times higher than in Canada.[68] While the reasons behind such a trend lie outside the scope of this study, one point seems quite clear: industrial turmoil in Canada was significantly less disruptive than in the United States. This fact was of substantial importance at Lethbridge, because the improbability of bloodshed afforded Deane the luxury of weighing both sides of the dispute.

Deane's background, perhaps, was just as important in determining his initial neutrality. Like many officers in the Mounted Police, Deane had extensive military training, having served as a lieutenant in the Royal Marines from 1866 to 1882, during which time he participated in the Second Ashanti War (1873–74), subjugating African tribesmen on the Gold Coast. He came to Canada and joined the NWMP in 1883, where one of his early assignments was an erudite one: to compile the first *Regulations and Orders* of the force. After a stint in Regina at the NWMP's Headquarters Division, he served from 1888 to 1898 as the commanding officer at Lethbridge.[69] According to one historian, Deane thought himself something of a gentleman, and this "sense of superiority extended to most human beings, including businessmen, and he therefore considered himself an admirable conveyor of reason and fairness."[70] Deane and his men thus stood on fairly equal ground with the bosses at the AR&CC, and so were not as likely to be awed or bullied by management.[71] While the shared cultural experiences and values of employers and police could be expected to produce amicable relations between the groups, it seems just as plausible that—secure in their status—the Mounties could form their own opinions about the lockout.

This quality of independent thinking appears in Deane's attempt to broker an agreement between the two sides. With the miners' consent, Deane attended a gathering three weeks into the lockout, hoping to pacify the workers with one or two small concessions approved by management. In

24. Richard Burton Deane of the North-West Mounted Police, 1898.
Courtesy of Glenbow Archives, NA-3668-27.

the course of the meeting, the superintendent became "our friend Capt. Deane" and "cheerfully consented" to accompany a group of miners to a meeting the next day with company management "in order to see fair play." After mediating a largely successful negotiation between the miners' representatives and the AR&CC's superintendent of mines (whom the workers despised), Deane was pleased with his accomplishments and returned to a meeting of all the miners with a proposal in hand.[72]

In the end, however, his efforts, went for naught, as "a miserable little firebrand" (in Deane's words) insisted at the gathering that the company's few concessions were no concessions at all and persuaded the miners not to accept anything less than a maximum wage cut of 5 percent. The company refused, and it was at this point that the workers' resolve began to falter. Most damaging to their solidarity was a notice that the company had posted a few days earlier, listing the 130 men invited to return to work on the company's terms.[73] Although none had signed up by the 9 March deadline, when the company sent out termination notices the next day, those previously selected for retention promptly returned to work. All others were ordered to vacate their homes on company property by 30 April.[74] These hardball tactics worked and the mines soon reopened, although about 150 workers not chosen for employment remained in the camp.

Deane looked favorably upon these developments for the most part, but he recognized that, even with the mines reopened, the lockout at the AR&CC was not concluded, noting that "the trouble now is to dispose of the men for whom there is no work." To be sure, Deane had ruminated on this dilemma for some time, and at the outset of the dispute he had urged Elliott Galt to provide free transportation to Great Falls, Montana, for unemployed miners and their families.[75] Given the bleak economic circumstances in the coal mines across the border, however, such an offer held little attraction to the workers, who rebuffed the proposal, along with Deane's suggestion that they find construction work on the CPR main line. But in early April, with the miners' solidarity broken and the chosen men reinstated, Deane managed to persuade "several deputations of Sclavs & Hungarians" that their best option was to head south.[76] With the departure of thirty-two men and their families on 2 April, the lockout effectively ended in victory for the AR&CC.

For his part, Galt was elated with the results, and from London the board of directors relayed the text of a minute passed at one of its meetings. The motion directed the company secretary "to convey to Captain Deane the thanks of the Board for his able and untiring efforts for the maintenance of law and order during the Lock out of the miners in February & March."[77] Galt had good reason to be grateful, since Deane's efforts had helped the company to resume production while ridding itself of potential malcontents who might have caused trouble if they had remained in Lethbridge without work. Moreover, the superintendent had effected this resolution "between masters and men" peacefully and without major complaint from the workers, who likely sensed Deane's private disapproval of the company's position and clearly appreciated his intercession on their behalf.[78] At the same time, the police presence—requested by mine administrators—conferred an air of legitimacy on the actions of the AR&CC and must have indicated to the miners that the state would not allow vital industrial production to cease, notwithstanding the workers' grievances.

§

In contrast to the studied impartiality exhibited by Deane in his handling of the disturbance at Lethbridge, Captain McMurry appears to have sided with T&PCC management from the moment of his arrival. To be certain, Adjutant General King issued pro forma instructions for McMurry to remain neutral, and the Ranger captain met with both camps shortly after he came to Thurber, assuring workers that they would have no trouble with the police so long as they obeyed the law.[79] And yet several details indicate that the Ranger squad was not an objective arbiter in the dispute. For instance, McMurry corresponded from the mines with King on stationery bearing the T&PCC letterhead, and he acquired provisions for his men and their horses at the company store.[80] Moreover, McMurry accepted Hunter's interpretation of the struggle as the direct result of worker indolence and the influence of dangerous outsiders, joining the Colonel in his assessment of the demonstrators as a lawless "mob."[81]

Several factors may help to explain the Rangers' support for the T&PCC relative to the Mounties' detachment at Lethbridge, starting with the Ranger captain's "instinctive bias against agitatory labor and in favor of management."[82] Sam "Soft Voice" McMurry had come to Texas from Tennessee after the Civil War and had likely developed his suspicion of unions from his work in supervising turbulent railroad camps in West Texas and the Panhandle during the 1880s. His views thus reflected the strident antilabor fulminations of his boss, Adjutant General King, and according to one historian may even have smoothed his ascent up the ranks to commanding officer. Furthermore, while Deane was contacted by Elliott Galt well before the situation at the Lethbridge mines spun out of control, McMurry first came to Thurber amid company reports of gunfire and intimidation of the workforce.

Once at the T&PCC, McMurry made little attempt to mediate the conflict, as Deane had tried to do at the AR&CC. Instead, his negative view of the striking miners led to an unequal application of the law and thus spawned a series of repressive measures, including arrests on charges of "rioting" or "intimidation" that dispersed crowds gathered to jeer at those miners refusing to quit work.[83] Yet more questionable was McMurry's decision to grant John L. Sullivan a leave of absence to "attend to some anarchists and dynamiters, who were giving the officials a lot of trouble at the mine." Like at least three other members of the squad, Sullivan enlisted in Hunter's private security detail at the conclusion of his Ranger tour of duty.[84]

Some suggestion of the implications of Ranger attempts to restore order at Thurber emerges in an examination of the divergent attitudes toward the police expressed by the company officials and the strikers, respectively. Considering that the Rangers shared Hunter's low opinion of the disaffected miners and sometimes incarcerated the most troublesome among them, it is not surprising that T&PCC management and its supporters praised the efforts of the police. For instance, a July 1889 editorial in the local newspaper—which backed Hunter vigorously while condemning the strikers—predicted that the police would deliver a victory to the Colonel, ending with the following taunt: "The rangers send their compliments to all the lawless cusses in the county."[85] Hunter was particularly fulsome, explaining in a missive to Austin several years later that "I rank the Texas Rangers as the best police force in the world, and I do not know what the State of Texas, with her vast frontier infested with so many desperadoes, would do without them."[86]

The strikers, on the other hand, took a dimmer view of the police, in contrast to their counterparts at Lethbridge, who actively sought Deane's assistance in representing their interests to management. One KOL official complained to the attorney general of Texas that workers at the T&PCC were "being abused, imposed upon, and mistreated by a company of state Rangers, placed there it appears for the purpose of bulldozing and assisting 'corporate greed.'"[87] A disgruntled few even lodged complaints against the Rangers alleging rough treatment by the police; in one case, a local judge found in the plaintiffs' favor but assessed a fine of only one dollar. McMurry himself acknowledged the miners' frustration with their apparent bias in favor of the company, writing to King in July 1889 that the strikers "claim they could soon get clear of 'Old Hunter' & the negroes [strikebreakers], were it not for the Rangers."[88]

Had the police limited their support of the T&PCC to expressions of sympathy for management's predicament or the occasional arrest of troublesome strikers, the miners might have had some success in slowing production and forcing Hunter to recognize the union. Instead, it was precisely the effort of Company B that broke the strike of 1888–89. With labor at the T&PCC in very short supply, Hunter began to look elsewhere for miners, especially the states of the industrial Midwest. He became frustrated, however, when one early recruitment drive ended in failure as 500 strikebreakers from Pittsburgh about to depart for Texas were convinced otherwise by the distribution of KOL circulars decrying living and working conditions at the T&PCC.[89] Finally, in early 1889, Hunter managed to sign up 172 men—most of them African Americans—at Brazil, Indiana, and prepared to transport them to Fort Worth, where he was to be met by the Rangers.

As McMurry explained in two different letters to Adjutant General King, he well understood that the successful importation of an outside workforce would "settle the so-called strike," and the Ranger captain vowed to expedite Hunter's efforts. To this end, McMurry schemed to get the replacement workers to Thurber with as little trouble as possible, knowing that KOL representatives would try their best to intercept the train at Fort Worth and convince the strikebreakers not to continue on to Thurber. Thus McMurry and two men accompanied Hunter to Dallas, where they met the train and made arrangements that, just short of the Fort Worth depot, the four cars carrying the strikebreakers would be detached and coupled to a new engine, which would then proceed directly to the mines. The plan worked well, for the labor activists only caught on to the ruse at the last moment, and because the train did not stop at the Fort Worth station they had no chance "to deliver themselves of their inflammatory speeches and distribute their lying documents."[90]

Upon reaching the mines, however, many of the fifty-four white workers refused to take up their tools, and instead joined the Knights. Three strikebreakers even published a letter in the local newspaper that summer, writing, "We would advise all miners to stay away, as we find a body of men here battling for their rights, and we are satisfied that they are justified in making the stand they are." The black miners, on the other hand, "remained faithful to their word," and according to Hunter "experience has shown they give less trouble and are easier to please than the foreign element which predominates among the white miners." Despite the defections and the high cost of importing workers—which Hunter bitterly calculated at $10,834—the addition of between 115 and 120 men helped the Colonel's cause considerably, since his labor force had dwindled to just thirty-five men before the arrival of the strikebreakers.[91]

25. Captain Sam McMurry's Ranger Company B at Thurber, Texas, 1889. Courtesy of the Texas Ranger Hall of Fame and Museum, Waco TX.

The importance of the Rangers to the smooth operation of the T&PCC became apparent that spring and summer, as production in the mines grew steadily. McMurry's letters to King from this period bear an unmistakably triumphant tone and suggest that the Ranger captain took an active interest in the company's success. For instance, in June 1889 he explained to the adjutant general that "everything is in much better shape here now than it has ever been," before going on to say that "I dont think [the strikers] can hold out much longer." In another report from the following month, McMurry noted that the company was getting out 350 tons of coal per day, almost doubling the daily output from February. Although there were periodic disturbances at the mines throughout the summer and fall, including the severe beating of two strikebreakers on 4 July, by November the mines were producing fully 500 tons per day.[92]

Even with estimated company losses of $80,000, the Rangers' assistance had put Hunter in a strong position from which to negotiate with the strikers.[93] Thus, when a member of the KOL executive board arrived in Thurber in June to discuss the situation, the Colonel "absolutely refused to treat with [him]," and the union official therefore urged the KOL's governing board to withdraw its endorsement of the strike, which it approved that November.[94] Adjutant General King quickly declared a victory on the company's behalf, which he credited to his elite police force. He wrote, "The protection given by the Rangers to this one interest and the prevention of its forced failure and bankruptcy is of sufficient importance to the present and future progress of industrial development of our State to compensate for the cost of all the Rangers for several years."[95]

Despite Hunter's victory, miner activism at Thurber did not cease entirely, and the summer of 1890 saw another unionization effort, at which point Hunter wrote again to the adjutant general for police support. The Colonel asked specifically for Captain McMurry, lending the impression that he had come to consider the Rangers something of his own private police force. He explained that: "As I have always called upon Gov. Ross and yourself in my troubles at these Mines as your Rangers has been my only protection as against the unlawful element that has prevailed against our enterprise . . . I ask you again for a little assistance if you can consistently give it." The Colonel got his wish when McMurry arrived five days later with a small squad that remained in Thurber off and on for the next several months.[96]

Mounties and Rangers at Lethbridge and Thurber, 1894–1906

Mountie impartiality and Ranger antiunion hostility both waned as the century drew to a close, so that the two constabularies experienced something of a chiasma in their dealings with militant workers and labor organizers. In Canada, two principal factors eroded the neutrality that guided NWMP actions in industrial disputes, the first of which was the growing strength of labor organizations in the West. In explaining this development, some historians have pointed to improvements in Canada's economy after 1896, which in the words of one scholar "provided the labour movement with new room to manoeuvre." Also important, it seems, was the deterioration of living and working conditions for industrial laborers on the Canadian frontier, especially as their wages did not keep pace with the soaring profits enjoyed by owners and managers during the nation's financial upturn.[97]

One indicator of growing labor militancy in the North-West was the incidence of strikes in the region, which jumped from 102 during the 1890s to 325 during the first decade of the twentieth century, a trend that was in keeping with developments nationwide.[98] Several of these events took place at the AR&CC, one of them coming in August 1897 when a group of workers seasoned in labor activism protested the unannounced closing of a company mine shaft and urged their fellow miners to lay down their tools. Although contract miners won some concessions from management, less skilled employees (such as loaders and drivers) did not, and these others held out. According to the leading historian of the Galt enterprises, Superintendent Deane interceded once again, although in contrast to his neutrality three years before, this time he "badgered" the strikers to get back to work. Since the 1894 lockout, "Deane, like many of his middle-class compatriots, was worried that the workers were becoming too powerful, and he took deep satisfaction when the workers returned to their jobs at the end of August without signing a formal agreement."[99]

In addition to concern about rising labor activism, or perhaps precisely because of it, the Canadian government began to formulate new guidelines for increased federal management of labor strife. Described by one scholar as "compelled compromise," this system—as reflected in the Railroad Labour Disputes Act of 1903—set the terms by which strikes or lockouts could be called, and provided for state intervention in the case of an impasse between workers and management. Although in theory both sides stood to gain from Ottawa's assistance, the legislation actually played into employers' hands, for measures such as the 1903 act were intended to get workers back on the job quickly in order to obviate any slowdowns in productivity.[100] While these laws had little to say explicitly about the role of the NWMP in work stoppages, as Ottawa's principal representatives on the frontier, the force was clearly expected to take an active role in resolving such conflicts.

The importance of these two developments and their implications for Mountie involvement in twentieth-century labor disputes became clear in the bitter 1906 strike at the Alberta Railway and Irrigation Company (AR&IC; the company was renamed in 1904 to denote Galt's consolidation of his rail, coal, and irrigation interests). The seeds for the strike had been sown by a pair of earlier defeats—the 1897 action, and another brief stoppage in 1903—that had taught miners at the AR&IC the high price of disunity among the workforce. In the wake of those setbacks, many Lethbridge miners turned for support to the United Mine Workers of America (UMWA).

Founded in 1890, the UMWA had built its reputation by organizing bituminous miners in Pennsylvania and the Great Lakes states, focusing on winning better wages and more hospitable employment conditions for its members.[101] The reach of the UMWA soon extended to the coalfields of the

North American West, and by 1906 the union had gained a foothold in the vicinity of the AR&IC, since Alberta laborers preferred it to the perceived radicalism of the Western Federation of Miners. District 18, covering the collieries of Alberta and eastern British Columbia, was established in November 1903 under the leadership of Welsh activist Frank Sherman and counted an initial membership of over 3,000. A little more than two years later, Local 574 was organized at Lethbridge and soon presented AR&IC management with a list of demands.[102]

As explained by the strike's foremost authority, the stakes were high for both sides in the dispute: the UMWA hoped to capitalize on several earlier successes by organizing the largest mine in the province, while company officials wanted to thwart unionization and thus keep costs and worker activism low.[103] Although the miners proposed a range of amendments to company policies, including an eight-hour workday and a minimum wage, their chief demand was union recognition.[104] AR&IC management consented to meet with UMWA representatives to discuss the matter, but then stated publicly even before the conference took place that the position of Local 574 was "unreasonable, and [company officials] do not hold any prospect of acceding to it."[105] It thus came as little surprise when General Manager P. L. Naismith rejected the miners' proposals and then rebuffed subsequent requests by the union to negotiate. In response, almost all of the 524 employees of the AR&IC quit work on 9 March in defiance of the company's position.

As before, management appealed for assistance to the RNWMP (the force had acquired the "Royal" prefix in 1904, courtesy of King Edward VII), and a Mountie squad arrived at the mines on 27 February, pledged to remain neutral. In contrast to the circumspection that had guided Superintendent Deane during the 1894 lockout, however, the Mounted Police now showed a strong inclination to view the situation from the company's perspective. For instance, three days after the declaration of the strike Naismith insisted in a letter to Commissioner A. B. Perry that the mere presence of the RNWMP would have a marked effect on his employees, hinting not so subtly at the coercive nature of such a police detail.[106] The commanding officer at Lethbridge, Superintendent J. O. Wilson, echoed this sentiment two days later in almost precisely the same language, explaining that "a show of force may prevent trouble."[107] Perry complied with Naismith's request, providing thirty-four men for strike duty and keeping forty-eight on call at nearby posts; all told, this commitment represented more than 10 percent of the RNWMP's total manpower.[108]

Although the presence of the "Hungarian and Slav element" as well as the detonation of a bomb outside the house of a miner who refused to join the union may have predisposed RNWMP brass to side with the company, deploying the Mounties in a "show of force" was problematic.[109] Just the year before, UMWA official L. P. Eckstein had expressed his concern to a member of Parliament that two Mounties had unwittingly assisted in the eviction from their company-owned homes of eleven Italian miners laid off by the West Canadian Coal Company at Lille, Alberta. After a prompt investigation, RNWMP comptroller Fred White determined that the police had only escorted the company manager to the houses of the miners in order to prevent any disturbance of the peace, and not to forcibly remove the workers. Nevertheless, White conceded: "We have had many cases where efforts have been made to use the Police Force for the collection of debits recovered by civil action. Also, as is apparent in the Lille case, an effort to use men in uniform, with all the semblance of the authority of law, to awe those against whom proceedings have been taken."[110] Despite his previous acknowledgement of corporate manipulation of the police, White did not object to Wilson's proposed "show of force" at Lethbridge.

Other features of the police presence confirm the increasingly close relationship between the RNWMP and AR&IC management and lend credence to the concerns of UMWA officials and miners alike that the Mounties were not honest brokers but rather sympathized with the company.[111] For one thing, within a few days of their arrival at the mines, members of the RNWMP detachment had taken up residence near the coal works in converted boxcars belonging to the AR&IC and enjoyed meals provided by the company. Wilson explained that management had even furnished the police with a fire hose for use against the strikers (if necessary), although the superintendent quickly added that he did not anticipate any such trouble. More revealing, perhaps, was Wilson's decision to swear in eleven company employees as "special constables" charged with policing the mines and defending property and equipment from potential saboteurs.[112] Perry worried that this might seem "indiscreet" given the circumstances, but evidently allowed Wilson's order to stand.[113]

Furthermore, for one of the first times in its history, the RNWMP conducted low-level espionage. As Wilson explained in a confidential letter to Commissioner Perry, a Constable Gorski—who was fluent in several languages—had joined the union sometime in the middle of March "in order to find out what the strikers intended to do." Wilson was mortified when he discovered this and expressed special concern that were Gorski found out, the miners would assume he had been placed there by the company. Wilson thus sent Gorski back to RNWMP headquarters immediately and "instructed him not to let on he is in the Police nor to mention the strike to anyone en route to Regina."[114] In another case of apparent police spying, the force collected information on the earnings of several of the strike leaders, probably in the hopes of exposing them as men of some financial means and thus challenging their credibility as labor activists.[115]

The most valuable duty performed by the RNWMP during the strike was to keep the mines operational by protecting those men willing to work. At first, this directive involved escorting workers to and from the mines, a job of critical importance according to Naismith, who explained to Comptroller White that "every day the property is worked the strikers are losing ground."[116] This was not lost on the protesters and their families, who lined the route that led from camp to the mines and chided the men who crossed their pickets. The Mounties responded by declaring that anyone who followed or otherwise harassed replacement workers would be arrested.[117] The increased vigilance of the police led subsequently to charges of abuse, such as those filed by two miners who alleged that a detachment of five police had drawn their weapons to break up a parade, holding one striker hostage until the crowd promised to disperse.[118] On occasion, Mountie detachments also met trainloads of arriving workers to prevent interference by strikers.[119]

By the middle of April, one month after the strike had begun, the situation had settled into a stalemate, with the police maintaining a protective watch over the eighty-five men at work and keeping protesters at bay. There were, to be certain, periodic disturbances, including several explosions near mine entrances and at the houses of strikebreakers (no injuries were reported); however, it is clear that from mid-April onward, each side hoped to triumph by simply outlasting the other. But where the strikers hoped to prevail in spite of the Mounties, management believed victory was impossible without police assistance. The company's reliance on the force can be seen in Naismith's indignant response to RNWMP headquarters upon being informed in July of a drastic reduction in police owing to the lull in striker activity. As Naismith bitterly complained: "Consider removal now would be received as intimation by strikers that they are at liberty to arbitrate. . . . Please delay this. You must protect us."[120]

The actions of the RNWMP during the 1906 strike resembled nothing so much as the Ranger intervention at Thurber in 1888–89. Although the Mounties steadfastly insisted upon their neutrality, their efforts at Lethbridge mirrored to a considerable degree those of Sam McMurry's squad at the T&PCC seventeen years earlier, and thus suggest the RNWMP's evolving role in labor disputes as the nineteenth century gave way to the twentieth. For example, both constabularies took much of their early reading of the conflicts from company management and exhibited a reflexive suspicion of the striking workers. Moreover, the two forces accepted the companies' largesse—whether in the form of provisions, room, or board—creating among the miners an impression of police favoritism for the corporations. Most significantly, it was precisely the state-sanctioned intervention of the Mounties and Rangers in 1888–89 and 1906, respectively, that permitted the two collieries to keep functioning, even at a reduced rate of production, thus allowing management to resist the workers' demands.[121]

Ultimately, it was public pressure—fueled by outrage over the coal shortage during the onset of a brutally cold winter—that brought the strike to a conclusion in November 1906. Deputy Minister of Labour Mackenzie King brokered an agreement whereby the strikers won some of their requests, including a 10 percent wage increase and a grievance procedure.[122] Nevertheless, it is difficult to see in the resolution anything less than a significant victory for the AR&IC, since the miners lost on three of their most steadfast demands: union recognition, a closed shop, and a checkoff system deducting union dues directly from employee paychecks.[123] In effect, this left the miners where they had found themselves before the strike: at the mercy of management and without the institutional muscle of a labor organization to defend or advance their interests.

§

Whereas the relative deterioration of Mountie neutrality in industrial disputes at the AR&IC was the consequence of structural factors that had redefined the relationship between labor and the Canadian state, lessening Ranger animosity toward striking T&PCC workers owed more to contingent circumstances. This was evident in the summer of 1894, when tensions between miners and the company reemerged over the issue of unionization. In early June a group of Thurber miners convened at the local Knights of Labor Hall to discuss recent wage cuts by Colonel Hunter. At the meeting, labor organizers urged the attendees to call a strike protesting the reductions in pay. Meanwhile, law enforcement officials—tipped off by a company informant—surrounded the establishment and arrested those inside on charges of unlawful assembly. Worried that another effort to organize his workforce was underway, Hunter wrote to Adjutant General W. H. Mabry—King's successor—and requested the appointment of five Special Rangers (nonmembers issued Ranger commissions to provide them with state authority) to patrol the company grounds. Hunter specifically named at least two former members of Company B in the missive.[124]

In sharp contrast to the aggressive response of his predecessor in 1888 and again in 1890, Mabry refused Hunter's appeal and instead sent captains W. J. "Bill Jess" McDonald and W. H. Owen to investigate, instructing McDonald "to preserve the peace without arbitrary actions towards the men because they may be strikers."[125] Mabry's prudence, it turned out, reflected the circumspection of his boss, Governor James S. Hogg, who had an extensive legal and political record as a foe of monopolies and other forms of corporate greed.[126] As the adjutant general subsequently explained in a confidential message to McDonald, "Gov Hogg is averse to using the strong arm of the state to intimidate workmen whose wages may be below what justly can be paid them as living wages."[127]

Mabry made clear his expectations of McDonald—and in the process revealed the changes in Ranger strike duty at Thurber—a few days later when he rejected McDonald's initial briefing on the situation, insisting that he had not gone into enough "particulars" to suit Hogg and his attorney general. He thus instructed the Ranger captain to file a "full and impartial report of the grievances on the part of the men employed by the Coal Company, or other persons connected with the mines." Even after McDonald had submitted a satisfactory second report and (along with Hunter) requested additional police, Mabry demurred, explaining, "Owing to the Governor's dislike to any appearance of coercion, until it is necessary to maintain peace, law & order, no rangers will be sent to that point at present."[128] Although Hunter managed eventually to install two Special Rangers at the mines, the moderation of state officials marked a conspicuous departure from previous arrangements between Austin and the T&PCC and by contrast illuminated the nature of the constabulary's one-sided involvement at Thurber up to that point.

If the service of a different governor, adjutant general, and Ranger captain produced small but significant changes in police intervention at the T&PCC in 1894, shifting conditions such as these led to even greater Ranger restraint during the strike of 1903. A resurgent UMWA pushed even harder that summer to unionize the Thurber miners, buoyed by a string of victories in Arkansas, Indian Territory, and northern Texas, including the organization of miners at Alba, Bridgeport, Lyra, Rock Creek, and Strawn, all within seventy miles of Thurber. When T&PCC officials discovered that activists had infiltrated the town and planned a union drive to coincide with Labor Day, General Manager William K. Gordon contacted Governor S. W. T. Lanham to ask that he send "three or four of your Ranger Boys" to keep an eye on the situation. Moreover, Gordon promised to furnish the police with horses and to pick up all their expenses.[129]

Although Lanham did not inspire the same degree of corporate distrust as James Hogg, Lanham's adjutant general—John A. Hulen—was no less adamant than W. H. Mabry that the Rangers should "keep the peace, and in no event take sides with any faction that may possibly arise."[130] Hulen, however, was evidently less reluctant than Mabry to send police to Thurber, and thus a small squad arrived at the mines on 5 September led by Captain John H. Rogers, one of the so-called Christian Rangers who was known to carry his Bible along with his guns. While his correspondence to Hulen betrayed some of the same suspicion of the strikers expressed by Bill McDonald and especially Sam McMurry, Rogers was evenhanded in performing his duties. For instance, when on 8 September a group of Rangers approached a meeting of more than 2,000 people who supported unionization, the police merely asked the miners not to detonate any celebratory explosives and then quickly departed.[131] And in stark contrast to his predecessors, Rogers even conceded that the T&PCC might have to recognize the union in order to survive, a fact brought home to the Ranger captain by the defection of at least 500 miners in mid-September.[132]

Of course the increased strength of the UMWA and growing Ranger equanimity were not the only variables that favored the miners in 1903. On the advice of labor activists, the workers eschewed the occasional violence and drunkenness that had occurred during the strikes of 1888–89 and 1894, improving their image in the public eye. (This marks a critical departure from the events at Lethbridge, which grew more volatile over time and which served to alienate the public during the 1906 strike.)[133] Also important in their eventual success was the change in T&PCC leadership. In 1899 the

Colonel had turned over control of the company to Gordon and Hunter's son-in-law, Edgar Marston. While both men were deeply opposed to the labor movement—even in the midst of the strike, Gordon allegedly said he would "let the grass grow all over Thurber before he would recognize the union"—they were much better liked than Hunter.[134] Gordon especially proved himself worthy of his employees' esteem when, as the momentum swung toward the miners in 1903, he treated the departing strikers with fairness and did not lean upon the Rangers for further intervention.

In the end, the mass defections of the workforce crippled the company and brought management to terms. Gordon, who like Hunter had relied heavily on the importation of an outside workforce, had great difficulty in recruiting strikebreakers this time. In one celebrated case from the 1903 dispute, the company brought in several trainloads of replacement workers, only to see all but three of the men turn around before reaching the mines. The individuals who did make the trip to Thurber then joined the union, becoming known as the "$30,000 men" because they were all that was left from a crew of strikebreakers it had cost the company that much to transport to Texas.[135]

Sensing the company's defeat, Edgar Marston traveled from New York City to Thurber, where he conferred with union leaders for three days in late September. On the twenty-sixth, representatives of the two sides signed an agreement that awarded the miners an immediate 15 percent raise, biweekly paydays, an eight-hour workday, and, most importantly, union recognition. Negotiations went so well that afterward Captain Rogers referred to the disturbance as the "most quiet and orderly strike ever had, or that is of record anywhere."[136] Even labor periodicals—one of which had once referred to W. H. King as the "asinine general of Texas" for his repressive use of the Rangers at Thurber in the late 1880s—heaped praise on all involved in the settlement.[137] The T&PCC quickly became a closed shop with mandatory UMWA membership, and—in the words of Gomer Gower, a veteran of the entire fifteen-year struggle at Thurber—"one of the most pleasant mining communities in the entire country."[138]

The early twentieth-century strikes against the AR&IC and the T&PCC produced sharply different outcomes. At Lethbridge, the 1906 defeat marked the last gasp of unionization efforts by the UMWA at the Galt works. Negotiators lost on more than merely their bid for union recognition, since they consented to the inclusion of a nondiscrimination clause in the final settlement, guaranteeing equal treatment of all employees regardless of union affiliation and thus reducing the benefits and appeal of membership. Galt, meanwhile, wasted no time in shoring up the industry against future union encroachment. In October 1906, even before the strike against his company had ended, he met with other regional mine officials to form the Western Coal Operators' Association, "for the purpose of offensive and defensive protection of the coal interests of the Crow's Nest Pass and Alberta Coal Mines."[139] The organization also hired a detective from the Pinkerton Agency to monitor the comings and goings of the UMWA and its sympathizers.

More significantly, perhaps, the strike contributed to the passage of the Industrial Disputes Investigation Act (IDIA), which forbade work stoppages and lockouts in coal mines and public utilities until a board had first examined the disagreement and recommended a settlement. Although the act was initially applauded in Canadian labor circles, workers soon became convinced that it operated to management's advantage, since it "established a legal roadblock in the way of workers seeking to press their claims against employers who already held most of the cards."[140] The IDIA, moreover, provided law enforcement agencies with another weapon to use against recalcitrant workers: the accusation of conducting an "illegal" strike, which carried with it a mandatory criminal investigation. Indeed, only a few months after its enactment at least one Mountie officer inquired about the applicability of the IDIA in a minor disturbance at Lille, in southern Alberta, explaining that its use "may do some good and give some of these foreigners a lesson."[141]

In Thurber, conversely, conditions for miners at the T&PCC improved dramatically in the wake of the 1903 settlement. The company—once known derisively by employees as "Gordon's Kingdom"—relaxed its hold over the workforce, allowing miners to live outside the town, reforming the practices of the company store, and even taking down the barbed-wire fence Hunter had constructed in the late 1880s. In the words of one Texas labor activist, after the strike "Thurber was said to be the only little city wherein every worker was a dues-paying member of his respective union."[142] In stark contrast to its defeat in Alberta, the UMWA's sweeping victory at the T&PCC created fertile ground for unionism among bituminous coal miners statewide. Whereas before the strike only 300 such workers were organized, in the wake of the 1903 action UMWA membership in Texas soared, so that the union counted an estimated 2,200 members by 1909. Overall, more than 72 percent of all bituminous miners in the state sought organization between 1902 and the collapse of the industry in 1923, when oil supplanted coal as the dominant fossil fuel.[143]

Several factors may explain the different results in Alberta and Texas. First, one wonders whether perhaps Colonel Hunter's initial and unwavering hostility served to radicalize miners at the T&PCC, to the point that they would accept nothing less than union recognition, however long it took. Although Elliott Galt was no less opposed to worker organization at the AR&IC, he probably seemed more accessible to his employees than the Colonel did to his. For instance, it is hard, if not impossible, to imagine Hunter offering free transportation from Thurber for laid-off workers, as Galt had done in 1894 (admittedly, out of self-interest and at Superintendent Deane's suggestion). Of greater importance in shaping the upshot of the two disputes were the different labor conditions that prevailed on the respective frontiers by the early twentieth century. T&PCC management enjoyed little support from other mine operators in North Texas at this time, since smaller works at places like Lyra, Strawn, and Rock Creek had all accepted unionization. Manager William K. Gordon thus had few strikebreakers at his disposal. Galt, meanwhile, had managed to keep between 100 and 160 men at work, and even purchased some $70,000 of new equipment to demonstrate the company's confidence that it would prevail.[144]

These incongruent results, however, should not obscure a range of fundamental similarities between the companies, the worker actions against them, and the response of authorities in Ottawa and Austin. Founded within just a few years of each other by entrepreneurs who had immigrated from Great Britain, the AR&CC and the T&PCC came into being and later flourished because of the rapid industrial expansion of the late nineteenth century and a corresponding spike in the appetite for coal. European immigrants made up the majority of their workforces, although Slavs and Hungarians predominated at Lethbridge while Italians were the single most numerous ethnic constituency at Thurber. Living and working conditions in both locales were substandard, and when workers agitated for improvements, stridently antiunion company officials resisted and later appealed to state, territorial, and federal officials for assistance in maintaining law and order at the mines.

These parallels began to break down with the initial interventions of the police at the collieries. Under the leadership of Superintendent R. B. Deane, the Mounties tried to facilitate an agreement between labor and management, and while Deane's efforts may have aided the company by ridding Lethbridge of potential malcontents, it was also clear to the workers that the superintendent was mindful of worker interests as well. No such corollary could be found at Thurber, where Captain Sam McMurry and his Rangers made little secret of their support for the T&PCC. Class differences between the two men and their organizations more generally may help to account for this discrepancy. By comparison with his Ranger counterpart, Deane—who had been born in India and spent the last years of his retirement in Italy—was worldly and elite, and like other members of the NWMP he sought to "Canadianize the West." This duty, in the words of a leading historian of the force, involved the creation of a society that was "orderly and hierarchical . . . a place where powerful institutions and a responsible and paternalistic upper class would ensure true liberty and justice."[145] Such a perspective likely imbued him with a strong sense of duty to his inferiors, people such as the miners at the AR&CC, whom he was bound by social obligations to protect and also to assimilate into the mainstream of Anglo-Canadian society.

McMurry, on the other hand, though described by one historian as "a cool and calculating professional," did not boast as exalted or sophisticated a background as Deane. Rather, he had worked his way up the ranks through a series of gritty Ranger assignments, from service against Mexicans in the Nueces Strip to patrolling work camps of West Texas during the boom years of railroad construction in the early to mid-1880s.[146] It was in that capacity that he had developed a deep suspicion of industrial workers and their advocates, unalloyed by the patronizing concern exhibited by Deane. The Rangers, moreover, were much more likely to be the objects rather than the purveyors of paternalist sentiment, as seen in their dealings with company management. Though Hunter leaned heavily on the police from time to time, he left little doubt as to who was really in charge at Thurber, considering himself—in the words of one former miner—to be the town's "undisputed lord and master."[147] This perspective outlived Hunter's tenure, as General Manager William K. Gordon referred to the police as the governor's "Ranger boys." That many former Rangers found work with the company after leaving the force only enhanced their subordinate status, while at the same time winning their loyalty and eroding their neutrality.

Broader trends also shaped early police involvement at Lethbridge and Thurber, especially the relationship between the constabularies and the authorities they served. In Ottawa, federal officials were concerned that the type of labor violence seen in the United States might have an adverse effect on the perception of Canada among other industrial nations, and thus were loath to employ the more confrontational tactics assumed by the Rangers (or even the U.S. state militias). The Mounties were therefore subject to levels of scrutiny from which the Rangers were largely exempt, as indicated by Comptroller Fred White's investigation of alleged Mountie misconduct at Lille in 1905. In Texas, on the other hand, state officials seem either to have been unaware of or not especially bothered by Ranger efforts on behalf of the T&PCC in the late 1880s. Given the support of the community for industrial production and the antipathy to the workers expressed by local law enforcement officials, the Rangers were, in effect, free to address the problems at Thurber as they or the adjutant general saw fit.

Over time, a handful of structural and contingent differences gradually inverted the nature of the constabularies' antistrike duties and helped to produce divergent results in the definitive worker actions against the coal companies in the early 1900s. In Canada, a growing tendency toward state intervention in work disputes deepened the involvement of the Mounted Police at Lethbridge. At the same time, the rising power of the labor movement in Canada alienated some Mounties, who saw in its challenges a subversion of the natural relationship between "masters and men," one clearly defined by the notions of the social order that predominated in the force at this time. Opposing developments were underway at the other end of the Plains, where personnel changes in some of the most powerful state offices forced a relaxation of the Rangers' tight control of worker agitation at Thurber. Under the leadership of different governors and adjutants general, a set policy of police antilabor bias was replaced by increased circumspection, marking a reversal from the Ranger interventions of the late 1880s.

None of this, of course, is meant to suggest that there was much difference in the reasons why authorities in Ottawa and Austin sent their rural police to Lethbridge and Thurber in the first place. As the physical arm of the state, the police were dispatched to safeguard capitalist enterprises deemed vital to the future of their respective political entities. And although their methods and perspectives may have changed over time, the results of the constabularies' efforts over a similar fifteen-year period were comparable:

by delaying or preventing unionization at the most important collieries in Texas and Alberta, the Rangers and Mounties helped to smooth industrialization on the Great Plains. Consider that, by the end of the nineteenth century, Texas had more miles of railroad than any state in the United States, and that in Canada it was now possible to travel by rail across the prairies and all the way to Vancouver. Coal had, quite literally, fueled these developments, which were in turn facilitated by the vigilance of rural police, whose service had prevented the total disruption of this indispensable energy supply during the most critical years of industrial expansion.

Furthermore, the work of the Mounties and Rangers at Lethbridge and Thurber presaged their wider involvement in labor disputes as the twentieth century progressed. For the RNWMP, this tendency was fully in evidence even as the 1906 strike at the AR&IC dragged on. That July, the Mounted Police attended to a brief disturbance in southeastern Alberta and remained on call during August in anticipation of a possible strike at Hillcrest Mines in the extreme southwestern corner of the province.[148] Then in September the general manager of the Crow's Nest Pass Coal Company in Fernie, British Columbia, appealed directly to the RNWMP comptroller for a squad of fifty Mounties to keep the peace during a strike against the company. The prospective intercession of the force was especially complex, for at that time the Mounties still had no jurisdiction beyond the borders of Alberta and Saskatchewan (save for the Yukon and portions of the Arctic). In the end, an RNWMP superintendent traveled to Fernie and held meetings with the manager and two members of the company visiting from Toronto, and together they made plans for how best to end the dispute.[149]

The intervention of the Mounties in British Columbia proved a sure sign of things to come, as the industrial turmoil of the period following the First World War occasioned a reorganization of the force and the dramatic expansion of its power. In 1918 federal officials became convinced that Bolshevism had taken root in many working-class communities, especially those with large contingents of eastern Europeans. In response, Ottawa enlisted the RNWMP to furnish intelligence and to enforce federal regulations in the region stretching from the Great Lakes westward to the Pacific, thus extending the authority of the force to include Manitoba and British Columbia. The Mounted Police developed a network of spies and infiltrated worker organizations suspected of harboring radicals. The culmination of their antilabor efforts in the West came during the Winnipeg General Strike of 1919, when members of the force helped defeat the action by arresting several of its leaders.[150] In the wake of the strike, government officials decided to create a new federal police force and thus imbued the Mounties—thereafter known as the Royal Canadian Mounted Police (RCMP)—with Dominion-wide jurisdiction.[151]

Like the Mounties, after 1900 the Rangers found themselves called on by officials with increasing frequency to handle labor troubles. In 1904, the year following the decisive worker action against the T&PCC, Captain John Brooks and members of Ranger Company A traveled to the South Texas town of Minera in order to monitor another coal strike. As Captain Brooks explained in his report for the year: "The disturbance caused by the strike was soon quieted and the men returned to work. The agitators were discharged and ordered to leave the mines." However, the blowing of the Spindletop gusher three years before had created a new line of work for the Rangers, one that would eventually supplant strike duty in the state's coalfields: keeping order in the rowdy oil boomtowns that grew up practically overnight in petroleum-rich East Texas. According to one authority on the force, Ranger squads dispatched to places such as Batson imported the techniques they had learned in policing unruly railroad camps on the opposite side of the state twenty years before, using aggressive action when necessary to keep the peace.[152]

It was this inclination of the Rangers to settle with force threats to the state's economic health that led the police into the biggest scandal in their history. In 1918, against the chaotic backdrop of the irredentist Plan de San Diego uprising from three years before, the Rangers helped Anglos keep a tight grip on their Mexican laborers. Specifically, members of the force terrorized those workers who responded to the overtures of labor contractors to leave the state in search of safety and higher wages.[153] Such violence, which was part of a larger campaign of torture and assassination directed against thousands of South Texas Mexicans, precipitated a state investigation of the constabulary in 1919 that recommended a reorganization of the force, in stark contrast to the massive expansion of the Mounties' jurisdiction the following year.[154] This decision to curb the Rangers' grasp suggested that there were, in fact, occasional backlashes to state intervention on behalf of capital in its struggles against labor and leftist dissent, a lesson that the newly empowered RCMP would not learn for another sixty years.[155] Of course, by that time the Rangers themselves were in need of a refresher course, given their brutal suppression of striking agricultural workers in the Rio Grande Valley during the 1960s.[156]

Epilogue

"Deeds, Real and Imagined"

In 2001 the student newspaper of Texas Tech University reported that school administrators had decided on a new policy of "honoring the rare commitment of the historic Texas Rangers of the Old West by providing scholarships for the children of active rangers."[1] Although Texas Tech had been founded in the Panhandle town of Lubbock in 1923—long after the constabulary had aided local ranchers by thwarting fence cutters or breaking the landmark cowboy strike of 1883—the decision by university officials to recognize the Rangers spoke to the enduring admiration of the force in many parts of the Lone Star State. It was not always thus, however. In fact, during the first decade of the twentieth century, a number of residents of Amarillo—just up the road from Lubbock—complained bitterly about the presence of a Ranger squad in their town, with one newspaper editorialist insisting that the extension of rail lines and phone service to the Panhandle had rendered the constabulary all but obsolete.[2] Though absent the anti-police animus, similar questions dogged the Mounties as well in this era, to the extent that in his 1916 memoir legendary NWMP officer R. B. Deane wrote that "the Force is now on an unquestionable down-grade and should be abolished before its reputation is quite gone."[3]

Despite such calls for their demise, events conspired to keep the constabularies in the field. Though reduced in size after the state investigation into their actions in South Texas during the decade of the Mexican Revolution, the Rangers were called upon by Austin to smash liquor smuggling along the Rio Grande border and also to police the oil boomtowns that sprouted up throughout East Texas during the 1920s. In 1935 the force was folded into the amorphous Texas Department of Public Safety, where today its one hundred members make up the state's chief investigative agency.[4] The

Mounties' survival, on the other hand, was more dramatic. Ottawa had almost completely phased out the RNWMP by the end of the First World War, but reinvigorated the constabulary by charging it with investigating the upsurge in labor militancy that occurred in 1918. Following the massive Winnipeg General Strike in 1919, the federal government—terrified by the specter of bolshevism—invested the force with Dominion-wide responsibilities and renamed it the Royal Canadian Mounted Police (RCMP) to reflect its national jurisdiction. Today, the constabulary consists of 22,000 members, who serve in every one of Canada's provinces and territories, from Ontario to Nunavut.[5]

While these modern incarnations of the Rangers and Mounties still exert a powerful hold on the popular imagination—witness the accolades surrounding the publication of storied Ranger Joaquin Jackson's 2005 memoir—most attention directed to the constabularies is oriented toward their earlier histories.[6] For instance, nostalgia permeates such places as the Texas Pioneer, Trail Driver and Texas Rangers Memorial Museum in San Antonio. Every spring, retired members of the force gather "to swap stories and remember those Rangers and their deeds, real and imagined, who had gone before."[7] Similarly, the price tags that dangle from commercial memorabilia celebrating the Mounties (including T-shirts and stuffed animals) carry promotional literature that emphasizes the force's illustrious past over its present-day activities. Thus one miniature brochure reads: "Since their adventurous beginnings in 1873 opening up the Western frontier and maintaining peace and order, the Royal Canadian Mounted Police continue to be one of Canada's most dynamic and recognizable symbols."[8]

There are several reasons why the nineteenth-century service of the constabularies is recalled and romanticized while the modern work of the police garners much less attention. On the most basic level, the fundamental association of the Rangers and Mounties with the "frontier" period of North American history guarantees a certain level of popular interest and cultural immortality, especially when one considers the powerful narratives of Western exceptionalism common to both Texas and Canada. (Such enthusiasm emerges even in odd places, as suggested by the Ford Motor Company's top-of-the-line King Ranch editions of select truck and SUV models, which come complete with the "Running W" brand of the ranch stitched onto the seats and consoles of their all-leather interiors.) Visitors to the Texas Ranger Hall of Fame and Museum in Waco or one of the myriad

Mounted Police forts scattered throughout Alberta and Saskatchewan are likely drawn as much by the opportunity to revisit a bygone era as they are inspired by the myths and legends of the forces themselves.

The Mounties and Rangers from this more distant era stand out today as clear defenders of right against wrong, a perspective that seems much easier to sustain when applied to a place and a time often characterized as "wild" or "lawless." The myth of the late nineteenth-century Ranger as "straight as an arrow and unflinchingly fair" thus corresponds comfortably with the cliché that the Mounties "always got their man" (inevitably a miscreant). And yet despite these historical claims to the constabularies' evenhanded enforcement of the law, one historian of the RCMP has suggested that public adoration of a constabulary is so unusual as to constitute "a perversion," arguing that such affection is usually (and perhaps more properly) bestowed upon an army.[9] One associates military forces, after all, with nation building and the defense of a commonwealth and its institutions. Constabularies, on the other hand, conjure images of the (sometimes excessive) exercise of state power, directed against an *internal* threat. To put it more bluntly: armies serve to defend or extend the geopolitical interests of a nation-state, while constabularies perform the less celebrated and certainly more controversial function of enforcing norms within civil society.

This is a critical observation, for it helps to explain the grip of the nineteenth-century Rangers and Mounties on both the general and academic imaginations in the intervening years. In essence, the constabularies served less as police forces than as small, highly effective paramilitary organizations. To be sure, they performed many of the duties more traditionally associated with typical police institutions, including the apprehension of criminals and the enforcement of codes of public order. But during the last third of the nineteenth century their central responsibilities involved the conquest of new territory and the establishment of the sovereignty of Austin and Ottawa over contested regions. This they achieved by vanquishing nonwhite peoples and crushing perceived threats to economic development on the frontier. By incorporating the hinterlands of Texas and western Canada, the Rangers and Mounties smoothed the development of modern, capitalist state entities.

This distinction between the affection bestowed upon armies and the skepticism typically engendered by the police may also explain the more muted nature of our enthusiasm for the twenty-first-century versions of the Rangers and Mounties. It is, of course, much harder to mythologize the use of the cell phone and squad car in lieu of the horse and rifle. But there is perhaps another reason of deeper significance. Once the Rangers and the Mounties had conquered their respective North American frontiers, the nature of their assignments experienced a subtle if fundamental shift. Having played a critical role in the incorporation of the far edges of the Great Plains, they were now called upon to police the industrial societies that bloomed in Texas and on the Canadian Prairies. Maintaining state power—through domestic surveillance, urban strikebreaking, and the prosecution of unpopular wars against the narcotics trade—would earn fewer accolades and considerably more cynicism than the absorption of the frontier.

Notes

Introduction

1. A brief discussion of the names used to describe the Mounted Police seems in order here. When founded in 1873, the constabulary had jurisdiction only in the North-West Territories, and hence was called the North-West Mounted Police (NWMP). This appellation endured until 1904, at which time King Edward VII of England saw fit to add the prefix "Royal" to name of the force (RNWMP). The constabulary assumed its present name—the Royal Canadian Mounted Police (RCMP)—in 1920, when it was invested with Dominion-wide responsibilities in the wake of the Winnipeg General Strike of the year before. As the present study concerns only the years 1875–1910, I refer to the force throughout as the North-West Mounted Police except for moments in the final chapter (which covers the period after 1904 but before 1920).

2. See Webb, *The Texas Rangers*, 549. For more on the insurrection, see Johnson, *Revolution in Texas*.

3. Letter from Fred Boardman to W. P. Webb, 11 April 1919, Center for American History at the University of Texas, Austin, Walter Prescott Webb Papers (cited hereafter as WPW), box 2M275.

4. See, e.g., Utley, *Lone Star Justice*, 301; and J. Jennings, "The Plains Indians and the Law," 64.

5. There are several notable exceptions, including "Intersections: Studies in the Canadian and American Great Plains," a special issue of *Great Plains Quarterly*; Sterling Evans, "Dependent Harvests"; and Wishart, *Encyclopedia of the Great Plains*, which takes a continental view of the region.

6. A small but growing number of historians have begun to consider the northern borderlands in recent years. See, e.g., the following: LaDow, *The Medicine Line*; McManus, *The Line Which Separates*; McCrady, *Living with Strangers*; and several of the essays in Higham and Thacker, *One West, Two Myths*.

1. Instruments of Incorporation

1. See Saskatchewan History and Folklore Society, *Wake the Prairie Echoes*, 1–5.

2. Letter from Mary Saunders Curry to L. P. Sieker, [n.d.], Texas State Library and Archives (cited hereafter as TSLA), Adjutant General Records (cited hereafter as AGR), Ranger Records (cited hereafter as RR), box 401-1159, folder 29.

3. See Utley, *Lone Star Justice*, 345 n. 10.

4. My definition of the Great Plains derives mostly—but not entirely—from geographer Wishart's description of the region found in his *Encyclopedia of the Great Plains*,

xii–xviii. We differ on where to draw the line in Texas. Wishart marks the southeastern boundary of the Plains at the Balcones Escarpment, which he considers a cultural fault line between the West and the South. While I agree that East Texas—with its Piney Woods and its history as a major cotton-producing region—belongs to the South, I would argue that the topography and the range-cattle culture of South Texas link it to the Plains.

5. Alberta and Saskatchewan attained provincial status (and their present boundaries) in 1905. Before that time, they were part of the North-West Territories, and in 1882 they were divided into districts. The District of Alberta made up the lower half of the present-day province, and Saskatchewan (roughly equal in size to the District of Alberta) was split into two sections: the Districts of Assiniboia and Saskatchewan, with the former contiguous to the 49th parallel.

6. For a helpful and recent look at the postwar period in Texas, see Moneyhon, *Texas after the Civil War.*

7. Immanuel Wallerstein has been the most influential proponent of world-systems theory, which helps to inform my own understanding of such developments in nineteenth-century North America. Adherents to this paradigm attribute sweeping social and economic changes to the rise of an aggressively capitalist political economy that emerged in western Europe during the sixteenth century and which spread throughout the rest of the globe through a series of successive "incorporations." In this way, the labor and resources of peripheral regions were absorbed into an international market economy controlled by core areas, defined as places possessing a powerful state apparatus, a diversified workforce, and mechanisms intended to ensure the accretion of wealth in private hands. For a useful distillation of the central features of the world-system, see Wallerstein, "World-Systems Analysis." Critics of world-systems theory argue that the model is highly deterministic, and as such obscures the historical experiences of people living on the periphery. The most rigorous critique of Wallerstein's model can be found in Stern, "Feudalism, Capitalism." In this book, I have attempted to steer a course between these viewpoints. On the one hand, I accept the premise that there was indeed a burgeoning system of international capitalism that knitted outlying regions of the globe to more developed metropolitan areas, a process that accelerated rapidly during the industrial era of the late nineteenth century. On the other hand, I investigate the absorption of the frontier from the perspective of the periphery rather than the core, which illuminates the experiences of the marginalized and admits of structural and contingent differences that played out at the local level. For a careful discussion of these developments in the North American West, see Robbins, *Colony and Empire.*

8. See, e.g., Glueck, *Minnesota and Manifest Destiny.* For more on nineteenth-century American filibustering, see May, *Manifest Destiny's Underworld.*

9. Horrall, "Sir John A. Macdonald."

10. Utley, *Lone Star Justice,* 143–59. The unit created in April was called the Frontier Battalion and was charged with containing Indians in the northern and western parts

of the state. The constabulary was augmented later in the year by the establishment of the Special Force of Rangers, which directed its efforts against Mexican "bandits" in South Texas. There has been some debate about the relationship of the Special Force to the Texas Rangers, because the unit was first formed as Washington County Volunteer Militia Company A. However, as the company served under the direction of the adjutant general and because its members considered themselves Rangers, most historians—including this author—have done so as well. See Utley, *Lone Star Justice*, 158; and Robinson, *The Men Who Wear the Star*, 182.

11. It is worth noting that beginning in 1880 command of the NWMP was divided between the commissioner (who was in charge of field operations) and the comptroller (who handled the constabulary's finances and served as the primary liaison between the force and other government departments). See Macleod, *The North-West Mounted Police*, 41.

12. Deane, *Mounted Police Life in Canada*, 137.

13. Gillett, *Six Years with the Texas Rangers*, 15.

14. Horrall, "Sir John A. Macdonald," 182. For evidence of the thoughts of NWMP officials on the RIC, see Canada, Parliament, "Annual Report of the Department of the Interior for the Year Ended 31st December, 1880, Part II, North-West Mounted Police Force, Commissioner's Report 1880," *Sessional Papers*, 1880–81, XIV, vol. 3, no. 3, p. 3.

15. Quoted in Utley, *Lone Star Justice*, 15. As Utley goes on to explain, while there is no evidence that Austin actually realized his plans, the Rangers nevertheless date their existence to 1823. For more on Austin, see Cantrell, *Stephen F. Austin*.

16. Utley, *Lone Star Justice*, 147.

17. Given the spare nature of Ranger enlistment rolls, it is challenging to determine their backgrounds before joining the force. A rare sample of demographic information on some 60 enlistees offers a few answers, though. Of this number, forty-five men—or 75 percent—listed farmer, ranger, cowboy, or ranch hand as their previous occupations, with the most common states of former residence (besides Texas) including Missouri, Mississippi, and Tennessee. Frontier Battalion Enlistment Rolls, 1877–83, TSLA, AGR, RR, box 401-1160, folder 21.

18. Utley, *Lone Star Justice*, 148–49.

19. Macleod, *The North-West Mounted Police*, 73.

20. Macleod, *The North-West Mounted Police*, 82–86.

21. Contrary to popular belief, the color was not meant to inspire confidence in the natives, but rather reflected the founders' deep-seated Anglophilia. See Morton, "Calvary or Police."

22. For more on the historical significance and material culture of NWMP forts, see Hildebrant, *Views from Fort Battleford*.

23. Macleod, "Canadianizing the West," 102; Macleod, *The North-West Mounted Police*, 5.

24. J. Jennings, "The Plains Indians and the Law," 58.

25. Deane, *Mounted Police Life in Canada*; Steele, *Forty Years in Canada*; Gillett, *Six Years with the Texas Rangers*; N. A. Jennings, *A Texas Ranger*.

26. For more on the NWMP motto (which is written in French as *Maintiens le droit*), see Kelly and Kelly, *The Royal Canadian Mounted Police*, 51. For the derivation of the informal Ranger motto, see Utley, *Lone Star Justice*, 257.

27. McMurtry, *In a Narrow Grave*, 40.

28. Macleod, *The North-West Mounted Police*, 207.

29. Dawson, "'That Nice Red Coat,'" 35. For information on the dime novel more generally and especially its socially coercive functions, see Denning, *Mechanic Accents*. For more on popular representations of the Mounties, see Francis, *National Dreams*, 29–51.

30. For a synopsis of the show—and many other entertainments featuring the NWMP—see Drew, *Lawmen in Scarlet*, 223–24.

31. Utley, *Lone Star Justice*, 297.

32. For more on *Rose Marie*, see Brégent-Heald, "Romantic Encounters."

33. Dawson, "'That Nice Red Coat,'" 130. For more on representations of the Mounties (and Canada more generally) by American movie studios, see Berton, *Hollywood's Canada*.

34. Utley, *Lone Star Justice*, 297.

35. *North West Mounted Police* remains an isolated example of cross-border collaboration between celluloid Rangers and Mounties, though this may be due principally to the direness of De Mille's picture. (In 1978 two movie critics included the film in a list of the fifty worst movies of all time. See Medved and Dreyfuss, *The Fifty Worst Films*, 165–69.)

36. Curiously, both movies star Alfred Molina as the villain; he plays Snidely Whiplash in *Dudley Do-Right* and John King Fisher in *The Texas Rangers*.

37. Official merchandise is available in four brands: RCMP Elite (traditional), RCMP Country (for sportsmen), MacLean of the Mounties (aimed at teens), and Lil' Mountie (a product line for infants). See Dawson, *The Mountie*, ix, 171–72.

38. Notes in author's possession.

39. Walden, *Visions of Order*.

40. See the work of Paredes, esp. *"With His Pistol in His Hand."*

41. For the best alternative view of Ranger history, see Samora, Bernal, and Peña, *Gunpowder Justice*. For more on the Plan de San Diego, see Johnson, *Revolution in Texas*. Filmmaker Kirby Warnock has treated the same themes in his documentary film *Border Bandits* (2004). A different—and some might say more forgiving—perspective on the Ranger role in these events is offered by Harris and Sadler, *The Texas Rangers*.

42. See Sallot, *Nobody Said No*. A fuller indictment of the Mounted Police can be found in L. Brown and C. Brown, *An Unauthorized History of the RCMP*.

43. Walden, *Visions of Order*, 2.

2. Subjugating Indigenous Groups

1. The total number in the scouting party was twenty-six, but five men remained behind to guard the Rangers' horses. For a complete account of this engagement, see letter from George W. Baylor to John B. Jones, 9 February 1881, Texas State Library and Archives (cited hereafter as TSLA), Adjutant General Records (cited hereafter as AGR), General Correspondence (cited hereafter as GC), box 401-400, folder 11.

2. There was some minor disagreement on the total number of Indians killed, wounded, and captured; the figures above are those listed in the *Report of the Adjutant-General of the State of Texas, February 28, 1882,* 38.

3. Carter, *Aboriginal People,* 174–75.

4. See Anderson, *The Conquest of Texas.*

5. Quoted in Dempsey, *Red Crow, Warrior Chief,* 98.

6. Robinson, *The Men Who Wear the Star,* 155; see also McPherson, *Battle Cry of Freedom,* 404–10.

7. Robinson, *The Men Who Wear the Star,* 151.

8. Petition from San Saba County to E. M. Pease, 5 October 1868, in Winfrey and Day, *Indian Papers of Texas,* 4:289. For a vivid description of Anglo worries about Indian raids in North Texas, see J. E. Wagner, "Memories of Oklahoma," typescript manuscript, J. E. Wagner Collections, Western History Collections, University of Oklahoma.

9. List of horses killed and stolen in Parker County, 9 June 1867, and list of persons killed and wounded in Parker County, 9 June 1867, in Winfrey and Day, *Indian Papers of Texas,* 4:218–23; letter from W. Fanning to J. W. Throckmorton, 7 February 1867, in ibid., 4:154–55, quotation on 155.

10. Letter from P. Gallagher to E. J. Davis, 24 January 1870, in Winfrey and Day, *Indian Papers of Texas,* 4:297.

11. Letter from H. Secrest to J. W. Throckmorton, 8 April 1867, in Winfrey and Day, *Indian Papers of Texas,* 4:183–84, quotation on 183.

12. *Annual Report of the Secretary of the Interior, 1871,* 42nd Congress, 2nd session, 919–20.

13. Kavanaugh, *Comanche Political History*; Hämäläinen, "The Western Comanche Trade Center," 494; Newcomb, *The Indians of Texas,* 160–63; and Flores, "Bison Ecology," 469.

14. For more information on the Kiowas, see Blue Clark, *Lone Wolf v. Hitchcock*; Mayhall, *The Kiowas*; Corwin, *Comanche and Kiowa Captives*; and Richardson, *Law and Status.*

15. Flores, "Bison Ecology," 471.

16. See Isenberg, *The Destruction of the Bison*; and Flores, "Bison Ecology."

17. Klos, "'Our People Could Not Distinguish.'"

18. For population estimates, see *Annual Report of the Secretary of the Interior, 1869,* 41st Congress, 2nd session, 826–27.

19. *Annual Report of the Secretary of the Interior, 1865,* 39th Congress, 1st session, 717.

20. *Annual Report of the Secretary of the Interior, 1869*, 41st Congress, 2nd session, 504; *Annual Report of the Secretary of the Interior, 1870*, 41st Congress, 3rd session, 728.

21. *Annual Report of the Secretary of the Interior, 1869*, 41st Congress, 2nd session, 835.

22. *Annual Report of the Secretary of the Interior, 1872*, 42nd Congress, 3rd session, 515.

23. Robinson, *The Men Who Wear the Star*, 155–67; Gammel, *The Laws of Texas*, 8 (part 1): 86–91, quotation on 86.

24. For a succinct treatment of these developments, see Carter, *Aboriginal People*, esp. 31–61.

25. Friesen, *The Canadian Prairies*, 137.

26. Letter from Lawrence Clarke to Alexander Morris, 10 July 1875, National Archives of Canada (cited hereafter as NAC), Record Group (cited hereafter as RG) 18, series A-1, vol. 6, file 333.

27. Letter from G. A. French to deputy minister of justice, 17 August 1875, NAC, RG 18, series A-1, vol. 6, file 333.

28. Letter from G. A. French to minister of justice, 6 August 1875, NAC, RG 18, series A-1, vol. 6, file 333.

29. See Milloy, *The Plains Cree*.

30. A note on the member tribes of the Blackfoot Confederacy seems in order here. The name "Blackfoot" comes from the Indians' term for themselves, *Sik-sik-a*, meaning "black foot" or "black feet," which likely referred to their moccasins, because they were either painted black or discolored by prairie fires. The Bloods were known also as the *Kai-nai*, or "many chiefs," while "Peigan"—or *Pi-kuni*—translates into "scabby robes." This last group was divided into North and South divisions, with the former living in southern Alberta and the latter in northern Montana (where they are known as the "Piegan"). It is also worth noting that Indians and scholars north of the U.S.-Canada border use the term "Blackfoot"—which I have adopted—while those on the American side use the plural, or "Blackfeet." See Dempsey, "The Blackfoot Nation," 385–87. In describing the relationships between the three groups, one scholar has explained that "a common language, common customs, a tradition of common origin, and frequent inter-marriage prevented open warfare between them, despite frequent feuds; against their own enemies they presented a united front. Yet even in their own eyes the union was too imperfect to require a common name, and the use of the term Blackfoot to cover all three tribes was really an unwarrantable extension by the early whites." Jenness, *The Indians of Canada*, 319.

31. Jenness, *The Indians of Canada*, 317.

32. Ewers, *The Blackfeet*, 260–61; and Milloy, *The Plains Cree*, 116–18. In a sense, this détente paralleled the situation in the south-central United States, where a grand alliance of Comanches, Kiowas, Southern Cheyennes, and Southern Arapahos emerged in the 1840s.

33. The legislation providing for the transfer of the HBC territory contained several

provisions designed to weaken Indian resistance to white settlement in the North-West, the most important of which empowered Indian Affairs officials to remove the natives' elected leaders "for dishonesty, intemperance or immorality." See J. R. Miller, *Skyscrapers Hide the Heavens*, 152–53.

34. William A. Dobak has argued that by the 1870s, Canadian Indians killed annually one-third more buffalo than they required, in large part to satisfy the demands of the trade in bison robes. See his "Killing the Canadian Buffalo," 52.

35. A. Morris, *The Treaties of Canada*, 169–70.

36. A. Morris, *The Treaties of Canada*, 173–75, quotation on 174.

37. A. Morris, *The Treaties of Canada*, 247–49, quotations on 249. Scollen exaggerated when he claimed that the Blackfoot barred the entry of whites into their territory, since American, Canadian, and European traders had lived among the Blackfoot for years.

38. Letter from S. A. Darion to minister of the interior, 28 May 1874, NAC, RG 10, vol. 3610, reel C-10106, file 3461.

39. T. T. Smith, "U.S. Army Combat Operations," 509.

40. For an account of the engagement at Walker Creek, see Utley, *Lone Star Justice*, 3–12. Utley argues that this battle was pivotal in the development of the Rangers from a squad of mounted volunteers into an established fighting force.

41. *Report of the Adjutant-General of the State of Texas for the Year 1875*, 3.

42. Letter from A. M. McFarland to John B. Jones, 22 January 1874, TSLA, AGR, Ranger Records (cited hereafter as RR), box 401-1158, folder 17; clipping from the *Weekly State Gazette*, 8 August 1874, TSLA, AGR, RR, box 401-1158, folder 17.

43. Quoted in Procter, *Just One Riot*, 1.

44. Klos, "'Our People Could Not Distinguish.'"

45. There were 135 Indian battles involving federal troops during this period and 54 in which the Rangers took part (although the Ranger figure actually applies only to the years from 1870 to 1881, as the force was generally inactive during the Civil War). See *Special Report of the Adjutant-General of the State of Texas, September 1884*, appendix; T. T. Smith, "U.S. Army Combat Operations," 503. At times, especially in the early months of Reconstruction, the number of federal troops in Texas was much higher than 4,500. The Frontier Force (1870–74) consisted of fourteen companies of about 50 men each, for a total of 700 Rangers, while enlistment in the six companies of the Frontier Battalion fluctuated between approximately 300 and 450 Rangers from 1874 to 1881.

46. *Special Report of the Adjutant-General of the State of Texas, September 1884*, appendix; T. T. Smith, "U.S. Army Combat Operations," 527. Yet another measure of Ranger brutality emerges in the small number of Indians they took as captives. Whereas U.S. Army records indicate that 214 Indian women and children were taken prisoner in post–Civil War skirmishes in Texas, the corresponding figure for the Rangers was 6, suggesting that killing was preferred to captivity as a method of removal.

47. See Frontier Battalion Enlistment Rolls, 1877–1883, TSLA, AGR, RR, box 401-1160, folder 21. Gary Anderson emphasizes the importance of intense Anglo-Texan racism to

the white-Indian violence that characterized much of nineteenth-century Texas history. See *The Conquest of Texas*.

48. Letter from Mrs. G. W. Arrington to J. Evetts Haley, 18 July 1926, Panhandle Plains Historical Museum (cited hereafter as PPHM).

49. See Alonso, *Thread of Blood*. William D. Carrigan makes a similar point about anti-Indian violence in Texas, arguing that prestige accrued to men who killed natives. See his *The Making of a Lynching Culture*, 31–47.

50. For more on the army's post–Civil War presence in Texas, see Richter, *The Army in Texas*.

51. Winfrey and Day, *Indian Papers of Texas*, 4:177–80, quotation on 179.

52. Robinson, *The Men Who Wear the Star*, 166–67.

53. "Account of Engagement with Comanche Indians," *San Antonio Herald*, 16 February 1875, in Winfrey and Day, *Indian Papers of Texas*, 4:369–72, quotation on 372. For more on the Peace Policy, see Utley, *The Indian Frontier*, 127–96.

54. Thomas Smith makes this point in "U.S. Army Combat Operations," 529.

55. Letter from citizens of Clarendon, Donley County, unaddressed, 30 December 1878, TSLA, AGR, GC, box 401-394, folder 8. This letter is incorrectly filed among correspondence from 1876.

56. Macleod, *The North-West Mounted Police*, 3.

57. Ewers, *The Blackfeet*, 32; and Isenberg, *The Destruction of the Bison*, 103–4. For more on the liquor trade among Indians and its deleterious social effects, see Mancall, *Deadly Medicine*.

58. For more on the development of the liquor trade in the Rocky Mountain Northwest, see Paul Sharp's classic *Whoop-Up Country*.

59. A. Morris, *The Treaties of Canada*, 247–49, quotation on 248. Specific information on the influence of alcohol among the Blackfoot can be found in Dempsey, *Firewater*.

60. For the best account of the incident, see Philip Goldring, "Whisky, Horses, and Death." The slaughter is often erroneously cited as the reason for the formation of the NWMP; while it certainly sped their deployment, plans for the constabulary predated the events in the Cypress Hills by several years.

61. Quoted in Dempsey, *Crowfoot*, 78 n. 2.

62. Canada, Parliament, "Report of the Secretary of State of Canada for the Year Ended 31st December, 1876, Appendix D, North-West Mounted Police," *Sessional Papers*, 1877, X, vol. 7, no. 9, p. 25. See also Dempsey, *Firewater*, 184–200. It is important to note that, despite their orders to end liquor trafficking, many Mounties were themselves great consumers of alcohol. See, e.g., Morgan, "The North-West Mounted Police," 56–59. For their part, U.S. officials marveled at the Canadian success in eradicating the liquor trade, with one observer advocating the adoption of Ottawa's tactics. See letter from William Alberson to Edward W. Smith, 1 March 1875, NAC, RG 18, series A-1, vol. 8, file 490.

63. Letter from S. A. Darion to minister of the interior, 28 May 1874, NAC, RG 10, vol. 3610, reel C-10106, file 3461.

64. Carter, "Categories and Terrains," 151–53. For more on the Sioux in Canada, see McCrady, *Living with Strangers.*

65. See telegram from E. A. Meredith to J. A. Provencher, 27 August 1875, NAC, RG 18, series A-1, vol. 6, file 333.

66. Letter from S. A. Darion to minister of the interior, 28 May 1874, NAC, RG 10, vol. 3610, reel C-10106, file 3461.

67. Lux, *Medicine That Walks,* 16–19.

68. For a helpful examination of Canadian treaty making in comparative perspective, see St. Germain, *Indian Treaty-Making Policy.*

69. A. Morris, *The Treaties of Canada,* 272.

70. Treaty 7 Elders and Tribal Council et al., *The True Spirit and Original Intent of Treaty 7,* 9, 117, 134, 379; St. Germain, *Indian Treaty-Making Policy,* 74. Macleod's Indian name is also sometimes rendered as *Stamixotokan.*

71. It is worth quoting here directly from Carter, *Aboriginal People,* 126, to give a better sense of the native perspective: "The relationship with the Crown was understood to consist of mutual, ongoing sharing arrangements that would guarantee each other's survival and stability. The concept of *wi taski win,* or sharing the blessing of the land in mutual harmony, provided that the sharing arrangements would be fair to each of the parties, enabling both to enjoy the prosperity of the land and *pim atchi hoowin,* or make a living."

72. Carter, *Aboriginal People,* 117–18, quotation on 117.

73. Isenberg, *The Destruction of the Bison,* 130–43, quotation on 130.

74. *Annual Report of the Secretary of the Interior, 1874,* 43rd Congress, 3rd session, 528.

75. For more on Mackenzie, see Pierce, *The Most Promising Young Officer.* J. L. Haley offers a thorough account of the conflict in *The Buffalo War.*

76. For Jones's account of the Lost Valley fight, see his letter to William Steele, 14 July 1874, TSLA, AGR, GC, box 401-392, folder 5.

77. *Report of the Adjutant-General of the State of Texas for the Year 1874,* 5. As Utley explains, the Kiowas had a very different account of the engagement—making no mention, for instance, of any Indian deaths—that he finds more credible. See *Lone Star Justice,* 150.

78. *Annual Report of the Secretary of the Interior, 1875,* 44th Congress, 1st session, 773.

79. *Report of the Adjutant-General of the State of Texas for the Year 1875,* 5.

80. Letter from John B. Jones to William Steele, 9 May 1875, TSLA, AGR, GC, box 401-393, folder 6.

81. Letter from Emanuel Deibbs to O. M. Roberts, 11 June 1879, Center for American History at the University of Texas, Austin, Texas Adjutant General Records (cited hereafter as TAGR), box 2Q401, folio 13.

82. See, e.g., letter from A. M. Patch, 4th Calvary, to post adjutant, 22 January 1879, TSLA, AGR, GC, box 401-398, folder 2. For more on such army policies and the tensions they generated with Texas residents and officials, see Southern Plains Indian Agencies Collection, Western History Collection, University of Oklahoma, book 26.

83. Letter from I. B. Sadler to O. M. Roberts, 3 February 1879, in Winfrey and Day, *Indian Papers of Texas*, 4:412.

84. See letter from R. Coke to O. M. Roberts, 18 February 1879, and letter from S. B. Maxey to O. M. Roberts, 27 March 1879, in Winfrey and Day, *Indian Papers of Texas*, 4:418–19, 420–21.

85. Letter from J. W. Davidson, 10th Cavalry, to assistant adjutant general, 11 January 1879, TSLA, AGR, GC, box 401-398, folder 1.

86. S. L. Smith, *The View from Officers' Row*, 113–38. For a sense of the historical roots of the conflict between settlers and army officials in Texas, see Klos, "'Our People Could Not Distinguish,'" 613–14.

87. Letter from J. Pope to O. M. Roberts, 2 April 1879, in Winfrey and Day, *Indian Papers of Texas*, 4:421–22, quotations on 422.

88. Letter from G. W. Arrington to John B. Jones, 19 December 1878, in Winfrey and Day, *Indian Papers of Texas*, 4:405–6, quotation on 406.

89. Letter from D. W. Roberts to John B. Jones, 15 June 1879, TSLA, AGR, GC, box 401-398, folder 9.

90. Letter from John B. Jones to O. M. Roberts, 15 February 1879, in Winfrey and Day, *Indian Papers of Texas*, 4:417.

91. Letter from G. W. Arrington to John B. Jones, 18 June 1879, TAGR, box 2Q401, folio 13.

92. Letter from Nicholas Nolan to post adjutant, 8 January 1879, TSLA, AGR, GC, box 401-398, folder 1; letter from J. A. Wilcox to assistant adjutant general, TSLA, AGR, GC, 17 January 1879, box 401-398, folder 2; and letter from G. W. Arrington to John B. Jones, 20 January 1879, in Winfrey and Day, *Indian Papers of Texas*, 4:409–11.

93. House Resolution 5040, in Winfrey and Day, *Indian Papers of Texas*, 4:443–44, quotations on 444.

94. La Vere, *The Texas Indians*, 214–16. Victorio appears to have reconsidered this decision in June 1879, when he presented himself at the Mescalero Agency in New Mexico and promised to stay. However, when territorial authorities attempted to arrest him for theft and murder, he left again, this time for good. See *Annual Report of the Secretary of the Interior, 1879*, 46th Congress, 2nd session, 20.

95. For more on the contributions of black troops in opposing Victorio, see Leiker, *Racial Borders*.

96. While George Baylor was no friend to the Indians, his brother John was a particularly vicious racist, who edited an anti-Indian newspaper called *The White Man* and, among other outrages, attacked the Brazos Reserve in 1859, murdering and scalping an octogenarian Indian man despite orders from U.S. soldiers to desist. See Klos, "'Our People Could Not Distinguish,'" 609, 612–13.

97. For a detailed account of this scouting expedition, see Gillett, *Six Years with the Texas Rangers*, 151–60.

98. Gillett, *Six Years with the Texas Rangers*, 167.

99. Utley, *Lone Star Justice*, 214–15. Baylor, among others, was quite disappointed to have missed out on this battle, and reported to Austin, "You can well imagine my disgust at not being 'in at the death' of the old villain after having rode so many miles on his track, especially as it turned out to be such an easy matter to take him in." See letter from G. W. Baylor to John B. Jones, 11 November 1880, TAGR, box 2Q401, folio 11.

100. Letter from G. W. Baylor to John B. Jones, 9 February 1881, TSLA, AGR, GC, box 401-400, folder 11.

101. *Report of the Adjutant-General of the State of Texas, December 31, 1882*, 26–27.

102. For examples, see letter from S. A. McMurry to W. H. King, 15 September 1881; and letter from G. W. Baylor to W. H. King, 30 September 1881, both in TAGR, box 2Q401, folio 12.

103. Carter, *Aboriginal People*, 116–17. A major component of this process involved the imposition of physical and social boundaries that circumscribed the movement and behavior of the Blackfoot. See McManus, *The Line Which Separates*, 57–105.

104. In describing the unprecedented concentration of powers in the NWMP and the absence of a nonindependent judiciary, J. Jennings explains that "the potential for abuse was theoretically unlimited. Yet it was precisely this authority which protected the Indians of the Plains from what Alexis de Tocqueville . . . warned would be the greatest failing of democracy—the unlimited power of the majority." See his study "The North-West Mounted Police," 5–6.

105. Waiser, *The North-West Mounted Police*, 32.

106. The confusion and fear likely experienced by Indians in NWMP custody are brought vividly to life in Dempsey, *Charcoal's World*, 10.

107. The fine for selling alcohol to Indians was $300, six months in jail, and the confiscation of property; sale to whites, however, often occasioned only a $50 fine. See J. Jennings, "The North-West Mounted Police," 86.

108. Baker, *Pioneer Policing in Southern Alberta*, 33; Hubner, "Horse Stealing and the Borderline," 53.

109. For more on the importance of horses to Plains Indians, see Holder, *The Hoe and the Horse*; Ewers, *The Horse in Blackfoot Indian Culture*; and Hämäläinen, "The Rise and Fall of Plains Indian Horse Cultures."

110. See Ewers, *The Horse in Blackfoot Indian Culture*, 171–215; and Milloy, *The Plains Cree*, 69–82.

111. Canada, Parliament, "Annual Report of the Department of the Interior for the Year Ended 31st December, 1880; Part II, North-West Mounted Police Force, Commissioner's Report 1880," *Sessional Papers*, 1880–81, XIV, vol. 3, no. 3, p. 31. For other examples of police concern about the international dimension of Indian horse theft, see letters from C. E. Denny to Edgar, 15 June 1882 and 15 November [1885?], Glenbow Alberta Institute (cited hereafter as GAI), Edgar Dewdney Fonds, M-320, series 15.

112. LaDow, *The Medicine Line*, esp. 43–72. See also Hogue, "Disputing the Medicine Line."

113. Canada, Parliament, "Annual Report of the Department of the Interior for the Year Ended 31st December, 1880; Part II, North-West Mounted Police Force, Commissioner's Report 1880," *Sessional Papers*, 1880–81, XIV, vol. 3, no. 3, p. 33.

114. Hubner makes this point in "Horse Stealing and the Borderline."

115. Indians accounted for 57 of 106 such cases between 1878 and 1889. See Waiser, *The North-West Mounted Police*, 24–26.

116. After a high of 48 arrests for horse theft in 1885 (of which Indians accounted for 60 percent), only 38 such arrests were made in the following three years (12 of which involved natives). In 1889, however, 21 cases of horse stealing were reported, 15 of them involving Indians. Waiser, *The North-West Mounted Police*, 24–26, 33.

117. Dobak, "Killing the Canadian Buffalo." For a Eurocanadian perspective on Indian starvation, see Edgar Dewdney, Journal from 1879 Trip to the North-West, entries for 14, 17, 18, and 19 July, GAI, Edgar Dewdney Fonds, M-320, series 13.

118. Canada, Parliament, "Annual Report of the Minister of the Interior for the Year Ended 30th June 1881, Part III, North-West Mounted Police Force, Report of the Commissioner 1881," *Sessional Papers*, 1882, XV, vol. 8, no. 18, p. 11.

119. Hogue, "Disputing the Medicine Line," 97–102. For more on later Cree removals, see Hogue, "Crossing the Line."

120. Canada, Parliament, "Annual Report of the Minister of the Interior for the Year Ended 30th June 1882, Part II, North-West Mounted Police Force, Report of the Commissioner 1882," *Sessional Papers*, 1883, XVI, vol. 10, no. 23, pp. 3–7.

121. Canada, Parliament, "Report of the Commissioner of the North-West Mounted Police Force 1883," *Sessional Papers*, 1884, XVII, vol. 11, no. 125, p. 16.

122. Carter, "Categories and Terrains," 155–56.

123. Letter from L. Vankoughnet to superintendent general of Indian affairs, 15 November 1883, NAC, RG 18, series B-1, vol. 1009, file 628.

124. Canada, Parliament, "Report of the Commissioner of the North-West Mounted Police Force 1887," *Sessional Papers*, 1888, XXI, vol. 17, no. 28, p. 47.

125. Canada, Parliament, "Report of the Commissioner of the North-West Mounted Police Force 1888," *Sessional Papers*, 1889, XXII, vol. 13, no. 17, p. 48.

126. Notes of an interview between chiefs of the Bloods and North Peigans with P. R. Neale, 2 February 1888, NAC, RG 18, series A-1, vol. 19, file 249.

127. See Pettipas, *Severing the Ties That Bind*.

128. Letter from Hayter Reed to L. W. Herchmer, 30 May 1896; letter from E. Brown to officer commanding Depot District, 13 June 1896; and letter from A. McNeill to Hayter Reed, 12 June 1896, all in NAC, RG 18, series B-1, vol. 1354, file 76.

129. Deane explained, "It feeds the naturally cruel nature of the spectators, it panders to the lust of both sexes, and unsettles the marital relations of the Indians themselves; and last, though not least, it acts as an incentive to the triumphant participant to evince a courage to which he is far from feeling in the commission of some lawless act." Baker, *Pioneer Policing in Southern Alberta*, 15.

130. Extract from Report of R. B. Deane, June 30, 1898, NAC, RG 18, series A-1, vol. 154, file 443.

131. Baker, *Pioneer Policing in Southern Alberta*, 98.

132. Letter from J. A. Smart to Fred White, 4 February 1901, NAC, RG 18, series A-1, vol. 205, file 136.

133. Milloy, "A National Crime," xv.

134. Milloy, "A National Crime," 23–47.

135. For more on the role of oblate priests in the residential school system, see Huel, *Proclaiming the Gospel*, 99–175.

136. Milloy, "A National Crime," 91.

137. For examples of police concern, see letter from L. W. Herchmer to comptroller, 30 June 1895, and letter from Hayter Reed to Fred White, 12 July 1895, NAC, RG 18, series A-1, vol. 110, file 517.

138. An Ordinance Relating to Industrial Institutions for Indian Children, and letter from NWMP assistant commissioner to Superintendent A. H. Griesbach, 4 October 1893, NAC, RG 18, series B-1, vol. 1284, file 352.

139. Letter from C. Constantine to Officer Commanding B Division at Qu'Appelle, January 1, 1895, NAC, RG 18, series A-1, vol. 103, file 63.

140. For examples, see letter from Father C. Claude to Superintendent J. H. McIllree, 6 November 1888, NAC, RG 18, series A-1, vol. 26, file 961; letter from Fred White to NWMP Commissioner, 29 January 1895, NAC, RG 18, series A-1, vol. 110, file 489; letter from J. H. McIllree to Fred White, 4 February 1902, NAC, RG 18, series A-1, vol. 228, file 137.

141. Tobias, "Indian Reserves in Western Canada," 98.

142. Quoted in La Vere, *Contrary Neighbors*, 216.

143. Samek, *The Blackfoot Confederacy*, 113–14.

144. *Report of the Adjutant-General of the State of Texas, December 31, 1882*, 26.

145. Canada, Parliament, "Report of the Commissioner for the North-West Mounted Police Force 1883," *Sessional Papers*, 1884, XVII, vol. 11, no. 125, p. 13.

146. Examples of this triumphalism abound. See, e.g., Macleod, *The North-West Mounted Police*, 143–50; J. Jennings, "The Plains Indians and the Law"; and Morton, "Cavalry or Police."

147. J. Jennings, "The Plains Indians and the Law," 64.

3. Dispossessing Peoples of Mixed Ancestry

1. There has been considerable debate among scholars concerning the most accurate way to render the term "Métis," with some preferring the lowercase *m* and still others choosing to omit the accent mark over the *e*. I have chosen "Métis" in accordance with the production guidelines stipulated by the University of Nebraska Press, but preserved the spelling used by other scholars where appropriate. For more on this discussion, see Peterson and Brown, *The New Peoples*, 3–16.

2. Letter from Gabriel Dumont and M. L. Riboulet to George Demanche, 1 December

1887, National Archives of Canada (cited hereafter as NAC), Record Group (cited hereafter as RG) 18, series A-1, vol. 23, file 653.

3. In this chapter and throughout the text of this book, I have followed David Montejano's example and used "Mexican" to refer to both Texas Mexicans and Mexicans born south of the Rio Grande, except at moments where I have found it necessary to emphasize national origin. See Montejano, *Anglos and Mexicans*, 10. "Tejano" refers exclusively to Texas-born Mexicans.

4. For a discussion of this transition situated in a broad North American context, see Adelman and Aron, "From Borderlands to Borders."

5. For a brief synopsis of the origins and characteristics of the two groups as well as a fascinating attempt to compare their histories from the perspective of the community study, see Faragher, "Americans, Mexicans, Métis."

6. Quoted in the *Texas Observer*, 9 June 1967, 23.

7. Despite the central importance of Mexicans and Métis to the decisions behind the deployments of the rural police forces, the nature of their missions in this regard is but poorly understood. Historians of the Rangers tend to regard their violence against Mexicans as either a justified response to Mexican "banditry" or the excesses of a virulent Anglo-Texan racism. Walter Prescott Webb, in *The Texas Rangers*, defended the Rangers' actions in the Nueces Strip, explaining famously that "affairs on the border [between Anglos and Mexicans] cannot be judged by standards that hold elsewhere" (252). Larry McMurtry takes issue with this apology, insisting that "torture is torture, whether inflicted in Germany, Algiers, or along the Nueces Strip." See his *In a Narrow Grave*, 41. Recent works, though more circumspect on the subject of Ranger abuses in South Texas, do not adopt a sufficiently critical perspective on police characterizations of Mexicans as cattle thieves or "bandits." See, e.g., Wilkins, *The Law Comes to Texas*; Robinson, *The Men Who Wear the Star*; and Utley, *Lone Star Justice*. On the other hand, revisionist historians who indict the Rangers in the most excoriating terms focus almost exclusively on the racism of the police and pay little attention to the specific socioeconomic contexts in which these mistreatments took place. See Samora, Bernal, and Peña, *Gunpowder Justice*; and Mirandé, *Gringo Justice*. One notable exception to this rule is Montejano, *Anglos and Mexicans*, who attributes Ranger excesses of the late nineteenth century to a combination of prejudice and the white desire for social and economic hegemony in the trans-Nueces. Both popular and academic historians of the Mounted Police, on the other hand, limit their discussions of the Métis to the role played by the NWMP in putting down the 1885 North-West Rebellion, and rarely distinguish between the concerns of the First Nations and peoples of mixed ancestry. See Kelly and Kelly, *The Royal Canadian Mounted Police*; Horrall, *The Pictorial History*; and Macleod, *The NWMP and Law Enforcement*. Turner's immense two-volume study, *The North-West Mounted Police, 1873–1893*, discusses interactions between the force and the Métis, but in keeping with the narrative style of the book offers little in the way of interpretation or analysis.

8. Two iconic (but dated) studies of the Métis are Giraud, *The Metis in the Canadian*

West; and Stanley, *The Birth of Western Canada*. For excellent surveys of more recent literature on the Métis, see Madill, "Riel, Red River, and Beyond"; J. R. Miller, "From Riel to the Métis"; and Pannekoek, "Metis Studies."

9. For more on French contracted servants, see Podruchny, *Making the Voyageur World*.

10. J. Foster, "The Plains Metis," 420–23. See also Friesen, *The Canadian Prairies*, 66–90. For an extended examination of Métis identity as explored through the history of a single family, see Devine, *The People Who Own Themselves*.

11. See Ens, *Homeland to Hinterland*, 9–56.

12. J. Foster, "The Plains Metis," 426–30, and Woodcock, *Gabriel Dumont*, 32–38.

13. Ens, *Homeland to Hinterland*, 79–81; Dobak, "Killing the Canadian Buffalo."

14. Friesen, *The Canadian Prairies*, 114–19. To be sure, other Canadian scholars have offered an alternative view, most notably Pannekoek, who argues that that divisions between the French and English halves of the settlement were the root cause behind the turmoil of the late 1860s. See esp. his "The Rev. Griffiths Owen Corbett," and also *A Snug Little Flock*. Spry, among many others, has challenged such assertions in "The Métis and Mixed-Bloods."

15. This description of Mexican origins in Texas relies on the first chapter of De León's *The Tejano Community*, 1–22.

16. Vezzetti, "Steamboats on the Lower Rio Grande," 78.

17. Population estimates come from Montejano, *Anglos and Mexicans*, 31. Following the American victory in 1848, Mexicans living in territory ceded to the United States were given one year to decide between two options: they could either liquidate their property holdings and move to Mexico, or they could choose to become American citizens. Those remaining in U.S. territory after one year were considered to have elected U.S. citizenship. See Weber, *Foreigners in Their Native Land*, 143. For more on the treaty and its historical implications, see Griswold del Castillo, *The Treaty of Guadalupe Hidalgo*.

18. For a fascinating reconsideration of popular and academic scholarship on the events of 1835–36, see Crisp, *Sleuthing the Alamo*.

19. De León, *They Called Them Greasers*, 49–53. See also Schwartz, *Across the River to Freedom*.

20. De León, *They Called Them Greasers*, xi.

21. Limón, *American Encounters*, 11–13; Weber, *Foreigners in Their Native Land*, 152. For more on the roots and ideology of the *Herrenvolk*, see Frederickson, *White Supremacy*.

22. For an excellent study of differing Anglo and Mexican notions of property, see Montoya, *Translating Property*.

23. For context, see De León and Stewart, *Tejanos and the Numbers Game*.

24. De León, *They Called Them Greasers*, 82–83.

25. Montejano, *Anglos and Mexicans*, 41–74. Alonzo, in *Tejano Legacy*, has challenged Montejano's claims, arguing that Mexican land loss in Texas only accelerated in the last quarter of the nineteenth century. While this may have been true for many wealthy

Mexicans, it seems clear that the majority of small landowners (and more than a few of the landed elite as well) suffered significant dispossession by white lawyers immediately following the war. The bitter, thirty-year (1849–79) legal battle surrounding the Espiritu Santo land grant—which Anglos had illegally appropriated in order to found the town of Brownsville—is but one example of such legal chicanery. See "Brownsville Town Tract Litigation, 1849–1879," Texas State Library and Archives (cited hereafter as TSLA), Harbert Davenport Collection, box 2-23/214, folder 6.

26. Camarillo and Castillo, *Furia y Muerte*, 7–8.

27. Weber, *Foreigners in Their Native Land*.

28. Rueck, "Imposing a 'Mindless Geometry.'"

29. Carter, *Aboriginal People*, 105–6.

30. Riel, "Declaration of the People of Rupert's Land and the North West," *Collected Writings*, 1:42–45.

31. Friesen, *The Canadian Prairies*, 119–28. Scott alone was executed (following a trial), probably because of his defiance while incarcerated.

32. Minnesota was at the center of this annexationist intrigue for several decades in the mid-nineteenth century. See Gluek, *Minnesota and the Manifest Destiny*.

33. Carter, *Aboriginal People*, 107.

34. For more information, see Flanagan, "Louis Riel and the Dispersion." See also Ens, "The Border, the Buffalo."

35. Ens, *From Homeland to Hinterland*, 148–49.

36. The cause behind the dispersal of the Red River Métis after 1870 is the subject of a passionate and ongoing debate. Ens, *From Homeland to Hinterland*, argues that the Métis were lured westward by the robe trade, which eventually weakened their ties to Red River. Sprague, *Canada and the Métis*, on the other hand, insists that the federal government deliberately dispossessed the Métis. My own interpretation, as should be evident, is more in sympathy with Sprague than Ens, especially in light of Ottawa's subsequent use of the NWMP to force the Métis to conform to government objectives before 1885 and after. For more on this controversy, see Carter, *Aboriginal People*, 109–11.

37. Friesen, *The Canadian Prairies*, 201.

38. The conflict, still vividly remembered along the border, has been treated in a number of secondary works, most of a deeply partisan nature. Woodman's *Cortina* reflects the Anglo perspective on the events, condemning Cortina as an opportunistic murderer. Goldfinch, in *Juan N. Cortina*, and Canales, in *Juan N. Cortina Presents His Motion*, adopt a much more sympathetic approach, seeing in Cortina's rebellion the culmination of a decade of Mexican frustrations following the Treaty of Guadalupe Hidalgo. For a fascinating view of the conflict through the eyes of a U.S. Army officer, see J. D. Thompson's edition of Heintzelman, *Fifty Miles and a Fight*. See also Thompson's *Juan Cortina*. Thompson is currently at work on the first full-length biography of Cortina.

39. Goldfinch, *Juan N. Cortina*, 42.

40. U.S. Congress, *Difficulties on the Southwestern Frontier*, House Executive Docu-

ment 52, 36th Congress, 1st session (1860), 70–72, emphasis in original. Given that Cortina—unlike Riel—was illiterate, there is some doubt about the authorship of the document.

41. Unsurprisingly, perhaps, Texas led the nation in the lynching of Mexicans between 1848 and 1928, accounting for 282 of the 597 reported victims of such crimes. It is important to note that both of these figures are conservative estimates. See Carrigan and Webb, "The Lynching of Persons," figures on 415.

42. For more, see Ford, *Rip Ford's Texas*.

43. For the best description of Ranger involvement in the Cortina War, see Utley, *Lone Star Justice*, 107–19. Ford had a complex relationship with Cortina, described by historian Jerry Thompson as "love-hate." Although the Ranger captain inveighed against Cortina in his 1885 memoir, he also took credit (in the same volume) for having saved his adversary from a Mexican firing squad in the mid-1870s. See J. D. Thompson, *Juan Cortina*, 2–3. For Ford's reference to the Cortinistas as a "foreign horde," see letter from J. S. Ford to Governor Runnels, 22 November 1859, Center for American History at the University of Texas, Austin, Walter Prescott Webb Papers (cited hereafter as wpw), box 2R291, vol. 4.

44. Letter from Stephen Powers to Governor Runnels, 23 October 1859, wpw, box 2R291, vol. 4.

45. Montejano, *Anglos and Mexicans*, 32–33. For damage estimates, see U.S. Congress, *Troubles on the Texas Frontier*, House Executive Document 81, 36th Congress, 1st session (1860), 77.

46. *Troubles on the Texas Frontier*, 14.

47. For more on the relationship between Métis parishioners and Catholic clergy, see two works by Huel: *Proclaiming the Gospel*, and *Archbishop A. A. Taché*.

48. Letter (translation) from Augustin Bralant, et al., to Alexander Morris, 11 September 1874, Canada, Parliament, *Sessional Papers*, 1885, XVIII, vol. 13, no. 116, p. 7. The extensive correspondence in this file—published as a Sessional Paper in 1885 but covering a twelve-year period beginning in 1873—is extremely useful in charting Métis concerns about their lands in the North-West and Ottawa's subsequent response.

49. Letter from Alexander Morris to Augustine Brabant [*sic*], et al., 16 September 1874, Canada, Parliament, *Sessional Papers*, 1885, XVIII, vol. 13, no. 116, p. 8.

50. For evidence of the perspective of federal and territorial officials, see copy of a resolution passed by the Council of the North-West Territories in legislative session on 2 August 1878, Canada, Parliament, *Sessional Papers*, 1885, XVIII, vol. 13, no. 116, pp. 35–36; and letter from David Laird to J. S. Dennis, 13 March 1879, Canada, Parliament, *Sessional Papers*, 1885, XVIII, vol. 13, no. 116, p. 82.

51. Letter from George McKay, et al., to the governor general of the Dominion of Canada, September 1878, Canada, Parliament, *Sessional Papers*, 1885, XVIII, vol. 13, no. 116, pp. 29–31, quotation on 29. It is worth noting that many of the signatories of this document had English surnames, suggesting that this particular settlement was populated largely by Eurocanadians and Country-born rather than Francophone Métis.

52. Osgood, *The Day of the Cattleman*, 27–33.

53. J. D. Young and Dobie, *A Vaquero of the Brush Country*, 56.

54. Ford, *Rip Ford's Texas*, 408.

55. *New York Times*, 14 October 1874.

56. *Depredations on the Frontiers of Texas*, 42nd Congress, 3rd session, no. 39, 1–63; Kelsey, "A Statement of Facts," 3.

57. Mexico, *Report of the Committee of Investigation Sent in 1873 by the Mexican Government*, 27–32. It is important to note that this report, just like many of the contemporaneous U.S. congressional investigations of trouble along the Texas-Mexico border (including *Depredations on the Frontiers of Texas*), was deeply partisan in nature.

58. Friend, "W.P. Webb's Texas Rangers," 321.

59. Memorial to the Hon. E. B. Pickett, president of the Constitutional Convention of the State of Texas, 24 November 1875, TSLA, Adjutant General Records (cited hereafter as AGR), General Correspondence (cited hereafter as GC), box 401-393, folder 15.

60. Letter from John A. Macdonald to William Macdougall, 12 December 1869, NAC, Sir John A. Macdonald Papers, vol. 516, reel C-28.

61. Macleod, *The North-West Mounted Police*, 8–9.

62. It is worth noting that it was strict Mounted Police policy that no Indians or Métis be placed in a position of authority or supervision over whites. See letter from Fred White to Cora Hughes, 2 March 1911, NAC, RG 18, series A-1, vol. 408, file 180.

63. Dempsey, *Jerry Potts*. Novelist Guy Vanderhaeghe offers a rich—if fictional—rendering of Potts in *The Last Crossing*.

64. Carter, *Capturing Women*, 175–78.

65. Letter from J. M. Walsh to R. W. Scott, 6 September 1876, NAC, RG 18, series A-1, vol. 9, file 69.

66. Letter from G. A. French to minister of justice, 8 April 1875, NAC, RG 10, vol. 3621, reel C-10108, file 4735.

67. Canada, Parliament, "Annual Report of the Department of the Interior for the Year Ended 30th June, 1881; Part III, North-West Mounted Police Force, Report of the Commissioner 1881," *Sessional Papers*, 1882, XV, vol. 8, no. 18, p. 23.

68. The matter of Métis landholding is a complex one. Although at the time of the Manitoba Act the Métis were promised 1.4 million acres of land for their children, confusion surrounded the actual business of allotment. In order to streamline the process, Ottawa offered scrip with which the Métis could then buy federal lands; this system, however, was ripe for exploitation by speculators. See Friesen, *The Canadian Prairies*, 197–201; and Carter, *Aboriginal People*, 157.

69. Letter (confidential) from Lawrence Clarke to Alexander Morris, 10 July 1875, NAC, RG 18, series A-1, vol. 6, file 333.

70. Copy of the laws and regulations established for the colony of St. Laurent on the Saskatchewan, 10 December 1873, NAC, RG 18, series A-1, vol. 6, file 333. As Woodcock explains, the Métis themselves avoided the term "provisional government" because of

its negative associations with the resistance of 1869–70, preferring instead "colony" or "community." See Woodcock, *Gabriel Dumont*, 96.

71. For a careful description of the encounter, see Woodcock, *Gabriel Dumont*, 103–10.

72. Letter from Selby Smyth to minister of justice, 27 July 1875, NAC, RG 18, series A-1, vol. 6, file 333; letter from Selby Smyth, unaddressed, 6 August 1875, NAC, RG 18, series A-1, vol. 6, file 333.

73. Woodcock, *Gabriel Dumont*, 109–10.

74. Letter from G. A. French to minister of justice, 6 August 1875, and letter from G. A. French to minister of justice, 14 September 1875, NAC, RG 18, series A-1, vol. 6, file 333.

75. Kelly and Kelly, *The Royal Canadian Mounted Police*, 78.

76. See letter from Lindsay Russell, deputy minister of the interior, to Charles Nolin, 13 October 1882, Canada, Parliament, *Sessional Papers*, 1885, XVIII, vol. 13, no. 116, p. 46.

77. Letter (translation) from V. Végréville to E. Deville, chief inspector of surveys, 19 January 1884, Canada, Parliament, *Sessional Papers*, 1885, XVIII, vol. 13, no. 116, pp. 64–65, quotation on 65.

78. Letter from Gabriel Dumont, et al., to Sir John A. Macdonald, minister of the interior, 4 September 1882, Canada, Parliament, *Sessional Papers*, 1885, XVIII, vol. 13, no. 116, p. 47.

79. Copy of a petition from Rev. Father André of Duck Lake to His Honor the Lieutenant-Governor in Council, undated, Canada, Parliament, *Sessional Papers*, 1885, XVIII, vol. 13, no. 116, p. 98.

80. Letter from Lawrence Clarke to James A. Grahame, 20 May 1884, NAC, RG 18, series A-1, vol. 12, file 20, part I.

81. Telegram from L. N. F. Crozier to Fred White, 8 July 1884, Canada, Parliament, *Sessional Papers*, 1885, XVIII, vol. 13, no. 116, p. 98; letter from L. N. F. Crozier to Fred White, 24 July 1884, NAC, RG 18, series A-1, vol. 12, file 20, part I.

82. Letter from Fred White to minister of interior, 3 September 1884, Canada, Parliament, *Sessional Papers*, 1885, XVIII, vol. 13, no. 116, pp. 101, and 100–13.

83. Letter from W. A. Brooks to officer commanding at Battleford, 21 August 1884, Canada, Parliament, *Sessional Papers*, 1885, XVIII, vol. 13, no. 116, p. 102. Riel's role in the events that followed is—as with much of Métis history—the subject of considerable debate, with some scholars laying the blame for the North-West Rebellion squarely at his feet. What is certain is that by the time he returned to Canada in 1884 he believed that he had been chosen by God to lead a religious revival, with the Métis as a chosen people. How that may have shaped the ensuing conflict is beyond the scope of this study, but there can be no doubt that deepening Métis concerns over their land tenure had created conditions ripe for another insurgency. For more, see Carter, *Aboriginal People*, 150–57.

84. Letter from Francis Dickens to officer commanding at Battleford, 9 November 1884, Canada, Parliament, *Sessional Papers*, 1885, XVIII, vol. 13, no. 116, pp. 107–8. Dickens—who had served for several years in India as a member of the Bengal Mounted

Police—was a ne'er do well, often described by his superior officers as drunk and indolent. Dickens—and historians—were done a great disservice by the publication of humorist Eric Nicol's *Dickens of the Mounted*. Nicol's book is often taken at face value by its readers, as the author apparently intended, creating considerable confusion and irritation. For more on the book and the reaction it provoked, see Thacker, "The Mystery of Francis Jeffrey Dickens."

85. Letter from G. H. Keenan to L. N. F. Crozier, 4 October 1884, NAC, RG 18, series A-1, vol. 12, file 20, part I; letter from L. N. F. Crozier to A. G. Irvine, 14 August 1884, Canada, Parliament, *Sessional Papers*, 1885, XVIII, vol. 13, no. 116, pp. 100–101, quotation on 101.

86. Perhaps the best single volume on the affair is Beal and Macleod, *Prairie Fire*. For the NWMP account of the conflict, see Canada, Parliament, "Report of the Commissioner of the North-West Mounted Police Force 1885," *Sessional Papers*, 1886, XIX, vol. 6, no. 8a, pp. 20–47.

87. This description is drawn from Woodcock, *Gabriel Dumont*, 173–74.

88. Wallace, *A Trying Time*, 149; Friesen, *The Canadian Prairies*, 231.

89. Debate over Indian involvement in the North-West Rebellion has raged since the time of the events themselves, but many historians seem now to believe that the insurrection was almost entirely a Métis affair. See, e.g., J. Foster, "The Plains Metis," 435; and J. R. Miller, *Skyscrapers Hide the Heavens*, 188. For a sense of the First Nations' perspective on the events, see Stonechild, "The Indian View."

90. Flanagan, *Riel and the Rebellion*, 3–4.

91. Friesen, *The Canadian Prairies*, 227.

92. Morton, *The Last War Drum*, indicts the police for their cowardice, while J. Jennings, "The North-West Mounted Police," 266, argues for the deemphasis of the rebellion in accounts of the NWMP.

93. J. Jennings, "The North-West Mounted Police," 266.

94. On the relationship of the Special Force to the Texas Rangers, see chap. 1, n. 10, above.

95. Utley, *Lone Star Justice*, 57–86. For wider context on atrocities committed by U.S. troops in Mexico during the conflict, see Paul Foos, *A Short, Offhand, Killing Affair*.

96. For more on McNelly, see Robinson, *The Men Who Wear the Star*, 182–83; and Wilkins, *The Law Comes to Texas*, 84–87. For a recent full-length biographical study, see Parsons and Little, *Captain L. H. McNelly*.

97. Durham, *Taming the Nueces Strip*, 130.

98. W. R. Morrison uses this phrase to describe Mountie efforts in the far northern reaches of the Dominion. See his *Showing the Flag*.

99. Letter from L. H. McNelly to William Steele, June 1875 [n.d.], TAGR, box 2Q400, folio 8, emphasis in the original. There are conflicting reports on the total numbers of Mexicans killed in the battle and displayed afterward in the square. Durham, *Taming the Nueces Strip*, thought the actual number was sixteen, while the Brownsville city marshal said later that he had collected only eight bodies, "all we could find, though not all that

were killed." See testimony of Joseph P. O'Shaunessy before F. J. Parker, U.S. Circuit Court, Eastern District of Texas, 16 June 1875, TAGR, box 2Q400, folio 8. The numbers cited above reflect McNelly's version of events.

100. Notice from the Office of the Inspector of Hides and Animals at Brownsville, 17 June 1875, TAGR, box 2Q400, folio 8.

101. For his part, Vetencourt was charged with making threats and attempting to assault a Brownsville resident, and because he could not pay the $500 bond he was committed to the county jail. Transcript in Justice Court, Precinct No. 2, Cameron County, Texas, 16 and 18 June 1875, TAGR, box 2Q400, folio 8.

102. In the spring of 2004, McNelly was "tried" at Baylor University Law School for his invasion of Mexico, and was found "mostly not guilty" by the members of the jury. For more information on the trial, see "Texas Ranger Facing 'Trial' for 1875 Event," *Waco Tribune*, 8 May 2004.

103. Robinson, *The Men Who Wear the Silver Star*, 200–204. Utley explains that other participants in the raid estimated the dead at five or six times this number. *Lone Star Justice*, 166.

104. Webb, *The Texas Rangers*, 263–65.

105. Diego García, mayor of Camargo, Tamaulipas, wrote to Sergeant John H. Wilkinson of the Eighth U.S. Cavalry that the crossing of the U.S. troops "infringes upon the laws and friendly relations existing between the United States and Mexico," and insisted that the American forces withdraw. See letter from Diego García to J. H. Wilkinson, 19 November 1875, TSLA, AGR, GC, box 2-23/963. On the U.S. side, Colonel J. H. Potter, acting on direct orders from Washington, wrote from Fort Brown to demand McNelly's retreat and to prohibit further army assistance. See telegram from J. H. Potter to A. J. Alexander, 20 November 1875, TSLA, AGR, GC, box 2-23/963.

106. Telegram from L. H. McNelly to William Steele, 22 November 1875, TSLA, AGR, GC, box 401-393, folder 10.

107. Letter from L. H. McNelly to William Steele, May 1875 [n.d.], TAGR, box 2Q400, folio 8.

108. N. A. Jennings, *A Texas Ranger*, 211. King continued to serve as McNelly's benefactor even after the Ranger captain's death, fronting the $3,000 needed to construct McNelly's tomb in Mt. Zion cemetery in Burton, Texas. See "The Fall of a Lawman and His Tomb," *Dallas Morning News*, 10 February 2002.

109. Webb, *The Texas Rangers*, 278; Durham, *Taming the Nueces Strip*, 134.

110. The quotation comes from the foreword by Joe B. Frantz to Procter, *Just One Riot*, viii.

111. Wallace noted that he instituted this practice "without authority of law." See letter from Warren Wallace to William Steele, 22 August 1874, TAGR, box 2Q400, folio 8. See also Utley, *Lone Star Justice*, 161. Among the grievances filed against Wallace was his alleged use of *la ley fuga*, "the fugitive law," in which law enforcement officers shoot a suspect "in the act of escape." Wallace himself admitted that he used torture to obtain confessions and intelligence. See letter from Warren Wallace to William Steele, 21 August 1874, TAGR, box 2Q400, folio 8.

112. N. A. Jennings, *A Texas Ranger*, 151–52.

113. U.S. Congress, *Texas Border Troubles*, House Miscellaneous Document 64, 45th Congress, 2nd session (1878), 130–31.

114. Royce, in "Jesus Sandoval," relates a different account of the events inspiring Sandoval's anti-Mexican vigilance, in which a party of Cortina raiders burned his ranch and raped his wife and daughter.

115. See Webb, *The Texas Rangers*, 242–43. Sandoval served a little more than eighteen months with the Rangers. For more information on him, see Parsons, *"Pidge."*

116. To be sure, Utley takes a different view, arguing that the Mexican government's forced exile of Cortina to the interior of Mexico was the real reason that the raids came to an end. See *Lone Star Justice*, 167–68. I find this unpersuasive for several reasons. First, Utley himself notes only a few pages earlier that "the mere presence of Rangers curtailed the depredations of stock thieves," making explicit mention of the activities of Wallace, among others (161). More importantly, Cortina—while certainly the most powerful raider along the border—was hardly the only individual bent on (re)claiming Texas cattle. Thus the almost total disappearance of Mexican cattle raids after the mid-1870s cannot be explained simply by his absence from the frontier.

117. Graf, "The Economic History of the Lower Rio Grande Valley," 644.

118. The figure of 900,000 comes from the introduction by Ben Procter to the reissue of N. A. Jennings's memoir, *A Texas Ranger*, xxxiii, while the smaller number can be found in the *Special Report of the Adjutant-General of the State of Texas, September 1884*, appendix.

119. Durham, *Taming the Nueces Strip*, 127.

120. U.S. Congress, *El Paso Troubles in Texas*, House Executive Document 93, 45th Congress, 2nd session (1878), 50.

121. U.S. Congress, *El Paso Troubles in Texas*, House Executive Document 93, 45th Congress, 2nd session (1878), 68.

122. See Romero, "El Paso Salt War," 123–25.

123. There are numerous accounts of the Salt War, most of them told in histories of the Rangers in the nineteenth century. My abbreviated description relies in large part on the narrative offered by Utley in *Lone Star Justice*, 188–206.

124. U.S. Congress, *El Paso Troubles in Texas*, House Executive Document 93, 45th Congress, 2nd session (1878), 24–25. It is worth noting that before their bitter disagreement over the salt lakes, Cardis and Howard had formed an alliance to mount a Democratic challenge to Republican rule in the El Paso area.

125. Letter from Charles Kerber to John B. Jones, 8 November 1877, TAGR, box 2Q400, folio 9b.

126. Newspaper clipping, *Galveston News*, 20 December 1877, in WPW, box 2R294, vol. 3.

127. See telegrams from John B. Jones to William Steele, 12 and 14 November 1877, TSLA, AGR, GC, box 401-396, folder 10. Jones appears also to have relied on Howard, with whom he was in correspondence, to help him enlist men for Company C. See letter from Charles Howard to John B. Jones, 15 November 1877, TAGR, box 2Q400, folio 9b.

128. See Utley, *Lone Star Justice*, 195–96; and U.S. Congress, *El Paso Troubles in Texas*, House Executive Document 93, 45th Congress, 2nd session (1878), 26.

129. Some observers were mortified that the U.S. Army had to intervene. As one editorialist in the *Charleston News and Courier* put it: "It is pitiful that a State which could roll up a 100,000 majority for the Democratic ticket cannot keep the peace within its own borders without whining for United States troops! In case that Texas has not force enough to put down the 'greaser' Americans, South Carolina will help, and so will every other Southern State. We do not propose to play into the hands of the 'strong government' party. Apparently, Texas does." Undated clipping, TSLA, AGR, Ranger Records, box 401-1158, folder 28.

130. U.S. Congress, *El Paso Troubles in Texas*, House Executive Document 93, 45th Congress, 2nd session (1878), 4, 87.

131. Romero, "El Paso Salt War," 132–33.

132. See J. Jennings, "The North-West Mounted Police," 98.

133. For more on Métis persistence in the North-West following the 1885 rebellion, see Payment, "Batoche after 1885."

134. For an excellent consideration of this historical and ongoing contest, see Limón, *Dancing with the Devil*.

135. For evidence of such concerns and the response of the NWMP, see letter from Fred White to Lawrence Vankoughnet, 29 March 1888, and letter from Fred White to commissioner, 3 April 1888, NAC, RG 18, series A-1, vol. 22, file 386. For more on Métis communities in Montana, see M. H. Foster, *We Know Who We Are*.

136. For a discussion of native efforts to exploit the 49th parallel during the late nineteenth century, see LaDow, *The Medicine Line*.

137. Letter from John Cotton to commissioner, 29 February 1888, NAC, RG 18, series A-1, vol. 17, file 147; letter from W. H. Conway to Sergeant Gordon, 4 March 1890, NAC, RG 18, series A-1, vol. 38, file 9.

138. Letter from R. B. Deane to W. B. Macleod, 16 April 1903, NAC, RG 18, series A-1, vol. 253, file 294.

139. See, e.g., Carter, "Categories and Terrains."

140. For examples, see telegram from W. M. Herchmer to Fred White, 2 January 1890, NAC, RG 18, series A-1, vol. 38, file 9; and John Cotton, monthly report from Prince Albert for January 1891, NAC, RG 18, series A-1, vol. 49, file 141.

141. See E. Young, *Catarino Garza's Revolution*.

142. In 1888 Garza wrote a blistering series of editorials in his paper, *El Comercio Mexicano*, accusing Sebree of the murder of Abraham Resendez, a suspected thief who was in Sebree's custody when he was killed. Several months later a Ranger squad arrested Garza on a libel charge stemming from the publication of his articles on Sebree. While Garza was free on $500 bail, Sebree shot and wounded him at Rio Grande City, touching off a huge pro-Garza demonstration demanding that Sebree be brought to justice. See E. Young, *Catarino Garza's Revolution*, 65–74.

143. See letter from J. A. Brooks to Thomas Scurry, 18 May 1902, TSLA, AGR, GC, box 401-469, folder 1; letter from J. A. Brooks to Thomas Scurry, 2 June 1902, WPW, box 2R289, vol. 15; letter from J. A. Brooks to Thomas Scurry, 4 October 1902, TSLA, AGR, GC, box 401-472, folder 17.

144. The notice is wrenching, since it mentions *su inconsolable madre*—his inconsolable mother. Death notice for Alfredo de la Cerda, 4 October 1902, TSLA, AGR, GC, box 401-472, folder 18.

145. Utley, among others, has argued that the Rangers' actions were justified by self-defense. See *Lone Star Justice*, 276–77. While this interpretation is difficult either to sustain or refute, evidence abounds of provocative police behavior in the Brownsville area both before and after the events, lending credence to Mexican skepticism of the Ranger version. First, Baker admitted that on the day he killed Rámon de la Cerda, he had accosted Reyes Silguero and left him tied to a tree for thirty-six hours, believing that he was a cattle thief (in fact, Silguero was a fence rider for the King Ranch). Moreover, after Baker's June examining trial, Ranger Captain J. A. Brooks conceded that he had beaten the leader of a crowd that had gathered to jeer Baker, and following Baker's October arraignment in the death of Alfredo de la Cerda, Brooks wrote candidly to the adjutant general that, owing to the ill will of the Mexicans, "I am satisfied that we will be compelled to kill some of these people to protect ourselves." Finally, the Mexican ambassador to the United States was so concerned by the events that he mentioned the case specifically in a letter to the U.S. State Department complaining of Ranger excesses. See letter from adjutant general to Joseph D. Sayers, 11 November 1902, WPW, box 2R289, vol. 15; letter from J. A. Brooks to Thomas Scurry, 20 June 1902, TSLA, AGR, GC, box 401-472, folder 16; letter from J. A. Brooks to Thomas Scurry, 5 October 1902, TSLA, AGR, GC, box 401-472, folder 17; letter from Mexican ambassador to U.S. State Department [translation], 11 February 1904, WPW, box 2R289, vol. 16 [enclosed in letter from John Hay to Governor of Texas, 16 February 1904]; undated and untitled document of charges against the Rangers, WPW, box 2R289, vol. 15.

146. Letter from John Cotton to commissioner, 19 March 1894, NAC, RG 18, series A-1, vol. 93, file 210.

147. Letter from F. J. A. Demers to L. W. Herchmer, 20 January 1900, NAC, RG 18, series A-1, vol. 179, file 106.

148. It is worth noting that some Métis expressed interest in serving on the Canadian side during the conflict and inquired about joining the Mountie detachments in action there. In response to one such request, the NWMP comptroller explained that only those who were "intelligent, educated and would pass as white men could be taken on the same as other applicants." Quoted in Macleod, *The North-West Mounted Police*, 149.

149. See Macleod, *The North-West Mounted Police*, 106–9.

150. Dusenberry, "Waiting for a Day."

151. Paredes, *A Texas-Mexican Cancionero*, and *"With His Pistol in His Hand,"* 3. Cortez became a hero to many Tejanos for resisting arrest on a charge of horse theft, dur-

ing which he killed a white sheriff. This prompted a huge manhunt, which ended in the apprehension of Cortez just miles from the Rio Grande. He was sentenced to life in prison, but received a pardon in 1913 and died three years later at age forty. For his part, Paredes—who spent almost his entire career as a professor at the University of Texas–Austin—nursed a deep skepticism of the Rangers that lasted until his death in 1999. See Graham, "Don Graham's Texas Classics."

152. See Johnson, *Revolution in Texas.*

153. For more on Canales, see Ribb, "José Tomás Canales and the Texas Rangers."

4. Defending the Cattleman's Empire

1. *Macleod Gazette,* 9 March 1886.

2. I have adapted the term "bonanza ranching" from Pursell, *The Machine in America,* 109–28.

3. This description relies heavily on the work of historical geographer Terry G. Jordan. See his *North American Cattle-Ranching Frontiers*; and also his *Trails to Texas.*

4. Jordan, *Trails to Texas,* 126; Jordan, *North American Cattle-Ranching Frontiers,* 215–18.

5. Osgood, *The Day of the Cattleman,* 27–33; Jordan, *North American Cattle-Ranching Frontiers,* 222.

6. Bruch, *Banister Was There,* 1–12.

7. Gillett, *Six Years with the Texas Rangers.*

8. Some Texas and most Canadian cattle companies added an "e" to the end of "ranch," suggesting perhaps their British origin, or at least a deeply ingrained Anglophilia.

9. Brayer, "The Influence of British Capital." Profit estimates come from Merrill, *Public Lands and Political Meaning,* 20. For more on Goodnight, see J. E. Haley, *Charles Goodnight.*

10. Dempsey, *The Golden Age of the Canadian Cowboy,* 7; Breen, *The Canadian Prairie West,* 9–11; and Simon M. Evans, *Prince Charming Goes West,* 33–61. For a rich first-hand account of the early days of Canadian ranching, see Ings's autobiographical *Before Fences.*

11. Jameson, *Ranches, Cowboys and Characters,* 7; Breen, "The Mounted Police," 116; and Dempsey, *The Golden Age,* 7.

12. Breen, "The Mounted Police," 117; Gardiner, *Letters from an English Rancher,* 13; and Jameson, *Ranches, Cowboys and Characters,* 16.

13. Breen, "The Mounted Police," 118; Breen, *The Canadian Prairie West,* 17–18; and McCullough, "Not an Old Cowhand," 32–33. For more on the Bar U, see Simon Evans, *The Bar U and Canadian Ranching History.*

14. Breen, "The Mounted Police," 121–25. For a representative example of a report concerning a flying patrol, see letter from M. Baker to officer commanding at Calgary, 12 May 1890, National Archives of Canada (cited hereafter as NAC), Record Group (cited hereafter as RG) 18, series A-1, vol. 42, file 495. For an excellent description of life on

a working Canadian ranch at the end of the nineteenth century, see Craig, *Ranching with Lords and Commons*. Craig's remembrances of his managerial service to the Oxley Ranch shed light on all aspects of the industry, from daily life to the raising of investment capital.

15. See Diary of W. F. Cochrane, Glenbow-Alberta Institute (cited hereafter as GAI), Cochrane Family Fonds.

16. Breen, "The Mounted Police," 120–21. For more on the Ranchmen's Club, including the membership roster, see the pamphlet titled "Constitution, Rules and Regulations of the Ranchmen's Club," GAI, A. E. Cross Family Fonds, M289, box 10, file 96. It is worth noting that the metropolitan cultural flavor of southern Alberta's ranch society was not unique to Canada and was in fact found throughout the greater North American West. See Elofson, *Cowboys, Gentlemen and Cattle Thieves*, and esp. his *Frontier Cattle Ranching*.

17. See letter from W. F. Cochrane to James Cochrane, 19 December 1884, Cochrane Family Fonds, Cochrane Ranche Letter Book, 1884–85.

18. Monthly report from Macleod, May 1890, NAC, RG 18, series A-1, vol. 41, file 238.

19. Canada, Parliament, "Annual Report of the Minister of the Interior for the Year Ended 30th June, 1881, Part II, North-West Mounted Police Force, Report of the Commissioner 1881," *Sessional Papers*, 1882, XV, vol. 8, no. 18, p. 24.

20. For examples of U.S. cattle infringing on Canadian pasture, see letter from Z. I. Wood to officer commanding at Maple Creek, 5 May 1894, NAC, RG 18, series A-1, vol. 105, file 184; memo respecting the drifting of cattle across the boundary line in the N.W. Territories, 30 November 1895, NAC, RG 18, series A-1, vol. 105, file 184; monthly reports from Maple Creek, September and October 1897, NAC, RG 18, series A-1, vol. 127, file 9.

21. For a description of this policy, see Spector, *Agriculture on the Prairies*, 27–42.

22. Letter from A. B. Perry to deputy minister of agriculture, 14 October 1896, GAI, David Breen National Archives of Canada Ranching Collection, 1880–1926 (cited hereafter as NACRC), box 2, file 55.

23. Extract from report of R. B. Deane, 17 May 1895, NAC, RG 18, series A-1, vol. 105, file 184.

24. Letter from Fred White to Clifford Sifton, 10 November 1903, NACRC, box 2, file 62. This plan was raised—and dismissed—at regular intervals throughout the 1890s and early 1900s.

25. J. E. Haley, "And Then Came Barbed Wire," 80.

26. The literature on barbed wire and the fencing of the West is surprisingly large, with perhaps the best account found in Webb, *The Great Plains*, 270–318. Another useful source is McCallum and McCallum, *The Wire That Fenced the West*. For sales statistics, see Webb, *The Great Plains*, 309.

27. McCallum and McCallum, *The Wire That Fenced the West*, 72.

28. Dary, *Cowboy Culture*, 310. For more on East Texas livestock laws, see Gammel, *The Laws of Texas*, 8:1131–41.

29. Hendrix, "The Nester." For evidence of early tensions between settlers and ranchers, see "Reminiscences of J. H. Abbott," J. H. Abbott Papers, Western History Collections, University of Oklahoma, Norman.

30. August, "Cowboys v. Rancheros"; Holden, *The Spur Ranch*, 65.

31. Texas was allowed to retain its lands in order to pay off the debts it had accumulated during its period as a republic (1836–45). In 1850 state officials ceded 67 of the 216 million acres—including parts of New Mexico, Oklahoma, Kansas, Colorado, and Wyoming—to the U.S. government in exchange for $10 million, settling a boundary dispute. See T. L. Miller, *The Public Lands of Texas*.

32. For more on Reconstruction in Texas, see Campbell, *Grass-Roots Reconstruction*; Barr, *Reconstruction to Reform*; and Moneyhon, *Texas after the Civil War*.

33. J. E. Haley, *The xit Ranch*, 49–57.

34. T. L. Miller, *The Public Lands of Texas*, 145–84. Both of these statutes were subsequently revised several times. Donald Worster offers some provocative ideas about the ideology of development (and its problems as an explanatory paradigm) in "Two Faces West." It is important to note that John Ireland, who succeeded Oran Roberts as governor of Texas, attempted to slow the sale of public lands initiated by his predecessor.

35. Isenberg, "Environment and the Nineteenth-Century West."

36. *Report of the Adjutant-General of the State of Texas, December 1883*, 27.

37. Starrs, *Let the Cowboy Ride*, 110–24. The "Fifty Cent Act" passed in 1879 was effectively repealed three years later, but not before huge amounts of land had been purchased by individual ranchers and syndicates. See Abbe, "Ranching and Speculation."

38. Letter from Matthew H. Cochrane to John A. Macdonald, 17 December 1880, nacrc, box 1, file 13. Cochrane estimated his initial investment at $125,000.

39. Breen, *The Canadian Prairie West*, 18–19.

40. For more on the importance of Montana to the early economy of Alberta, see Klassen, *Eye on the Future*, 9–37.

41. For more on the National Policy, see Aitken, "Defensive Expansionism."

42. Canada, Parliament, "Annual Report of the Department of the Interior for 1880," *Sessional Papers*, 1880–81, vol. 3, no. 3, p. viii.

43. This developmental paradigm is known as the "Staples Thesis," promulgated by Canadian economist Harold Innis. For examples of this idea in practice, see his books *The Fur Trade in Canada*, and *The Cod Fisheries*.

44. Holden, *The Spur Ranch*, 64–65; Gard, *Rawhide Texas*, 75.

45. J. E. Haley, *The xit Ranch*, 87–88. The initials "xit" stood for "Ten in Texas," a reference to the fact that the ranch occupied land in parts of ten Texas counties. Dary, in *Cowboy Culture*, 317, provides a fascinating description of the process by which large ranchers strung wire.

46. Holt, "The Introduction of Barbed Wire," 70; letter from E. P. Earhart to J. Evetts Haley, 22 February 1927, Panhandle Plains Historical Museum (cited hereafter as pphm).

47. Holt, "The Introduction of Barbed Wire," 69.

48. Holden, *The Spur Ranch*, 68–73.

49. See letter from I. L. Elwood to D. N. Arnett, 2 August 1892, D. N. Arnett Papers, Southwest Collections, Texas Tech University, Lubbock, box 1, folder 5; letter from E. P. Earhart to J. Evetts Haley, 22 February 1927, PPHM. Many cowboys like Pie-Biter resented barbed wire for another reason: enclosure rendered the trail drive obsolete, forcing cowhands out of work.

50. Memoirs of W. R. Durham, Jr., 18 August 1936, PPHM.

51. Letter from N. Y. Bickell to J. E. Haley, 21 October 1926, PPHM.

52. The literature on enclosure is extensive. I have relied on Neeson, *Commoners*. See also Wrightson, *Earthly Necessities*; and E. P. Thompson, *Customs in Common*.

53. *Report of the Adjutant-General of the State of Texas, December 1883*, 25.

54. Gard, "The Fence-Cutters," 1–4.

55. See Holt, "The Introduction of Barbed Wire," 76. For use of the term "White Capper," see letter from A. E. Noel and R. M. Low to C. A. Culberson, 19 September 1898, Texas State Library and Archives (cited hereafter as TSLA), Adjutant General Records (cited hereafter as AGR), General Correspondence (cited hereafter as GC), box 401-449, folder 12.

56. Quoted in Holt, "The Saga of Barbed Wire," 39.

57. Utley, among others, takes this perspective, writing that "they [the cutters] were corrupted by alliance with cattle thieves and hide burners with their own sinister aims." See *Lone Star Justice*, 234.

58. Letter from James Keiffer to John Ireland, 23 September 1883, TSLA, AGR, GC, box 401-403, folder 7.

59. Letter from E. P. Earhart to J. Evetts Haley, 22 February 1927, PPHM.

60. Quoted in Holt, "The Introduction of Barbed Wire," 72.

61. Quoted in Holt, "The Introduction of Barbed Wire," 74.

62. Letter from W. H. King to C. B. McKinney, 13 January 1883, TSLA, AGR, GC, ledger 401-630, 211.

63. Letter from J. M. Lee to John Ireland, 29 July 1883, TSLA, AGR, GC, box 401-403, folder 2.

64. Letter from C. W. Powell to John Ireland, 2 August 1883, TSLA, AGR, GC, box 401-403, folder 4.

65. *Message of Governor John Ireland to the Eighteenth Legislature, Convened in Special Session, at the City of Austin, January 8, 1884*.

66. Gammel, *The Laws of Texas*, 9:566–67.

67. Breen, *The Canadian Prairie West*, 20.

68. See Card, *The Diaries of Charles Ora Card*, 51–53.

69. Simon Evans, *Prince Charming Goes West*, 45; quotation from Jameson, *Ranches, Cowboys and Characters*, 8.

70. Simon Evans, *Prince Charming Goes West*, 41.

71. *Macleod Gazette*, 24 August 1882.

72. *Macleod Gazette*, 23 September 1882.

73. See Ranelagh, *A Short History of Ireland*, 136.

74. Letter from F. Girard to H. Langevin, 18 November 1884, NACRC, box 2, file 47.

75. *Macleod Gazette*, 24 March 1883.

76. Canada, Parliament, "Annual Report of the Department of the Interior for 1883," *Sessional Papers*, 1884, vol. 7, no. 12, p. 4.

77. *Macleod Gazette*, 24 March 1883.

78. *Macleod Gazette*, 21 July 1885.

79. Brado, *Cattle Kingdom*, 182.

80. Breen, *The Canadian Prairie West*, 44–47.

81. Simon Evans, *Prince Charming Goes West*, 47–48.

82. Canada, Parliament, "Annual Report of the Department of the Interior for 1885," *Sessional Papers*, 1886, vol. 6, no. 8, p. 19.

83. Letter from William Pearce to H. Stanley Pinhorne, 27 September 1886, NACRC, box 1, file 24 (enclosed in letter from Pearce to minister of the interior, 11 November 1886).

84. Breen, "The Canadian Prairie West," 70.

85. See letter from William Pearce, unaddressed, 7 May 1889, NACRC, box 2, file 33. In this document (which appears to be a form letter), Pearce explained to settlers that the desired land was unsuitable for farming and that area leaseholders had expressed their concerns about the settlers' brush fires and barbed wire.

86. Letter from S. B. Steele to NWMP commissioner, 17 October 1891, NACRC, box 2, file 53.

87. See *Report of the Adjutant-General of the State of Texas, February 28, 1882*, 27.

88. State of Texas, *Message of Governor John Ireland.*

89. Examples abound. See, e.g., letter from F. N. Vallins to W. H. King, 14 April 1884, and letter from S. C. VanDevender to W. H. King, 3 May 1884, TSLA, AGR, GC, box 401-404, folders 5 and 11.

90. The most complete history of the fabled Pinkerton Agency makes no mention whatsoever of the agency's extensive work in Texas in 1884. See Morn, *"The Eye That Never Sleeps."*

91. Letter from Alan Pinkerton to John Ireland, 11 March 1884, TSLA, AGR, GC, box 401-404, folder 1.

92. The Runnels County cutters were apprehended destroying part of a 90,000-acre enclosure on the property of Colonel T. L. Odum, a Texas legislator. See Utley, *Lone Star Justice*, 235–36. For King's misgivings about the detectives, see letter from W. H. King to G. R. Freeman, 11 April 1884, TSLA, AGR, GC, ledger 401-631, 208–9. Letter from William Carlton to W. H. King, 10 June 1884, TSLA, AGR, GC, box 401-404, folder 16.

93. Letter from S. C. VanDevender to W. H. King, 3 May 1884, TSLA, AGR, GC, box 401-404, folder 11.

94. Letter from G. W. Baylor to W. H. King, 16 March 1884, TSLA, AGR, GC, box 401-404, folder 3.

95. Letter from G. B. Greer to John Ireland, 19 July 1884, TSLA, AGR, GC, box 401-405, folder 5. That Greer appears to have been a sheepman may have provided the cutters with added incentive to destroy his fence, since sheep grazed the range much more closely than cattle. See letter from G. B. Greer to L. P. Sieker, 26 August 1884, TSLA, AGR, GC, box 401-405, folder 9.

96. Report of P. F. Baird, 8 August 1884, enclosed in letter from L. P. Sieker to W. H. King, 8 August 1884, TSLA, AGR, GC, box 401-405, folder 8.

97. For arrest figures, see *Report of the Adjutant-General of the State of Texas, December 1884*, 28.

98. Letter from D. D. Sanderson to John Ireland, 10 January 1885, TSLA, AGR, GC, box 401-406, folder 1.

99. This description of the cattle industry in Brown County relies on Havins, *Something about Brown*, esp. 33–40.

100. Havins, *Something about Brown*, 37.

101. There is some debate about whether the scout was an Indian or a white man dressed as an Indian. But in an interview, Baugh's great-nephew George insisted that the scout was indeed a white man, a fact that deterred his relative from scalping the dead man but did not keep him from displaying his effects in the Baugh home. The slain man had his revenge, though, as his clothes promptly infested the Baugh house with lice. See T. C. Smith, *From the Memories of Men*, 26–27.

102. Aten, *Six and One-half Years*.

103. Aten's account is contained in a letter to L. P. Sieker, 11 June 1887, Center for American History at the University of Texas, Austin, Walter Prescott Webb Papers (cited hereafter as WPW), box 2R289, vol. 11. Havins offers a different version of events in *Something about Brown*, 39.

104. Quoted in Havins, *Something about Brown*, 40.

105. Quoted in T. C. Smith, *From the Memories of Men*, 29.

106. See T. C. Smith, *From the Memories of Men*; and letter from William Scott to L. P. Sieker, 12 December 1886, TSLA, AGR, Ranger Records, box 401-1160, folder 4.

107. Aten's letters, particularly a set of five missives from 1888, have received ample attention from Ranger historians, including Webb, *The Texas Rangers*; Wilkins, *The Law Comes to Texas*; and Utley, *Lone Star Justice*. Indeed, they usually form the basis for any study of the Frontier Battalion's efforts to eradicate fence cutting, although in most cases the letters have been used (and with great effect) to add color to a narrative.

108. Aten, *Six and One-half Years*, 20–22.

109. Letter from Ira Aten to L. P. Sieker, 31 August 1888, TSLA, AGR, GC, box 401-412, folder 19.

110. Letter from William Scott to W. H. King, 14 February 1887, TSLA, AGR, GC, box 401-409, folder 14.

111. Letter from Ira Aten to L. P. Sieker, 31 August 1888, TSLA, AGR, GC, box 401-412, folder 19.

112. Letter from Ira Aten to L. P. Sieker, 31 August 1888, TSLA, AGR, GC, box 401-412, folder 19.

113. Letter from Ira Aten to L. P. Sieker, 17 September 1888, TSLA, AGR, GC, box 401-413, folder 4.

114. Letter from Ira Aten to L. P. Sieker, 31 August 1888, TSLA, AGR, GC, box 401-412, folder 19.

115. Letter from Ira Aten to L. P. Sieker, 8 October 1888, TSLA, AGR, GC, box 401-413, folder 6.

116. Aten, *Six and One-half Years*, 22.

117. Letter from Ira Aten to L. P. Sieker, 15 October 1888, TSLA, AGR, GC, box 401-413, folder 6.

118. Breen, "The Canadian Prairie West," 72. For evidence of the expansion of stock-watering reserves, see orders-in-council issued on the following dates: 12 October 1889, 7 November 1890, 6 October 1891, 28 May 1892, 18 July 1894, 21 May 1895, and 23 January 1896, all in NAC, RG 15, vol. 1204, file 141376, part II.

119. Quoted in Breen, *The Canadian Prairie West*, 56.

120. Letter from William Pearce to secretary of the Department of the Interior, 23 October 1894, NAC, RG 15, vol. 1204, file 141376, part II.

121. Petition from the High River Stock Association to the minister of the interior, 2 April 1894, NAC, RG 15, vol. 1241, file 352945.

122. Letter from A. M. Burgess to T. Mayne Daly, 30 April 1894, NAC, RG 15, vol. 1241, file 352945.

123. See letter from Fred White to deputy minister of the interior, 12 June 1894, NAC, RG 18, series A-1, vol. 116, file 72; letter from John Hall to Fred White, 18 June 1894, NAC, RG 18, series A-1, vol. 116, file 72; and letter from William Pearce to John Hall, 27 July 1894, NAC, RG 15, vol. 1241, file 352945. It bears repeating that Pearce's Cato-like insistence concerning the protection of Alberta's stock interests was motivated to a great degree by his conviction that the region was simply not suited to farming.

124. See, e.g., letter from George B. Jonas to the minister of the interior, 19 June 1894; and petition to John Hall, undated, both in NAC, RG 15, vol. 1241, file 352945.

125. See letter from A. R. Cuthbert to S. B. Steele, 24 January 1895; letter, unaddressed, from R. Duthie, 12 March 1895; and letter from William Pearce to secretary of the Department of the Interior, 26 March 1895, all three in NAC, RG 15, vol. 1241, file 352945.

126. See NAC, RG 18, series A-1, vol. 101, file 23. For squatting by an ex-policeman, see letter from William Pearce to John Herron, 4 November 1895, NAC, RG 15, vol. 1204, file 141376, part II.

127. Letter from Lynwode Pereira to Fred White, 19 September 1895, NAC, RG 18, series A-1, vol. 116, file 72.

128. Breen, "The Canadian Prairie West," 73.

129. Canada, Parliament, "Report of the Commissioner of the North-West Mounted Police Force 1895," *Sessional Papers*, 1896, XXIX, vol. 11, no. 15, p. 38.

130. See monthly report of Sam Steele, November 1895, NAC, RG 18, series A-1, vol. 102, file 46.

131. See *Report of the Adjutant-General of the State of Texas, December 1888*, 47–48.

132. *Report of the Adjutant-General of the State of Texas, December 1888*, 41.

133. Letter from John N. Garner to W. H. Mabry, 13 November 1893, WPW, box 2R289, vol. 12.

134. Simon Evans, "The End of the Open Range Era," 72–74.

135. See letter from James A. Smart to Frank Oliver, 17 June 1897; and letter from Lynwode Pereira to William Pearce, 14 July 1897, both in NAC, RG 15, vol. 1204, file 141376, part III.

136. Simon Evans, "The End of the Open Range Era," 74.

137. Letter from A. Power to deputy minister of the interior, 21 November 1896, NAC, RG 18, series A-1, vol. 116, file 72.

138. Letter from Fred White to the secretary of the interior, 15 July 1905, NAC, RG 18, series B-1, vol. 1560, file 133.

139. For more on Populism in Texas, see Goodwyn, *Democratic Promise*.

140. Lower, *Western Canada*, 316; Havins, *Something about Brown*, 37.

141. Letter from Ira Aten to L. P. Sieker, 17 September 1888, TSLA, AGR, GC, box 401-413, folder 4.

142. Letter from G. W. Baylor to W. H. King, 16 March 1884, TSLA, AGR, GC, box 401-402, folder 3.

143. Letter from William Scott to W. H. King, 14 February 1887, TSLA, AGR, GC, box 401-409, folder 14.

144. Gard, "The Fence-Cutters," 9.

145. Duke and Frantz, *6,000 Miles of Fence*, 107.

146. Breen, "The Mounted Police," 135.

147. Simon Evans, "The End of the Open Range Era."

148. David C. Jones narrates the story of this migration and its outcome in his eloquent *Empire of Dust*. Figures from the appendix (pp. 254–56) indicate that between 1906 and 1921 the population of southwestern Saskatchewan jumped from 257,763 to 757,510, while southeastern Alberta grew from 185,195 to 588,454 over the same period. Alberta and Saskatchewan achieved provincial status in 1905.

149. See Worster, *Dust Bowl*, esp. the map on p. 30 for a sense of the damage in Texas.

5. Policing the Industrial Frontier

1. Hunter's tactics included a mandatory boycott of Lawson's establishment for all T&PCC employees "on pain of discharge," as well as various other forms of harassment. See Rhinehart, *A Way of Work*, 47–48.

2. Sullivan devotes three pages of his memoir to the skirmish. See Sullivan, *Twelve Years in the Saddle*, 30–32.

3. Leadbeater, "An Outline of Capitalist Development," 14–15.

4. The literature on Canadian railroad expansion is considerable; what follows is meant only to suggest some of the more important works. An extremely useful bibliography can be found in Owram, *Canadian History*, 133–36. Legget, *Railways of Canada*, offers a detailed and accessible survey. A dated but careful account of the shady corporate and governmental dealings that lay behind the construction of the CPR can be found in Myers, *A History of Canadian Wealth*. For a closer look at the social conditions that prevailed in the work camps and settlements along the main line of the CPR, see Dempsey, *The CPR West*. Den Otter, *Civilizing the West*, explores a single family's development and management of a western rail line and its subsidiary operations.

5. For more on the National Policy, see Aitken, "Defensive Expansionism."

6. The relationship between the railroad and regional coal companies is explored in den Otter, "Bondage of Steam."

7. Den Otter, *Civilizing the West*, 320–21.

8. Den Otter, *Civilizing the West*, 332–33. See also Seager, "Class, Ethnicity, and Politics," 307–8.

9. According to Bercuson, adding to the lethal nature of coal mining in the Canadian West—particularly in British Columbia—was the fact that the region's coal was fifteen times more gaseous than comparably graded bituminous in Pennsylvania, a condition discovered only after a series of explosions that killed hundreds of miners. See Bercuson, "Labour Radicalism," 169. It is worth noting that the mines at Lethbridge were comparatively low in explosive gases. For more on the perils of western mining, see Whiteside, *Regulating Danger*.

10. See Peck, *Reinventing Free Labor*; and McCormack, "The Western Working-Class Experience," 117–18. It would be a mistake, however, to assume that all immigrant miners were central Europeans whose first language was not English. Many, in fact, came from communities in the United Kingdom.

11. Avery, "*Dangerous Foreigners*," 8–9; McCormack, "The Western Working-Class Experience," 117.

12. Kealey, *Workers and Canadian History*, 334–35.

13. McCormack, *Reformers, Rebels, and Revolutionaries*, 12–13. Unlike most mining locales in the West, Lethbridge was in fact incorporated and boasted a range of shops that—at least in theory—offered miners an alternative to the company store.

14. Friesen, *The Canadian Prairies*, 297.

15. Den Otter, *Civilizing the West*, 273–74.

16. Quoted in R. C. Brown and Cook, *Canada, 1896–1921*, 116.

17. McCormack, *Reformers, Rebels, and Revolutionaries*, 10.

18. See U.S. Department of the Interior, *Report on Manufacturing Industries in the United States at the Eleventh Census*, 8. For my purposes, "western states" include Texas, Montana, Wyoming, Colorado, New Mexico, Idaho, Utah, Arizona, Washington, Oregon, Nevada, and California.

19. By 1900 Texas counted more than 12,000 factories and a wage-earning population of 48,000. See U.S. Department of the Interior, *Twelfth Census of the United States*, 862.

20. See U.S. Department of the Interior, *Report on Transportation Business in the United States at the Eleventh Census*, 4.

21. Zlatkovich, *Texas Railroads*, 7–9.

22. Henderson, "The Texas Coal Mining Industry," 208–10; Calderón, *Mexican Coal Mining Labor*, 17.

23. King, "Rascals and Rangers," 6–7.

24. Rhinehart, "'Underground Patriots,'" 511; Rhinehart, *A Way of Work*, 3; and Calderón, *Mexican Coal Mining Labor*, 237.

25. See Spratt, *The Road to Spindletop*, 263; and Powers, "The Subversion of 'Gordon's Kingdom,'" 26.

26. Figures from Rhinehart, *A Way of Work*, 11–13. Whereas in 1890 most of the names on the Johnson ledgers were English, Irish, Scottish, or Welsh, by 1900 native Italians alone constituted 41 percent of the miners at Thurber.

27. Marilyn Rhinehart offers a thorough and compelling description of the "the subterranean community" in *A Way of Work*, 18–39. My description of working conditions in the mines of Erath County relies heavily on her account. Quotation from p. 21.

28. Rhinehart, *A Way of Work*, 22–31.

29. Allen, *Chapters*, 20.

30. Fink, *Workingmen's Democracy*, xii. For more on the Knights—who have received an avalanche of academic treatment—see Voss, *The Making of American Exceptionalism*; and Weir, *Beyond Labor's Veil*.

31. The strike—which was directed against the Baltimore and Ohio Railroad—led to the deaths of more than a hundred people and the widespread destruction of railroad cars, locomotives, and buildings. See Foner, *The Great Labor Uprising*. For more on the KOL in Canada, see Kealey and Palmer, *Dreaming of What Might Be*.

32. Rhinehart, *A Way of Work*, 72.

33. See den Otter, *Civilizing the West*, 7–41.

34. Den Otter, *Civilizing the West*, 320–21.

35. Quoted in den Otter, *Civilizing the West*, 271.

36. R. B. Deane, monthly report, February 1894, National Archives of Canada (cited hereafter as NAC), Record Group (cited hereafter as RG) 18, series A-1, vol. 91, file 148.

37. Den Otter, *Civilizing the West*, 275.

38. R. B. Deane, monthly report, February 1894, NAC, RG 18, series A-1, vol. 91, file 148.

39. Despite their nearly identical names, the Texas and Pacific Railroad (T&PR) did not own the Texas and Pacific Coal Company (T&PCC); rather, the mining venture took its name from the fact that its property was located along the railroad's line.

40. Spratt, *Thurber*, ix–xii.

41. T&PCC Stockholders Report, 19 February 1890, University of Texas at Arlington—Special Collections Division, W. K. Gordon, Sr. Papers (cited hereafter as WKGP), AR421, box 2, folder 13; letter from Gomer Gower to Ben Owens, 4 November 1940, Center for American History at the University of Texas, Austin, Labor Movement in Texas Collection (cited hereafter as LMTC), box 2E 308, folder 14.

42. It is interesting to note that the fence around T&PCC property marked one of the first recorded uses of barbed wire as a boundary demarcating human settlement, a fact well recalled by North Texans of today. See letter to the editor, *Harper's Magazine*, June 2001, 86.

43. Letter from Gomer Gower to Ben Owens, 12 April 1940, and letter from Gomer Gower to Ben Owens, 12 November 1940, both in lmtc, box 2e308, folder 14, emphasis in the original. For more on Gower, who at the age of eleven immigrated from Wales with his family, see Rhinehart, "A Way of Work," 1–4.

44. Statistics from Allen, *Chapters*, 109–10; T&PCC Stockholders Report, 19 February 1890, wkgp, ar421, box 2, folder 13.

45. Allen, *Chapters*, 92; letter from Gomer Gower to Ben Owens, 4 November 1940, lmtc, box 2e 308, folder 14.

46. *Stephenville Empire*, 22 December 1888; telegram from J. J. Humphries to L. S. Ross, 13 December 1888, Texas State Library and Archives (cited hereafter as tsla), Adjutant General Records (cited hereafter as agr), General Correspondence (cited hereafter as gc), box 401-413, folder 13; monthly return for December 1888, Company B, tsla, agr, Ranger Records (cited hereafter as rr), box 401-1248.

47. It is worth pointing out that Deane's initial attempt at mediation was not the result of a directive from either Regina or Ottawa. However, given that he was in regular contact with his superiors and acted at Lethbridge in his capacity as a member of a territorial police force, his actions constituted federal intervention.

48. Quoted in den Otter, *Civilizing the West*, 251.

49. Among the other dispensations by the government to the cpr were $25 million in cash, and a twenty-six-year tax exemption on company lands. Leadbeater, "An Outline of Capitalist Development," 7–8. See also Myers, *A History of Canadian Wealth*, 150–300.

50. For an example of nwmp vigilance against alcohol consumption among railroad workers (in British Columbia, in this case), see the engaging (if florid and self-serving) memoir of legendary Mountie officer Samuel B. Steele, *Forty Years in Canada*, 186–87. For a description of nwmp duties concerning the supervision of work crews, see S. B. Steele, monthly report, July 1897, nac, rg 18, series a-1, vol. 126, file 3. For returning deserters, see Canada, Parliament, "Report of the Commissioner of the North-West Mounted Police Force 1890," *Sessional Papers*, 1891, XXIV, vol. 15, no. 19, pp. 30–31. Some workers had received a cash advance or its equivalent (such as transportation to the work site), which they were required to repay before quitting.

51. For nwmp strike duty, see nac, rg 18, series a-1, vol. 63, file 228; and nac, rg 18, series b-1, vol. 1511, file 198; Macleod, "Canadianizing the West," 104; L. Brown and C. Brown, *An Unauthorized History*, 28–29. While Macleod goes on to say that after 1885 the Mounties were scrupulous to avoid taking sides in labor disputes, my research—as indicated in the remainder of this chapter—suggests that this was not always the case.

52. Macleod makes precisely this point in "Canadianizing the West," 104.

53. See Morton, "Aid to the Civil Power," 407.

54. For more on the background of the NWMP officer corps, see Macleod, *The North-West Mounted Police*, 73–88.

55. Sidney Harring has argued that authorities in cities such as Buffalo, Chicago, Cleveland, and Milwaukee relied upon their constabularies to manage striking workers. See his *Policing a Class Society*, 101–48.

56. Harring, *Policing a Class Society*, 112. See also Dubofsky, *The State and Labor*, 1–35.

57. *Report of the Adjutant-General of the State of Texas, December 31, 1882*, 23.

58. Dubofsky, *Industrialism and the American Worker*, 34.

59. See Allen, *The Great Southwest Strike*.

60. *Report of the Adjutant-General of the State of Texas, December 1886*, 5. The Haymarket Riot—which occurred less than one month after the Southwest Strike—likely made an impact on King as well. See Avrich, *The Haymarket Tragedy*.

61. *Report of the Adjutant General of the State of Texas for 1889–90*, 27.

62. Officials in other states, however, had fewer qualms (or options) than their counterparts in Austin, and thus dispatched their militia units more than 150 times for strike duty between 1877 and 1903. Over the same period, federal troops intervened in four major labor disputes and several minor ones. For statistics on militia and army interventions, see Cooper, *The Army and Civil Disorder*, xiii–xv, 3–24. For more on the militia, see Riker, *Soldiers of the States*; and Hill, "The National Guard in Civil Disorders."

63. See Purcell, "The History of the Texas Militia," 257–309. That the only significant peacekeeping duty performed by the Texas National Guard between 1874 and 1903 was its handling of the Southwest Strike is perhaps the clearest indication of Austin's concerns about militia preparedness.

64. *Report of the Adjutant-General of the State of Texas, February 28, 1882*, 30; and *Report of the Adjutant-General of the State of Texas, December 31, 1882*, 26–27.

65. Canada, Parliament, "Report of the Commissioner of the North-West Mounted Police Force 1894," *Sessional Papers*, 1895, XXVIII, vol. 9, no. 15, p. 91; R. B. Deane, monthly report, February 1894, NAC, RG 18, series A-1, vol. 91, file 148.

66. Canada, Parliament, "Report of the Commissioner of the North-West Mounted Police Force 1894," *Sessional Papers*, 1895, XXVIII, vol. 9, no. 15, p. 91; R. B. Deane, monthly report, February 1894, NAC, RG 18, series A-1, vol. 91, file 148.

67. Figures are for 1901–5. Canada, *Report on Strikes and Lockouts in Canada from 1901 to 1912*, 238.

68. Baker, "The Miners and the Mounties," 141.

69. Deane, *Mounted Police Life in Canada*.

70. Baker, *Pioneer Policing in Southern Alberta*, 45–46.

71. In fact, the Mounties had enjoyed very friendly relations with the Galt company since the late 1880s, as suggested by occasional social visits paid to Sir Alexander by NWMP colonel James F. Macleod. See, e.g., letter from James F. Macleod to Mary Macleod, postmarked 18 January 1891, Macleod Fonds, Glenbow-Alberta Institute.

72. Letter from R. B. Deane to L. W. Herchmer, 9 March 1894, NAC, RG 18, series A-1, vol. 91, file 148.

73. At a meeting on 2 March, Galt had bumped the figure to a total of 200 men retained, if the two sides could effect a contract for the sinking of an air shaft. See R. B. Deane, weekly report, 2 February [*sic*] 1894, NAC, RG 18, series A-1, vol. 91, file 148.

74. See R. B. Deane, weekly report, 16 March 1894, NAC, RG 18, series A-1, vol. 91, file 148; and R. B. Deane, monthly report, March 1894, NAC, RG 18, series A-1, vol. 91, file 148.

75. The provisions were as follows: free transportation for single men in groups of at least fifty individuals for the week following 26 February; and free passes for married men and their families for the entire month of March. See R. B. Deane, monthly report, February 1894, NAC, RG 18, series A-1, vol. 91, file 148.

76. R. B. Deane, monthly report, April 1894, NAC, RG 18, series A-1, vol. 91, file 148. Deane interceded on their behalf and convinced Galt to temporarily revive the pass system.

77. R. B. Deane, monthly report, June 1894, NAC, RG 18, series A-1, vol. 91, file 148.

78. R. B. Deane, monthly report, March 1894, NAC, RG 18, series A-1, vol. 91, file 148.

79. For the adjutant general's directions that McMurry not choose sides, see letter from W. H. King to S. A. McMurry, 15 February 1889, TSLA, AGR, RR, ledger 401-1135, 579–80. On McMurry's meeting with union representatives, see Rhinehart, *A Way of Work*, 48–49.

80. For an example of McMurry's use of T&PCC stationery, see his letter to W. H. King, 6 April 1889, TSLA, AGR, GC, box 401-414, folder 5. For his use of the company store, see letter from S. A. McMurry to L. P. Sieker, 28 February 1889, TSLA, AGR, GC, box 401-413, folder 18.

81. McMurry adopted this term for the strikers as early as April 1889. See his letter to W. H. King, 6 April 1889, TSLA, AGR, GC, box 401-414, folder 5.

82. J. M. Morris, *A Private in the Texas Rangers*, 119. See 276–79 for a brief but useful biographical sketch of McMurry.

83. Letter from S. A. McMurry to W. H. King, 6 June 1889, Walter Prescott Webb Papers (cited hereafter as WPW), box 2R289, vol. 11. An examination of the monthly returns for Company B between 1888 and 1894 shows that arrests in Erath County averaged less than one per month during times of relative peace, but jumped as high as eight (June 1889) or even thirteen (December 1889) when workers gathered to protest company policies. See monthly returns, Company B, TSLA, AGR, RR, box 401-1248.

84. Sullivan, *Twelve Years in the Saddle*, 33. In an 1890 letter to King requesting further Ranger assistance at the mines, Hunter asked the adjutant general to "please send John Sullivan a permit to carry arms as he is one of the Captains old men now in the employ of their company." See letter from R. D. Hunter to W. H. King, 5 July 1890, WPW, box 2R289, vol. 11.

85. *Stephenville Empire*, 27 July 1889. The paper's support for the company likely stemmed from the enthusiasm of its owner (or editorial board) for capitalist develop-

ment in the region, as expressed in the following piece from 2 October 1890. Describing the T&PCC, the paper exhorted readers, "Let us not forget that Col. Hunter, by the development of these vast coal fields, has done more for Erath county than any living man." See also articles from 13 July 1889, 20 July 1889, and 9 October 1890.

86. Letter from R. D. Hunter to W. H. Mabry, 4 December 1894, WPW, box 2R289, vol. 13.

87. Quoted in Allen, *Chapters*, 93. Miner Gomer Gower insisted that while on a personal level the Rangers "were a pretty decent bunch of fellows," their presence "seriously hampered" the efforts of the strikers to dissuade strikebreakers from working the mines. See letter from Gomer Gower to Ben Owens, 4 November 1940, LMTC, box 2E308, folder 14.

88. Letter from S. A. McMurry to W. H. King, 6 June 1889, WPW, box 2R289, vol. 11; letter from S. A. McMurry to W. H. King, 2 July 1889, WPW, box 2R289, vol. 11.

89. T&PCC Stockholders Report, 19 February 1890, WKGP, AR421, box 2, folder 13.

90. Letter from S. A. McMurry to W. H. King, 2 February 1889; letter from S. A. McMurry to W. H. King, 17 February 1889; and letter from S. A. McMurry to W. H. King, 17 February 1889, all in TSLA, AGR, GC, box 401-413, folder 18.

91. *Stephenville Empire*, 22 July 1889; T&PCC Stockholders Report, 19 February 1890, WKGP, AR421, box 2, folder 13. For the estimate of the workforce before the arrival of the replacement workers, see letter from S. A. McMurry to W. H. King, 2 February 1889, TSLA, AGR, GC, box 401-413, folder 18.

92. Letter from S. A. McMurry to W. H. King, 6 June 1889, TSLA, AGR, GC, box 401-414, folder 12; letter from S. A. McMurry to W. H. King, 2 July 1889, TSLA, AGR, GC, box 401-414, folder 17; letter from S. A. McMurry to W. H. King, 8 July 1889, TSLA, AGR, GC, box 401-414, folder 17; and letter from S. A. McMurry to W. H. King, 13 November 1889, TSLA, AGR, GC, box 401-415, folder 16.

93. Hunter insisted that fighting the strike had cost $30,000, and that another $50,000 had been lost owing to delays in production. T&PCC Stockholders Report, 19 February 1890, WKGP, AR421, box 2, folder 13.

94. Rhinehart, *A Way of Work*, 79.

95. *Report of the Adjutant General of the State of Texas for 1889–90*, 28.

96. Letter from R. D. Hunter to W. H. King, 5 July 1890, WPW, box 2R289, vol. 11; letter from S. A. McMurry to W. H. King, 7 October 1890, TSLA, AGR, GC, box 401-417, folder 18.

97. Kealey, *Workers and Canadian History*, 423; McCormack, *Reformers, Rebels, and Revolutionaries*, 5; and Bercuson, "Labour Radicalism," 174.

98. Kealey, *Workers and Canadian History*, 346–48. It is worth noting that these figures accounted for 20 percent and 21 percent of the totals for all of Canada over the same two periods, suggesting that labor activism was on the rise throughout Canada.

99. Den Otter, *Civilizing the West*, 277–78.

100. Webber, "Compelling Compromise." See also Craven, *"An Impartial Umpire."*

101. Dulles and Dubofsky, *Labor in America*, 175–84.

102. Den Otter, *Civilizing the West*, 283–84.

103. Baker, "The Miners and the Mounties," 146.

104. *United Mine Workers Journal*, 9 August 1906.

105. Quoted in Streisel, "The Miners Strike Out," 3.

106. Naismith wrote, "I think it is of the utmost importance that a show of strength should be made at the commencement, otherwise they [the strikers] are liable to get beyond control and do most anything." See letter from P. L. Naismith to A. B. Perry, 12 March 1906, NAC, RG 18, series A-1, vol. 316, file 238, part II.

107. Telegram from J. O. Wilson to A. B. Perry, 14 March 1906, NAC, RG 18, series A-1, vol. 316, file 238, part II.

108. Baker, "The Miners and the Mounties," 147.

109. For police comment on foreign miners, see letter from C. Goodwin to J. O. Wilson, 1 March 1906, NAC, RG 18, series A-1, vol. 316, file 238, part II. For more on the explosion of 9 March, see letter from J. O. Wilson to RNWMP Commissioner, 9 March 1906, NAC, RG 18, series A-1, vol. 316, file 238, part II.

110. Letter from L. P. Eckstein to W. A. Galliher, 9 June 1905, NAC, RG 18, series A-1, vol. 300, file 517; letter from RNWMP Comptroller to W. A. Galliher, 29 June 1905, NAC, RG 18, series A-1, vol. 300, file 517.

111. See letter from F. H. Sherman to W. A. Galliher, 12 March 1906, NAC, RG 18, series A-1, vol. 316, file 238, part II; and resolutions passed by the Lethbridge Miners Union, 10 March 1906, NAC, RG 18, series A-1, vol. 316, file 238, part II.

112. Letter from J. O. Wilson to A. B. Perry, 15 March 1906, NAC, RG 18, series A-1, vol. 316, file 238, part II; letter from P. L. Naismith to Fred White, 23 March 1906, NAC, RG 18, series A-1, vol. 316, file 238, part II. It bears mentioning that in Canadian law of this period, any magistrate or justice of the peace could swear in a citizen as a special constable, and that Wilson did so in this capacity (and not as a police superintendent). Although AR&IC management could probably have found a civilian justice of the peace to do this for them, Wilson likely preferred to do it himself in order to retain tight control of the situation.

113. Letter from A. B. Perry to unknown correspondent [probably J. O. Wilson], undated, NAC, RG 18, series A-1, vol. 316, file 238, part II. Perry later wrote to Comptroller Fred White mentioning "Special Constables not employed by us but sworn in under Ordinance," drawing a fine distinction that apparently allowed the "specials," as they were called, to serve as police but at the company's liability. Telegram from A. B. Perry to Comptroller, 23 March 1906, NAC, RG 18, series A-1, vol. 316, file 238, part II.

114. Letter from J. O. Wilson to A. B. Perry, 20 March 1906, NAC, RG 18, series A-1, vol. 316, file 238, part I.

115. See undated note calculating the average earnings of the strike leaders per day for six months, NAC, RG 18, series A-1, vol. 316, file 238, part I. That this information was intended to damage the credibility of the strike leaders is conjecture. However, a case from the following year strongly supports my reading of the situation. During a strike at another Alberta coalfield, Comptroller Fred White asked Commissioner Perry to quietly

investigate rumors that UMWA official Frank Sherman was "quite beyond fearing the 'wolf at his door,' and further that his wealth has been acquired almost entirely through his associations as a labour organizer or strike agitator." See unsigned letter to A. B. Perry, 22 April 1907, NAC, RG 18, series A-1, vol. 337, file 318.

116. Letter from P. L. Naismith to Fred White, 23 March 1906, NAC, RG 18, series A-1, vol. 316, file 238, part II.

117. Letter from J. O. Wilson to Commissioner, 17 March 1906, NAC, RG 18, series A-1, vol. 316, file 238, part II.

118. Sworn testimony of John Harvey and William Gardner, miners, 17 March 1906, NAC, RG 18, series A-1, vol. 316, file 238, part II. Wilson effectively conceded the miners' allegations in a letter to Perry written on the same day, although Comptroller Fred White insisted to the prime minister that the testimony of Harvey and Gardner was false. See memo from Fred White to Sir Wilfrid Laurier, 16 March 1906, NAC, RG 18, series A-1, vol. 316, file 238, part II.

119. Letter from E. J. Camies to J. O. Wilson, 2 June 1906, NAC, RG 18, series A-1, vol. 316, file 238, part I.

120. Telegram from P. L. Naismith to A. B. Perry, 18 July 1906, NAC, RG 18, series A-1, vol. 316, file 238, part I.

121. Den Otter puts it this way: "By protecting company property and those men refusing to strike, the police tipped the balance in favour of the AR&IC." *Civilizing the West*, 289.

122. Baker, "The Miners and the Mediator." King also played a role in labor relations in the U.S. West, consulting with John D. Rockefeller in the wake of the 1914 Ludlow Massacre. See Gitelman, *Legacy of the Ludlow Massacre*, 264–329.

123. This interpretation is subject to debate, with those who insist that the strike was a success pointing to the fact that the miners had achieved financial parity with their counterparts in the Crow's Nest Pass, one of the stated goals of the action. Yet because the workers failed in their bid to win recognition of the union and thus to establish a closed shop at the AR&IC—the sine qua non of the strike—I deem it a failure, especially in light of what the T&PCC miners achieved in 1903. For a supportive view of this position, see Streisel, "The Miners Strike Out."

124. Rhinehart, *A Way of Work*, 81–82; letter from R. D. Hunter to W. H. Mabry, 5 June 1894, WPW, box 2R289, vol. 13.

125. Telegram from W. H. Mabry to W. J. McDonald, 7 June 1894, TSLA, AGR, Letter Press Book (cited hereafter as LPB) 401-653, p. 256. I am grateful to Harold Weiss for pointing me toward this correspondence. Considered one of the "Four Great Captains" of the late nineteenth and early twentieth centuries, McDonald had a colorful and storied career, which included service as a bodyguard to presidents Theodore Roosevelt and Woodrow Wilson. For more on McDonald, see Weiss, "'Yours to Command.'"

126. Before his election as governor, Hogg had served as the state's attorney general from 1887 to 1891, from which position he waged a spirited and successful campaign for railroad reform, earning the lasting enmity of Jay Gould. See Schmelzer, "Determining

the Extent of Power." For general information on Hogg, who was the first native-born governor of Texas, see Cotner, *James Stephen Hogg*.

127. Telegram from W. H. Mabry to W. J. McDonald marked "confidential," 11 June 1894, TSLA, AGR, LPB 401–653, p. 295. It appears that Hogg's reputation was of some concern to those who sided with the company, as suggested by a letter from a local attorney, who wrote to Mabry: "The impression was being made that Gov Hogg was opposed to corporations & that the agitators need not fear State interference—When they find that that the Governor and his officers are as ready to protect corporations in the peaceable possession of their property & in the enjoyment of their rights . . . I believe that these parties who are at the bottom of all of this trouble will subside." Letter from Henry M. Furman to W. H. Mabry, 8 June 1894, WPW, box 2R289, vol. 13.

128. Telegram from W. H. Mabry to W. J. McDonald, 12 June 1894; and telegram from W. H. Mabry to W. J. McDonald, 16 June 1894, TSLA, AGR, LPB 401–653, pp. 301, 347.

129. Rhinehart, *A Way of Work*, 84; letter from W. K. Gordon to S. W. T. Lanham, 30 August 1903, WPW, box 2R289, vol. 16.

130. Quoted in Rhinehart, *A Way of Work*, 86.

131. Rhinehart, *A Way of Work*, 88.

132. Letter from J. H. Rogers to J. H. Hulen, [n.d.], WPW, box 2R289, vol. 16.

133. See Streisel, "The Miners Strike Out," 6.

134. *United Mine Workers' Journal*, 17 September 1903. Gordon, in fact, was beloved by many of the striking miners, some of whom reportedly wept and expressed their affection for him even as they left Thurber in support of the 1903 strike. See Rhinehart, *A Way of Work*, 116. The daughter of a company employee provided a particularly poignant testimonial to Gordon's benevolence, remembering many years later how the general manager had once shut down production at one of the mines so that she could pass through the works in order to attend her last day of school. See letter from Bessie Reid to W. K. Gordon, Jr., 9 August 1969, WKGP, AR421, box 1, folder 12.

135. Letter from C. W. Woodman to Ben Owens, 22 April 1940, LMTC, box 2E308, folder 14.

136. *Biennial Report of the Adjutant General of Texas for the Years 1903 and 1904*, 161.

137. See Rhinehart, *A Way of Work*, 78; and *United Mine Workers' Journal*, 1 October 1903.

138. Quoted in Rhinehart, *A Way of Work*, xvi.

139. Streisel, "The Miners Strike Out," 6; den Otter, *Civilizing the West*, 299.

140. Craven, *"An Impartial Umpire"*; Fudge and Tucker, *Labour before the Law*; and Caragata, "The Labour Movement in Alberta," 110–11.

141. Letter from R. S. Belcher to officer commanding D Division, 18 July 1907, NAC, RG 18, series A-1, vol. 341, file 501. The assistant commissioner of the force did not think this was a good idea, however, believing that it was an unnecessary provocation for such a small work stoppage. For another such example, see letter from R. B. Deane to J. O. Wilson, 20 May 1909, NAC, RG 18, series A-1, vol. 374, file 341.

142. Letter from C. W. Woodman to Ben Owens, 22 April 1940, LMTC, box 2E308, folder 14.

143. Rhinehart, *A Way of Work*, 90; Calderón, *Mexican Coal Mining Labor*, 21. On the supplanting of coal by oil in Texas, see Allen, *Chapters*, 99.

144. Streisel, "The Miners Strike Out," 5.

145. Macleod, "Canadianizing the West," 110.

146. Morris, *A Private in the Texas Rangers*, 276.

147. Gomer Gower explained that "the Colonel had a dream of creating a vast empire over which he was the undisputed lord and master." See letter from Gomer Gower to Ben Owens, 12 November 1940, LMTC, box 2E308, folder 14.

148. The strike (which took place at Irvine) was a semicomic affair, though probably not for the workers. They walked out when, after the company cook was fired, the replacement hired by management showed up drunk and then refused to work, opting instead to walk the twenty-odd miles back to Medicine Hat. See NAC, RG 18, series A-1, vol. 321a, file 611. For the proposed stoppage at Hillcrest, Alberta, see NAC, RG 18, series A-1, vol. 321b, file 612.

149. NAC, RG 18, series A-1, vol. 322, file 685.

150. For more on the events of 1919, see Bercuson, *Confrontation at Winnipeg*.

151. Horrall, "The Royal North-West Mounted Police." For more on the general industrial turmoil of the period, see Kealey, "1919."

152. *Biennial Report of the Adjutant General of Texas for the Years 1903 and 1904*, 155; Utley, *Lone Star Justice*, 277–78.

153. See Johnson, *Revolution in Texas*, 162–65.

154. To be sure, two historians have recently questioned the net effect of the investigation on Ranger manpower, insisting that it was the end of World War I—and not the perception of Ranger excesses—that led to personnel reductions. This, of course, is open to debate, and at any rate does not change the fact that the legislature felt it necessary to examine the charges filed against the constabulary in the first place. See Harris and Sadler, *The Texas Rangers*, 460–61.

155. In 1979 the MacDonald Commission investigated alleged abuses of power by the RCMP, including the harassment, beating, and attempted assassination of leading Canadian communists. In light of these findings, the Mounties were stripped of their security role, which was assumed in 1982 by the newly created Canadian Intelligence Security Service. For more information on the investigation, see Sallot, *Nobody Said No*.

156. See Procter, "The Modern Texas Rangers."

Epilogue

1. *The University Daily*, 21 February 2001.

2. For a sampling of such letters, see TSLA, AGR, RR, box 401-1183, folder 7. And Panhandle residents were not the only Texans aggravated with the Rangers. In reporting on the beating of one of the "State's Cossacks" by a patron at a San Antonio tavern, one

South Texas newspaper added glibly, "There are some people who would recommend this bar as the place for the entire force to get its whiskey." See *Beeville Bee*, undated, untitled newspaper clipping (from November 1909), TSLA, AGR, RR, box 401-1183, folder 8.

3. Quoted in Atkin, *Maintain the Right*, 363.

4. Harris and Sadler, *The Texas Rangers*, 499–501.

5. Horrall, "The Royal North-West Mounted Police."

6. Jackson and Wilkinson, *One Ranger*.

7. *San Antonio Express-News*, 8 May 2000.

8. In author's possession.

9. Morton, "Cavalry or Police," 16.

Bibliography

Manuscript Collections

Center for American History at the University of Texas–Austin
    Labor Movement in Texas Collection
    Texas Adjutant General Records
    Walter Prescott Webb Papers

Glenbow-Alberta Institute, Calgary
    David Breen National Archives of Canada Ranching Collection
    Cochrane Family Fonds
    A. E. Cross Family Fonds
    Edgar Dewdney Fonds
    James Macleod Fonds
    New Walrond Ranche Letterbooks

National Archives of Canada, Ottawa, Ontario
    Department of Interior Records, Record Group 15
    Department of Justice Records, Record Group 13
    Indian Affairs Records, Record Group 10
    Sir John A. Macdonald Papers
    Royal Canadian Mounted Police Records, Record Group 18

Panhandle-Plains Historical Museum, Canyon, Texas
    G. W. Arrington Papers
    N. Y. Bickell Papers
    W. R. Durham, Jr. Memoirs
    E. P. Earhart Papers

Southwest Collections, Texas Tech University, Lubbock
    D. N. Arnett Papers

Texas State Library and Archives, Austin
    Harbert Davenport Collection
    Texas Adjutant General Records, General Correspondence, Record Group 401
    Texas Adjutant General Records, Ranger Records, Record Group 401

University of Texas–Arlington, Special Collections Division
  W. K. Gordon, Sr. Papers

Western History Collections, University of Oklahoma Library, Norman
  J. H. Abbott Papers
  Southern Plains Indian Agencies Collections
  J. E. Wagner Collections

Government Documents

CANADA

Canada. Parliament. *Sessional Papers. Annual Reports of the Commissioner of the (Royal) North-West Mounted Police Force.* 1876–1910.
———. *Sessional Papers. Annual Reports of the Department of the Interior.* 1880–1900.
———. *Sessional Papers.* Vol. 17, no. 116. 1885.
Report on Strikes and Lockouts in Canada from 1901 to 1912. Ottawa: Department of Labour, 1913.

MEXICO

Reports of the Committee Sent in 1873 by the Mexican Government to the Frontier of Texas. Translated. New York: Baker & Godwin, 1875.

TEXAS

State of Texas. *Message of Governor John Ireland to the Eighteenth Legislature, Convened in Special Session, at the City of Austin, January 8, 1884.* Austin: State Printer, 1884.
———. *Proceedings of the Joint Committee of the Senate and the House in the Investigation of the State Ranger Force.* 1919.
———. *Reports of the Adjutant General of the State of Texas.* 1874–1910.

UNITED STATES

U.S. Congress. *Difficulties on the Southwestern Frontier.* House Executive Document 52, 36th Congress, 1st session (Serial 1050), 1860.
———. *El Paso Troubles in Texas.* House Executive Document 93, 45th Congress, 2nd session (Serial 1809), 1878.
———. *Texas Border Troubles.* House Executive Document 64, 45th Congress, 2nd session (Serial 1820), 1878.
———. *Troubles on the Texas Frontier.* House Executive Document 81, 36th Congress, 1st session (Serial 1056), 1860.
U.S. Department of the Interior. *Annual Reports of the Secretary of the Interior.* 1872–81.
———. *Report on Manufacturing Industries in the United States at the Eleventh Census: 1890—Part I: Totals for States and Industries.* 1890.

————. *Report on Mineral Industries in the United States at the Eleventh Census.* 1890.

————. *Report on Transportation Business in the United States at the Eleventh Census: 1890—Part I: Transportation by Land.* 1890.

————. *Twelfth Census of the United States, Taken in the Year 1900: Manufactures, Part II—States and Territories.* 1900.

Published Primary Sources

Aten, Ira. *Six and One-half Years in the Ranger Service: The Memoirs of Ira Aten, Sergeant Company D, Texas Rangers.* Bandera TX: Frontier Times, 1945.

Card, Charles Ora. *The Diaries of Charles Ora Card: The Canadian Years, 1886–1903.* Edited by Donald G. Godfrey and Brigham Y. Card. Salt Lake City: University of Utah Press, 1993.

Craig, John Roderick. *Ranching with Lords and Commons.* Toronto: William Briggs, 1903.

Deane, R. Burton. *Mounted Police Life in Canada: A Record of Thirty-One Years' Service.* 1916; Toronto: Cole Publishing Co., 1973.

Durham, George, as told to Clyde Wantland. *Taming the Nueces Strip: The Story of McNelly's Rangers.* Austin: University of Texas Press, 1962.

Ford, John Salmon. *Rip Ford's Texas.* Edited by Stephen B. Oates. 1963; Austin: University of Texas Press, 1987.

Gammel, H. P. N., ed. *The Laws of Texas, 1822–1897.* 10 vols. Austin: Gammel Book Co., 1898.

Gardiner, Claude. *Letters from an English Rancher.* Edited by Hugh A. Dempsey. Calgary: Glenbow-Alberta Institute, 1988.

Gillett, James B. *Six Years with the Texas Rangers, 1875–1881.* 1921; Lincoln: University of Nebraska Press, 1976.

Heintzelman, Samuel Peter. *Fifty Miles and a Fight: Major Samuel Peter Heintzelman's Journal of Texas and the Cortina War.* Edited by Jerry Thompson. Austin: Texas State Historical Association, 1998.

Jennings, N. A. *A Texas Ranger.* 1899; Chicago: Lakeside Press, 1992.

Kelsey, John P. "A Statement of Facts Respecting the Reports About Cattle and Hide Stealing Upon the Rio Grande by Citizens of Mexico, and Respecting the Report of the U.S. Commissioners to Texas, Appointed Under Joint Resolution of Congress, May 7, 1872." In *Western Americana: Frontier History of the Trans-Mississippi West, 1550–1900.* New Haven: Research Publications, 1975.

Morris, Alexander. *The Treaties of Canada with the Indians of Manitoba and the North-West Territories.* Toronto: Willing & Williamson, 1890.

Riel, Louis. *The Collected Writings of Louis Riel.* G. F. G. Stanley, gen. ed. 5 vols. Edmonton: University of Alberta Press, 1985.

Steele, Samuel B. *Forty Years in Canada: Reminiscences of the Great North-West with Some Account of His Service in South Africa.* London: Herbert Jenkins, 1915.

Sullivan, W. J. L. *Twelve Years in the Saddle for Law and Order on the Frontier of Texas*. 1909; Lincoln: University of Nebraska Press, 2001.

Winfrey, Dorman H., and James M. Day, eds. *The Indian Papers of Texas and the Southwest, 1825–1916*. 5 vols. 1966; Austin: Texas State Historical Association, 1995.

Secondary Literature

Abbe, Donald. "Ranching and Speculation in Lynn County, Texas, 1876–1930." In *Working the Range: Essays in the History of Western Land Management and the Environment*, edited by John Wunder, 81–97. Westport CT: Greenwood Press, 1985.

Adelman, Jeremy, and Stephen Aron. "From Borderlands to Borders: Empires, Nation-States, and the Peoples In Between in North American History." *American Historical Review* 104, no. 3 (June 1999): 814–41.

Aitken, Hugh G. J. "Defensive Expansionism: The State and Economic Growth in Canada." In *The State and Economic Growth in Canada*, edited by Hugh G. J. Aitken, 79–114. New York: Social Science Research Council, 1959.

———, ed. *The State and Economic Growth in Canada*. New York: Social Science Research Council, 1959.

Allen, Ruth. *Chapters in the History of Organized Labor in Texas*. Austin: University of Texas Press, 1941.

———. *The Great Southwest Strike*. Austin: University of Texas Press, 1942.

Alonso, Ana María. *Thread of Blood: Colonialism, Revolution, and Gender on Mexico's Northern Frontier*. Tucson: University of Arizona Press, 1995.

Alonzo, Armando C. *Tejano Legacy: Rancheros and Settlers in South Texas, 1734–1900*. Albuquerque: University of New Mexico Press, 1998.

Anderson, Gary Clayton. *The Conquest of Texas: Ethnic Cleansing in the Lone Star State, 1820–1875*. Norman: University of Oklahoma Press, 2005.

Atkin, Ronald. *Maintain the Right: The Early History of the North-West Mounted Police*. New York: John Day, 1973.

August, Ray. "Cowboys v. Rancheros: The Origins of Western Livestock Law." *Southwestern Historical Quarterly* 96, no. 4 (April 1993): 457–88.

Avery, Donald. *"Dangerous Foreigners": European Immigrant Workers and Labour Radicalism in Canada, 1896–1932*. Toronto: McClelland & Stewart, 1979.

Avrich, Paul. *The Haymarket Tragedy*. Princeton: Princeton University Press, 1984.

Baker, William M. "The Miners and the Mediator: The 1906 Strike and Mackenzie King." *Labour/Le Travail* 11 (Spring 1983): 89–117.

———. "The Miners and the Mounties: The Royal North-West Mounted Police and the 1906 Lethbridge Strike." In *The Mounted Police and Prairie Society, 1873–1919*, edited by William M. Baker, 137–71. Regina: Canadian Plains Research Center, 1998.

———, ed. *The Mounted Police and Prairie Society, 1873–1919*. Regina: Canadian Plains Research Center, 1998.

—, ed. *Pioneer Policing in Southern Alberta: Deane of the Mounties, 1888–1914*. Calgary: Historical Society of Alberta, 1993.

Bakken, Gordon Morris, ed. *Law in the Western United States*. Norman: University of Oklahoma Press, 2000.

Barr, Alwyn. *Reconstruction to Reform: Texas Politics, 1876–1906*. 1971; Dallas: Southern Methodist University Press, 2000.

Barron, F. Laurie, and James B. Waldram, eds. *1885 and After: Native Society in Transition*. Regina: Canadian Plains Research Center, 1986.

Beal, Bob, and Rod Macleod. *Prairie Fire: The 1885 North-West Rebellion*. Edmonton: Hurtig Publishers, 1984.

Bercuson, David Jay. *Confrontation at Winnipeg: Labour, Industrial Relations, and the General Strike*. 1974; Montreal: McGill-Queen's University Press, 1990.

—. "Labour Radicalism and the Western Industrial Frontier: 1897–1919." *Canadian Historical Review* 58, no. 2 (June 1977): 154–75.

Berton, Pierre. *Hollywood's Canada: The Americanization of Our National Image*. Toronto: McClelland & Stewart, 1975.

Binnema, Theodore, Gerhard J. Ens, and R. C. Macleod, eds. *From Rupert's Land to Canada*. Edmonton: University of Alberta Press, 2001.

Brado, Edward. *Cattle Kingdom: Early Ranching in Alberta*. Vancouver: Douglas & McIntyre, 1984.

Brayer, Herbert O. "The Influence of British Capital on the Western Range Cattle Industry." *Journal of Economic History* 9 (1949): 85–98.

Breen, David H. "The Canadian Prairie West and the 'Harmonious' Settlement Interpretation." *Agricultural History* 47, no. 1 (1973): 63–75.

—. *The Canadian Prairie West and the Ranching Frontier, 1874–1924*. Toronto: University of Toronto Press, 1983.

—. "The Mounted Police and the Ranching Frontier." In *Men in Scarlet*, edited by Hugh A. Dempsey, 115–37. Calgary: McClelland & Stewart, 1974.

Brégent-Heald, Dominique. "Romantic Encounters: Film, Tourism, and the Spectacle of the 'Other' in *Rose Marie* (1936) and *Ride the Pink Horse* (1947)." Unpublished paper presented to the Western History Association, Annual Meeting, Scottsdale, Arizona, October 2005.

Brown, Lorne, and Caroline Brown. *An Unauthorized History of the RCMP*. Toronto: James Lewis & Samuel, 1973.

Brown, Robert Craig, and Ramsay Cook. *Canada, 1896–1921: A Nation Transformed*. Toronto: McClelland & Stewart, 1974.

Bruch, Leora. *Banister Was There*. Fort Worth: Branch-Smith, 1968.

Calderón, Roberto. *Mexican Coal Mining Labor in Texas and Coahuila, 1880–1930*. College Station: Texas A&M University Press, 2000.

Calloway, Colin G., ed. *New Directions in American Indian History*. Norman: University of Oklahoma Press, 1988.

Camarillo, Alberto, and Pedro Castillo. *Furia y muerte: Los bandidos chicanos.* Los Angeles: Aztlán Publications, 1973.

Campbell, Randolph B. *Grass-Roots Reconstruction in Texas, 1865–1880.* Baton Rouge: Louisiana State University Press, 1997.

Canales, José T. *Juan N. Cortina Presents His Motion for a New Trial.* 1951; New York: Arno Press, 1974.

Cantrell, Gregg. *Stephen F. Austin: Empresario of Texas.* New Haven: Yale University Press, 1999.

Caragata, Warren. "The Labour Movement in Alberta: An Untold Story." In *Essays in the Political Economy of Alberta,* edited by David Leadbeater, 99–137. Toronto: New Hogtown Press, 1984.

Carrigan, William D. *The Making of a Lynching Culture: Violence and Vigilantism in Central Texas, 1836–1916.* Urbana: University of Illinois Press, 2004.

Carrigan, William D., and Clive D. Webb. "The Lynching of Persons of Mexican Origin and Descent in the United States, 1848–1928." *Journal of Social History* 37, no. 2 (Winter 2003): 411–38.

Carroll, John Alexander, ed. *Reflections of Western Historians.* Tucson: University of Arizona Press, 1969.

Carter, Sarah. *Aboriginal People and Colonizers of Western Canada to 1900.* Toronto: University of Toronto Press, 1999.

———. *Capturing Women: The Manipulation of Cultural Imagery in Canada's Prairie West.* Montreal: McGill-Queen's University Press, 1997.

———. "Categories and Terrains of Exclusion: Constructing the 'Indian Woman' in the Early Settlement Era in Western Canada." *Great Plains Quarterly* 13, no. 3 (Summer 1993): 147–61.

Cherwinski, W. J. C., and Gregory S. Kealey, eds. *Lectures in Canadian Labour and Working-Class History.* Toronto: New Hogtown Press, 1985.

Clark, Blue. *Lone Wolf v. Hitchcock: Treaty Rights and Indian Law at the End of the Nineteenth Century.* Lincoln: University of Nebraska Press, 1994.

Cooper, Jerry M. *The Army and Civil Disorder: Federal Military Intervention in Labor Disputes, 1877–1900.* Westport CT: Greenwood Press, 1980.

Corwin, Hugh D. *Comanche and Kiowa Captives in Oklahoma and Texas.* Guthrie OK: Cooperative Publishing, 1959.

Cotner, Robert C. *James Stephen Hogg: A Biography.* Austin: University of Texas Press, 1959.

Craven, Paul. *"An Impartial Umpire": Industrial Relations and the Canadian State, 1900–1911.* Toronto: University of Toronto Press, 1980.

Crisp, James E. *Sleuthing the Alamo: Davy Crockett's Last Stand and Other Mysteries of the Texas Revolution.* New York: Oxford University Press, 2005.

Cronon, William, George Miles, and Jay Gitlin, eds. *Under an Open Sky: Rethinking America's Western Past.* New York: Norton, 1991.

Dary, David. *Cowboy Culture: A Saga of Five Centuries.* New York: Knopf, 1981.

Dawson, Michael. *The Mountie: From Dime Novel to Disney.* Toronto: Between the Lines, 1998.

————. "'That Nice Red Coat Goes to My Head Like Champagne': Gender, Antimodernism, and the Mountie Image, 1880–1960." *Journal of Canadian Studies* 32, no. 3 (Fall 1997): 119–39.

De León, Arnoldo. *The Tejano Community, 1836–1900.* Albuquerque: University of New Mexico Press, 1982.

————. *They Called Them Greasers: Anglo Attitudes Toward Mexicans in Texas, 1821–1900.* Austin: University of Texas Press, 1983.

De León, Arnoldo, and Kenneth L. Stewart. *Tejanos and the Numbers Game: A Socio-Historical Interpretation from the Federal Censuses, 1850–1900.* Albuquerque: University of New Mexico Press, 1989.

Dempsey, Hugh A. "The Blackfoot Nation." In *Native Peoples: The Canadian Experience,* edited by R. Bruce Morrison and C. Roderick Wilson, 381–413. 1986; Toronto: McClelland & Stewart, 1995.

————. *Charcoal's World.* Saskatoon: Western Producer Prairie Books, 1978.

————, ed. *The CPR West: The Iron Road and the Making of a Nation.* Toronto: McClelland & Stewart, 1984.

————. *Crowfoot: Chief of the Blackfeet.* Norman: University of Oklahoma Press, 1972.

————. *Firewater: The Impact of the Whisky Trade on the Blackfoot Nation.* Calgary: Fifth House Publishers, 2002.

————. *The Golden Age of the Canadian Cowboy.* Saskatoon: Fifth House Publishers, 1995.

————. *Jerry Potts, Plainsman.* Calgary: Glenbow Foundation, 1966.

————, ed. *Men In Scarlet.* Calgary: McClelland & Stewart West, 1974.

————. *Red Crow, Warrior Chief.* Lincoln: University of Nebraska Press, 1980.

Denning, Michael. *Mechanic Accents: Dime Novels and Working-Class Culture in America.* New York: Verso, 1987.

Deverell, William, ed. *A Companion to the History of the American West.* Oxford: Blackwell Publishing, 2004.

Devine, Heather. *The People Who Own Themselves: Aboriginal Ethnogenesis in a Canadian Family, 1660–1900.* Calgary: University of Calgary Press, 2004.

Dobak, William A. "Killing the Canadian Buffalo: 1821–1881." *Western Historical Quarterly* 27, no. 1 (Spring 1996): 33–52.

Drew, Bernard A. *Lawmen in Scarlet: An Annotated Guide to Royal Canadian Mounted Police in Print and Performance.* Metuchen NJ: The Scarecrow Press, 1990.

Dubofsky, Melvyn. *Industrialism and the American Worker, 1865–1920.* New York: Thomas Y. Crowell, 1975.

————. *The State and Labor in Modern America.* Chapel Hill: University of North Carolina Press, 1994.

Duke, Cordelia Sloan, and Joe B. Frantz. *6,000 Miles of Fence: Life on the XIT Ranch of Texas*. Austin: University of Texas Press, 1961.

Dulles, Foster Rhea, and Melvyn Dubofsky. *Labor in America: A History*. Wheeling IL: Harlan Davidson, 1984.

Dusenberry, Verne. "Waiting for a Day That Never Comes: The Dispossessed Métis of Montana." In *The New Peoples: Being and Becoming Métis in North America*, edited by Jacqueline Peterson and Jennifer S. H. Brown, 119–36. Winnipeg: University of Manitoba Press, 1985.

Elofson, Warren M. *Cowboys, Gentlemen and Cattle Thieves: Ranching on the Western Frontier*. Montreal: McGill-Queen's University Press, 2000.

———. *Frontier Cattle Ranching in the Land and Times of Charlie Russell*. Montreal: McGill-Queen's University Press, 2004.

Ens, Gerhard J. "The Border, the Buffalo, and the Métis of Montana." In *The Borderlands of the American and Canadian Wests: Essays on Regional History of the 49th Parallel*, edited by Sterling Evans, 139–54. Lincoln: University of Nebraska Press, 2006.

———. *Homeland to Hinterland: The Changing Worlds of the Red River Metis in the Nineteenth Century*. Toronto: University of Toronto Press, 1996.

Evans, Simon M. *The Bar U and Canadian Ranching History*. Calgary: University of Calgary Press, 2004.

———. "The End of the Open Range Era in Western Canada." *Prairie Forum* 8, no. 1 (Spring 1983): 71–87.

———. *Prince Charming Goes West: The Story of the E.P. Ranch*. Calgary: University of Calgary Press, 1993.

Evans, Simon M., Sarah Carter, and Bill Yeo, eds. *Cowboys, Ranchers, and the Cattle Business: Cross-Border Perspectives on Ranching History*. Calgary: University of Calgary Press, 2000.

Evans, Sterling, ed. *The Borderlands of the American and Canadian Wests: Essays on Regional History of the 49th Parallel*. Lincoln: University of Nebraska Press, 2006.

———. "Dependent Harvests: Grain Production on the American and Canadian Plains and the Double-Dependency with Mexico, 1880–1950." *Agricultural History* 80, no. 1 (Winter 2006): 35–63.

Ewers, John C. *The Blackfeet: Raiders on the Northwestern Plains*. Norman: University of Oklahoma Press, 1958.

———. *The Horse in Blackfoot Indian Culture*. Washington: Smithsonian Institution Press, 1980.

Faragher, John Mack. "Americans, Mexicans, Métis: A Community Approach to the Comparative Study of North American Frontiers." In *Under an Open Sky: Rethinking America's Western Past*, edited by William Cronon, George Miles, and Jay Gitlin, 90–109. New York: Norton, 1991.

Fink, Leon. *Workingmen's Democracy: The Knights of Labor and American Politics*. Urbana: University of Illinois Press, 1983.

Flanagan, Thomas. "Louis Riel and the Dispersion of the American Metis." *Minnesota History* 49, no. 5 (Spring 1985): 179–90.

———. *Riel and the Rebellion: 1885 Reconsidered.* 1989; Toronto: University of Toronto Press, 2000.

Flores, Dan. "Bison Ecology, Bison Diplomacy: The Southern Plains from 1800–1850." *Journal of American History* 78, no. 2 (September 1991): 465–85.

Foner, Philip S. *The Great Labor Uprising of 1877.* New York: Pathfinder, 1977.

Foos, Paul. *A Short, Offhand, Killing Affair: Soldiers and Social Conflict during the Mexican-American War.* Chapel Hill: University of North Carolina Press, 2004.

Foster, John. "The Plains Metis." In *Native Peoples: The Canadian Experience,* edited by R. Bruce Morrison and C. Roderick Wilson, 414–43. Toronto: McClelland & Stewart, 1986.

Foster, Martha Harroun. *We Know Who We Are: Métis Identity in a Montana Community.* Norman: University of Oklahoma Press, 2006.

Francis, Daniel. *National Dreams: Myth, Memory, and Canadian History.* Vancouver: Arsenal Pulp Press, 1997.

Frederickson, George M. *White Supremacy: A Comparative Study in American and South African History.* New York: Oxford University Press, 1981.

Friend, Llerena B. "W.P. Webb's Texas Rangers." *Southwestern Historical Quarterly* 74, no. 3 (January 1971): 293–323.

Friesen, Gerald. *The Canadian Prairies: A History.* Lincoln: University of Nebraska Press, 1984.

Fudge, Judy, and Eric Tucker. *Labour before the Law: The Regulation of Workers' Collective Action in Canada, 1900–1948.* Toronto: Oxford University Press, 2001.

Gard, Wayne. "The Fence-Cutters." *Southwestern Historical Quarterly* 51, no. 1 (July 1947): 1–15.

———. *Rawhide Texas.* Norman: University of Oklahoma Press, 1965.

Giraud, Marcel. *The Metis in the Canadian West.* Translated by George Woodcock. 2 vols. Edmonton: University of Alberta Press, 1986. [Originally published in 1945 as *Le Métis canadien: Son rôle dans l'histoire des provinces de l'ouest.*]

Gitelman, H. M. *Legacy of the Ludlow Massacre: A Chapter in American Industrial Relations.* Philadelphia: University of Pennsylvania Press, 1988.

Gluek, Alvin G., Jr. *Minnesota and the Manifest Destiny of the Canadian Northwest: A Study in Canadian-American Relations.* Toronto: University of Toronto Press, 1965.

Goldfinch, Charles W. *Juan N. Cortina: A Reappraisal.* 1949; New York: Arno Press, 1974.

Goldring, Philip. "Whisky, Horses, and Death: The Cypress Hills Massacre and its Sequel." *Canadian Historic Sites: Occasional Papers in Archaeology and History* 21 (1979): 41–70.

Goodwyn, Lawrence. *Democratic Promise: The Populist Moment in America.* New York: Oxford University Press, 1976.

Graf, LeRoy P. "The Economic History of the Lower Rio Grande Valley, 1820–1875." PhD diss., Harvard University, 1942.

Graham, Don. "Don Graham's Texas Classics: Border Skirmish." *Texas Monthly*, January 2000, 26.

Grey, Zane. *Lone Star Ranger: A Romance of the Border*. New York: Harper & Brothers, 1915.

Griswold del Castillo, Richard. *The Treaty of Guadalupe Hidalgo: A Legacy of Conflict*. Norman: University of Oklahoma Press, 1990.

Haley, J. Evetts. "And Then Came Barbed Wire to Change History's Course." *The Cattleman* 13, no. 10 (March 1927): 78–83.

———. *Charles Goodnight: Cowman and Plainsman*. Norman: University of Oklahoma Press, 1949.

———. *The XIT Ranch of Texas and the Early Days of the Llano Estacado*. 1929; Norman: University of Oklahoma Press, 1953.

Haley, James L. *The Buffalo War: The History of the Red River Indian Uprising of 1874*. Garden City NY: Doubleday, 1976.

Hämäläinen, Pekka. "The Rise and Fall of Plains Indian Horse Cultures." *Journal of American History* 90, no. 3 (December 2003): 833–62.

———. "The Western Comanche Trade Center: Rethinking the Plains Indian Trade System." *Western Historical Quarterly* 29 (Winter 1998): 485–513.

Harring, Sidney L. *Policing a Class Society: The Experience of American Cities, 1865–1916*. New Brunswick: Rutgers University Press, 1983.

Harris, Charles H. III, and Louis R. Sadler. *The Texas Rangers and the Mexican Revolution: The Bloodiest Decade, 1910–1920*. Albuquerque: University of New Mexico Press, 2004.

Havins, T. R. *Something about Brown: A History of Brown County, Texas*. Brownwood TX: Banner Printing, 1958.

Henderson, Dwight F. "The Texas Coal Mining Industry." *Southwestern Historical Quarterly* 68, no. 2 (October 1964): 207–19.

Hendrix, John M. "The Nester: He Originated in West Texas . . . And He's an Honored Citizen." *West Texas Today* (Panhandle Plains Historical Museum, Canyon, Texas), February 1934.

Higham, Carol, and Robert Thacker, eds. *One West, Two Myths: A Comparative Reader*. Calgary: University of Calgary Press, 2004.

Higham, Robin, ed. *Bayonets in the Streets: The Use of Troops in Civil Disturbances*. Lawrence: University Press of Kansas, 1969.

Hildebrandt, Walter. *Views from Fort Battleford: Constructed Visions of an Anglo-Canadian West*. Regina: Canadian Plains Research Center, 1994.

Hill, Jim Dan. "The National Guard in Civil Disorders: Historical Perspectives." In *Bayonets in the Streets: The Use of Troops in Civil Disturbances*, edited by Robin Higham, 61–84. Lawrence: University Press of Kansas, 1969.

Hoerder, Dirk, ed. *"Struggle a Hard Battle": Essays on Working-Class Immigrants*. Dekalb: Northern Illinois University Press, 1986.

Hogue, Michel. "Crossing the Line: Race, Nationality, and the Deportation of the 'Canadian' Crees in the Canada-U.S. Borderlands, 1890–1900." In *The Borderlands of the American and Canadian Wests: Essays on Regional History of the 49th Parallel*, edited by Sterling Evans, 155–71. Lincoln: University of Nebraska Press, 2006.

———. "Disputing the Medicine Line: The Plains Cree and the Canadian-American Border, 1876–85." In *One West, Two Myths: A Comparative Reader*, edited by Carol Higham and Robert Thacker, 85–108. Calgary: University of Calgary Press, 2004.

Holden, William Curry. *The Spur Ranch: A Study of the Inclosed Ranch Phase of the Cattle Industry in Texas*. Boston: Christopher Publishing House, 1934.

Holder, Preston. *The Horse and the Hoe on the Plains: A Study of Cultural Development among North American Indians*. Lincoln: University of Nebraska Press, 1970.

Holt, R. D. "The Introduction of Barbed Wire into Texas and the Fence Cutting War." *West Texas Historical Association Year Book* 6 (June 1930): 65–81.

———. "The Saga of Barbed Wire in the Tom Green Country." *West Texas Historical Association Year Book* 4 (June 1928): 32–51.

Horrall, S. W. "The North-West Mounted Police and Labour Unrest in Western Canada, 1919." *Canadian Historical Review* 61, no. 2 (1980): 169–90.

———. *The Pictorial History of the Royal Canadian Mounted Police*. Toronto: McGraw Hill-Ryerson, 1973.

———. "Sir John A. Macdonald and the Mounted Police Force for the Northwest Territories." *Canadian Historical Review* 53, no. 2 (June 1972): 170–200.

Hubner, Brian. "Horse Stealing and the Borderline: The NWMP and the Control of Indian Movement, 1874–1900." In *The Mounted Police and Prairie Society, 1873–1919*, edited by William M. Baker, 53–70. Regina: Canadian Plains Research Center, 1998.

Huel, Raymond J. A. *Archbishop A. A. Taché of St. Boniface: The "Good Fight" and the Illusive Vision*. Edmonton: University of Alberta Press, 2003.

———. *Proclaiming the Gospel to the Indians and the Métis*. Edmonton: University of Alberta Press, 1996.

Ings, Frederick William. *Before Fences: Tales from the Midway Ranch*. Calgary: McAra Printing, 1980.

Innis, Harold A. *The Cod Fisheries: The History of an International Economy*. New Haven: Yale University Press, 1940.

———. *The Fur Trade in Canada: An Introduction to Canadian Economic History*. 1930; New Haven: Yale University Press, 1962.

"Intersections: Studies in the Canadian and American Great Plains." Special issue, *Great Plains Quarterly* 3, no. 1 (Winter 1983).

Isenberg, Andrew C. *The Destruction of the Bison: An Environmental History, 1750–1920*. New York: Cambridge University Press, 2000.

———. "Environment and the Nineteenth-Century West; or Process Encounters Place."

In *A Companion to the History of the American West*, edited by William A. Deverell, 77–92. Oxford: Blackwell, 2004.

Jackson, H. Joaquin, and David Marion Wilkinson. *One Ranger: A Memoir*. Austin: University of Texas Press, 2005.

Jameson, Sheilagh. *Ranchers, Cowboys, and Characters: The Birth of Alberta's Western Heritage*. Calgary: Glenbow-Alberta Institute, 1987.

Jenness, Diamond. *The Indians of Canada*. 1932; Toronto: University of Toronto Press, 1977.

Jennings, John. "The North-West Mounted Police and Canadian Indian Policy, 1873–1896." PhD diss., University of Toronto, 1979.

———. "The Plains Indians and the Law." In *Men in Scarlet*, edited by Hugh A. Dempsey, 50–65. Calgary: Historical Society of Alberta/McClelland & Stewart West, 1974.

Johnson, Benjamin. *Revolution in Texas: How a Forgotten Rebellion and Its Bloody Suppression Turned Mexicans into Americans*. New Haven: Yale University Press, 2003.

Jones, David C. *Empire of Dust: Settling and Abandoning the Prairie Dry Belt*. 1987; Calgary: University of Calgary Press, 2002.

Jordan, Terry G. *North American Cattle-Ranching Frontiers: Origins, Diffusion, and Differentiation*. Albuquerque: University of New Mexico Press, 1993.

———. *Trails to Texas: Southern Roots of Western Cattle Ranching*. Lincoln: University of Nebraska Press, 1981.

Kavanaugh, Thomas. *Comanche Political History: An Ethnohistorical Perspective*. Lincoln: University of Nebraska Press, 1996.

Kealey, Gregory S. "1919: The Canadian Labour Revolt." *Labour/Le Travail* 13 (Spring 1984): 11–44.

———. *Workers and Canadian History*. Montreal: McGill-Queen's University Press, 1995.

Kealey, Gregory S., and Bryan D. Palmer. *Dreaming of What Might Be: The Knights of Labor in Ontario, 1880–1900*. New York: Cambridge University Press, 1982.

Kearney, Milo, ed. *Studies in Brownsville History*. Brownsville TX: Pan American University Press, 1986.

Kelly, Nora, and William Kelly. *The Royal Canadian Mounted Police: A Century of History, 1873–1973*. Edmonton: Hurtig Publishers, 1973.

King, Dick. "Rascals and Rangers." *True West* 22 (March–April 1975): 6–13, 40, 44.

Klassen, Henry C. *Eye on the Future: Business People in Calgary and the Bow Valley, 1870–1900*. Calgary: University of Calgary Press, 2002.

Klos, George. "'Our People Could Not Distinguish One Tribe from Another': The 1859 Expulsion of the Reserve Indians from Texas." *Southwestern Historical Quarterly* 97, no. 4 (April 1994): 599–619.

LaDow, Beth. *The Medicine Line: Life and Death on a North American Borderland*. New York: Routledge, 2001.

La Vere, David. *Contrary Neighbors: Southern Plains and Removed Indians in Indian Territory*. Norman: University of Oklahoma Press, 2000.

————. *The Texas Indians.* College Station: Texas A&M University Press, 2003.

Leadbeater, David, ed. *Essays in the Political Economy of Alberta.* Toronto: New Hogtown Press, 1984.

————. "An Outline of Capitalist Development in Alberta." In *Essays in the Political Economy of Alberta*, edited by David Leadbeater, 1–70. Toronto: New Hogtown Press, 1984.

Leggett, Robert F. *Railways of Canada.* Toronto: McClelland & Stewart, 1980.

Leiker, James N. *Racial Borders: Black Soldiers along the Rio Grande.* College Station: Texas A&M University Press, 2002.

Limón, José. *American Encounters: Greater Mexico, the United States, and the Erotics of Culture.* Boston: Beacon Press, 1998.

————. *Dancing with the Devil: Society and Cultural Politics in Mexican-American South Texas.* Madison: University of Wisconsin Press, 1994.

Lower, J. Arthur. *Western Canada: An Outline History.* Vancouver: Douglas & McIntyre, 1983.

Lux, Maureen K. *Medicine That Walks: Disease, Medicine, and Canadian Plains Native People, 1880–1940.* Toronto: University of Toronto Press, 2001.

Macleod, R. C. "Canadianizing the West: The North-West Mounted Police as Agents of the National Policy, 1873–1905." In *Essays on Western History*, edited by Lewis H. Thomas, 101–110. Edmonton: University of Alberta Press, 1976.

————. *The North-West Mounted Police and Law Enforcement, 1873–1905.* Toronto: University of Toronto Press, 1976.

Madill, Dennis F. K. "Riel, Red River, and Beyond: New Developments in Métis History." In *New Directions in American Indian History*, edited by Colin G. Calloway, 49–78. Norman: University of Oklahoma Press, 1988.

Mancall, Peter C. *Deadly Medicine: Indians and Alcohol in Early America.* Ithaca: Cornell University Press, 1995.

May, Robert E. *Manifest Destiny's Underworld: Filibustering in Antebellum America.* Chapel Hill: University of North Carolina Press, 2002.

Mayhall, Mildred P. *The Kiowas.* Norman: University of Oklahoma Press, 1962.

McCallum, Henry D., and Frances T. McCallum. *The Wire That Fenced the West.* Norman: University of Oklahoma Press, 1965.

McCormack, A. Ross. *Reformers, Rebels, and Revolutionaries: The Western Canadian Radical Movement, 1899–1919.* Toronto: University of Toronto Press, 1977.

————. "The Western Working-Class Experience." In *Lectures in Labour and Canadian Working-Class History*, edited by W. J. C. Cherwinski and Gregory Kealey, 115–26. Toronto: New Hogtown Press, 1985.

McCrady, David G. *Living with Strangers: The Nineteenth-Century Sioux and the Canadian-American Borderlands.* Lincoln: University of Nebraska Press, 2006.

McCullough, Alan B. "Not an Old Cowhand—Fred Stimson and the Bar U Ranch." In *Cowboys, Ranchers, and the Cattle Business: Cross-Border Perspectives on Ranching*

History, edited by Simon Evans, Sarah Carter, and Bill Yeo, 29–41. Calgary: University of Calgary Press, 2000.

McManus, Sheila. *The Line Which Separates: Race, Gender, and the Making of the Alberta-Montana Borderlands*. Lincoln: University of Nebraska Press, 2005.

McMurtry, Larry. *In a Narrow Grave: Essays on Texas*. New York: Touchstone, 1968.

———. *Lonesome Dove*. New York: Simon & Schuster, 1985.

McPherson, James M. *Battle Cry of Freedom: The Civil War Era*. New York: Oxford University Press, 1988.

Medved, Harry, and Randy Dreyfuss. *The Fifty Worst Films of All Time (and How They Got That Way)*. New York: Popular Library, 1978.

Merrill, Karen R. *Public Lands and Political Meanings: Ranchers, the Government, and the Property between Them*. Berkeley: University of California Press, 2002.

Miller, J. R. "From Riel to the Métis." *Canadian Historical Review* 69, no. 1 (March 1988): 1–20.

———. *Skyscrapers Hide the Heavens: A History of Indian-White Relations in Canada*. 1989; Toronto: University of Toronto Press, 2000.

Miller, Thomas Lloyd. *The Public Lands of Texas, 1519–1970*. Norman: University of Oklahoma Press, 1972.

Milloy, John S. *"A National Crime": The Canadian Government and the Residential School System, 1879–1986*. Winnipeg: University of Manitoba Press, 1999.

———. *The Plains Cree: Trade, War, and Diplomacy, 1790–1870*. Winnipeg: University of Manitoba Press, 1988.

Mirandé, Alfredo. *Gringo Justice*. Notre Dame IN: University of Notre Dame Press, 1987.

Moneyhon, Carl H. *Texas after the Civil War: The Struggle of Reconstruction*. College Station: Texas A&M University Press, 2004.

Montejano, David. *Anglos and Mexicans in the Making of Texas, 1836–1986*. Austin: University of Texas Press, 1987.

Montoya, María E. *Translating Property: The Maxwell Land Grant and the Conflict over Land in the American West, 1840–1900*. Berkeley: University of California Press, 2002.

Morgan, E. C. "The North-West Mounted Police: Internal Problems and Public Criticism, 1874–1883." *Saskatchewan History* 26, no. 2 (Spring 1973): 41–62.

Morn, Frank. *"The Eye That Never Sleeps": A History of the Pinkerton National Detective Agency*. Bloomington: Indiana University Press, 1982.

Morris, John Miller, ed. *A Private in the Texas Rangers: A.T. Miller of Company B, Frontier Battalion*. College Station: Texas A&M University Press, 2001.

Morrison, R. Bruce, and C. Roderick Wilson, eds. *Native Peoples: The Canadian Experience*. 1986; Toronto: McClelland & Stewart, 1995.

Morrison, William R. *Showing the Flag: The Mounted Police and Canadian Sovereignty in the North, 1894–1925*. Vancouver: University of British Columbia Press, 1985.

Morton, Desmond. "Aid to the Civil Power: The Canadian Militia in Support of Social Order, 1867–1914." *Canadian Historical Review* 51, no. 4 (December 1970): 407–25.

————. "Cavalry or Police: Keeping the Peace on Two Adjacent Frontiers, 1870–1900." In *The Mounted Police and Prairie Society, 1873–1919*, edited by William M. Baker, 3–16. Regina: Canadian Plains Research Center, 1998.

————. *The Last War Drum: The North-West Campaign of 1885*. Toronto: Hakkert, 1972.

Muise, D. A., ed. *Approaches to Native History in Canada: Papers of a Conference Held at the National Museum of Man, October 1975*. Ottawa: National Museums of Canada, 1977.

Myers, Gustavus. *A History of Canadian Wealth*. Chicago: Charles H. Kerr & Co., 1914.

Neeson, J. M. *Commoners: Common Right, Enclosure, and Social Change in England, 1700–1820*. New York: Cambridge University Press, 1993.

Newcomb, W. W. *The Indians of Texas: From Prehistoric to Modern Times*. Austin: University of Texas Press, 1961.

Nicol, Eric, ed. *Dickens of the Mounted: The Astounding Long-Lost Letters of Inspector F. Dickens, NWMP, 1874–1886*. Toronto: McClelland & Stewart, 1989.

Osgood, Ernest Staples. *The Day of the Cattleman*. Chicago: University of Chicago Press, 1929.

Otter, A. A. den. "Bondage of Steam: The C.P.R and Western Canadian Coal." In *The C.P.R. West: The Iron Road and the Making of a Nation*, edited by Hugh A. Dempsey, 190–207. Toronto: McClelland & Stewart, 1984.

————. *Civilizing the West: The Galts and the Development of Western Canada*. Edmonton: University of Alberta Press, 1982.

Owram, Doug, ed. *Canadian History: A Reader's Guide*, vol. 2: *Confederation to the Present*. Toronto: University of Toronto Press, 1994.

Pannekoek, Fritz. "Metis Studies: The Development of a Field and New Directions." In *From Rupert's Land to Canada*, edited by Theodore Binnema, Gerhard J. Ens, and R. C. Macleod, 111–28. Edmonton: University of Alberta Press, 2001.

————. "The Rev. Griffiths Owen Corbett and the Red River Civil War of 1869–70." *Canadian Historical Review* 57, no. 2 (June 1976): 133–49.

————. *A Snug Little Flock: The Social Origins of the Riel Resistance of 1869–70*. Winnipeg: Watson & Dwyer, 1991.

Paredes, Américo. *A Texas-Mexican Cancionero: Folksongs of the Lower Border*. 1976; Austin: University of Texas Press, 1995.

————. *"With His Pistol in His Hand": A Border Ballad and Its Hero*. 1958; Austin: University of Texas Press, 1996.

Parsons, Chuck. *"Pidge," a Texas Ranger from Virginia: The Life and Letters of Lieutenant T. C. Robinson, Washington County Volunteer Militia Company 'A.'* Wolfe City TX: Henington Publishing Co., 1985.

Parsons, Chuck, and Marianne E. Hall Little. *Captain L. H. McNelly, Texas Ranger: The Life and Times of a Fighting Man*. Austin: State House Press, 2001.

Payment, Diane. "Batoche after 1885, a Society in Transition." In *1885 and After: Native Society in Transition*, edited by F. Laurie Barron and James B. Waldram, 173–87. Regina: Canadian Plains Research Center, 1986.

Peck, Gunther. *Reinventing Free Labor: Padrones and Immigrant Protest in the North American West, 1880–1930.* New York: Cambridge University Press, 2000.

Peterson, Jacqueline, and Jennifer S. H. Brown, eds. *The New Peoples: Being and Becoming Métis in North America.* Winnipeg: University of Manitoba Press, 1985.

Pettipas, Katherine. *Severing the Ties That Bind: Government Repression of Indigenous Ceremonies on the Prairies.* Winnipeg: University of Manitoba Press, 1994.

Pierce, Michael D. *The Most Promising Young Officer: A Life of Randall Slidell Mackenzie.* Norman: University of Oklahoma Press, 1993.

Podruchny, Carolyn. *Making the Voyageur World: Travelers and Traders in the North American Fur Trade.* Lincoln: University of Nebraska Press, 2006.

Powers, William Preston, Jr. "The Subversion of 'Gordon's Kingdom': The Unionization of the Texas and Pacific Coal Mines at Thurber, Texas, 1888–1903." MA thesis, University of Texas at Arlington, 1989.

Procter, Ben H. *Just One Riot: Episodes of the Texas Rangers in the Twentieth Century.* Austin: Eakin Press, 1991.

———. "The Modern Texas Rangers: A Law-Enforcement Dilemma in the Rio Grande Valley." In *Reflections of Western Historians*, edited by John Alexander Carroll, 215–31. Tucson: University of Arizona Press, 1969.

Purcell, Robert Alan. "The History of the Texas Militia, 1835–1903." PhD diss., University of Texas, 1981.

Pursell, Carol. *The Machine in America: A Social History of Technology.* Baltimore: Johns Hopkins University Press, 1995.

Ranelagh, John O'Beirne. *A Short History of Ireland.* 1983; New York: Cambridge University Press, 1994.

Rhinehart, Marilyn. "'Underground Patriots': Thurber Coal Miners and the Struggle for Individual Freedom, 1888–1903." *Southwestern Historical Quarterly* 92, no. 4 (April 1989): 509–42.

———. "A Way of Work and a Way of Life: Coal Mining and Coal Miners in Thurber, Texas, 1888–1926." PhD diss., University of Houston, 1988.

———. *A Way of Work and a Way of Life: Coal Mining in Thurber, Texas, 1888–1926.* College Station: Texas A&M University Press, 1992.

Ribb, Richard H. "José Tómas Canales and the Texas Rangers: Myth, Identity, and Power in South Texas, 1900–1920." PhD diss., University of Texas at Austin, 2001.

Richardson, Jane. *Law and Status among the Kiowa Indians.* New York: J. J. Augustin, 1940.

Richter, William L. *The Army in Texas during Reconstruction, 1865–1870.* College Station: Texas A&M University Press, 1987.

Riker, William H. *Soldiers of the States: The Role of the National Guard in American Democracy.* Washington DC: Public Affairs Press, 1957.

Robbins, William. *Colony and Empire: The Capitalist Transformation of the American West.* Lawrence: University Press of Kansas, 1994.

Robinson, Charles M., III. *The Men Who Wear the Star: The Story of the Texas Rangers.* New York: Random House, 2000.

Romero, Mary. "El Paso Salt War: Mob Action or Political Struggle?" *Aztlán* 16, no. 1–2 (Spring & Fall 1987): 119–43.

Royce, Lynn R. S. "Jesus Sandoval: Real-Life 'Lone Ranger' on the Rio Grande." *Real West* 26, no. 191 (June 1983): 32–37.

Rueck, Daniel. "Imposing a 'Mindless Geometry': Surveyors versus the Canadian Plains, 1869–1885." Unpublished paper presented to the Midwest Association for Canadian Studies, Biennial Conference, Omaha, Nebraska, October 2004.

Sallot, Jeff. *Nobody Said No: The Real Story about How the Mounties Always Get Their Man.* Toronto: James Lorimer, 1979.

Samek, Hana. *The Blackfoot Confederacy, 1880–1920: A Comparative Study of Canadian and U.S. Indian Policy.* Albuquerque: University of New Mexico Press, 1987.

Samora, Julian, Joe Bernal, and Albert Peña. *Gunpowder Justice: A Reassessment of the Texas Rangers.* Notre Dame IN: University of Notre Dame Press, 1979.

Saskatchewan History and Folklore Society. *Wake the Prairie Echoes: The Mounted Police Story in Verse.* Saskatoon: Western Producer Book Service, 1973.

Schmelzer, Janet. "Determining the Extent of Power: Farmer's Loan and Trust Company at the Texas Railroad Commission." In *Law in the Western United States*, edited by Gordon Morris Bakken, 423–25. Norman: University of Oklahoma Press, 2000.

Schwartz, Rosalie. *Across the River to Freedom: U.S. Negroes in Mexico.* El Paso: Texas Western Press, 1975.

Seager, Allen. "Class, Ethnicity, and Politics in the Alberta Coalfields, 1905–1945." In *"Struggle a Hard Battle": Essays on Working-Class Immigrants*, edited by Dirk Hoerder, 304–24. Dekalb: Northern Illinois University Press, 1986.

Sharp, Paul F. *Whoop-Up Country: The Canadian-American West, 1865–1885.* Minneapolis: University of Minnesota Press, 1955.

Smith, Sherry L. *The View from Officers' Row: Army Perceptions of Western Indians.* Tucson: University of Arizona Press, 1990.

Smith, T. C. *From the Memories of Men.* Brownwood TX: T. C. Smith, 1954.

Smith, Thomas T. "U.S. Army Combat Operations in the Indian Wars of Texas, 1849–1881." *Southwestern Historical Quarterly* 99, no. 4 (April 1996): 500–531.

Spector, David. *Agriculture on the Prairies, 1870–1940.* Ottawa: Parks Canada, 1983.

Sprague, Douglas N. *Canada and the Métis, 1869–1885.* Waterloo, Ontario: Wilfrid Laurier Press, 1988.

Spratt, John S. *The Road to Spindletop: Economic Change in Texas, 1875–1901.* Dallas: Southern Methodist University Press, 1955.

———. *Thurber: The Life and Death of a Company Coal Town.* Austin: University of Texas Press, 1986.

Spry, Irene M. "The Métis and the Mixed-Bloods of Rupert's Land before 1870." In *The New Peoples: Being and Becoming Métis in North America*, edited by Jacqueline Peterson and Jennifer S. H. Brown, 95–118. Winnipeg: University of Manitoba Press, 1985.

Stanley, G. F. G. *The Birth of Western Canada: A History of the Riel Rebellions.* 1936; Toronto: University of Toronto Press, 1979.

Starrs, Paul F. *Let the Cowboy Ride: Cattle Ranching in the American West.* Baltimore: Johns Hopkins University Press, 1998.

Stern, Steve J. "Feudalism, Capitalism, and the World-System in the Perspective of Latin America and the Caribbean." *American Historical Review* 93, no. 4 (October 1988): 829–72.

St. Germain, Jill. *Indian Treaty-Making Policy in the United States and Canada, 1867–1877.* Lincoln: University of Nebraska Press, 2001.

Stonechild, A. Blair. "The Indian View of the 1885 Uprising." In *1885 and After: Native Society in Transition*, edited by F. Laurie Barron and James B. Waldram, 155–70. Regina: Canadian Plains Research Center, 1986.

Streisel, Luke. "The Miners Strike Out: The Lethbridge Coal Miners' Strike of 1906." *Alberta History* 52, no. 4 (Autumn 2004): 2–7.

Thacker, Robert. "The Mystery of Francis Jeffrey Dickens, N.W.M.P., and Eric Nicol's *Dickens of the Mounted." Great Plains Quarterly* 12, no. 1 (Winter 1992): 19–30.

Thomas, Lewis H., ed. *Essays on Western History.* Edmonton: University of Alberta Press, 1976.

Thompson, E. P. *Customs in Common.* New York: New Press, 1991.

Thompson, Jerry D., ed. *Juan Cortina and the Texas-Mexican Frontier.* El Paso: Texas Western Press, 1994.

Tobias, John L. "Indian Reserves in Western Canada: Indian Homelands or Devises for Assimilation?" In *Approaches to Native History in Canada: Papers of a Conference Held at the National Museum of Man, October 1975*, edited by D. A. Muise, 89–103. Ottawa: National Museums of Canada, 1977.

Treaty 7 Elders and Tribal Council, with Walter Hildebrant, Dorothy First Rider, and Sarah Carter. *The True Spirit and Original Intent of Treaty 7.* Montreal: McGill-Queen's University Press, 1996.

Turner, John Peter. *The North-West Mounted Police, 1873–1893.* 2 vols. Ottawa: Edmond Cloutier, 1950.

Utley, Robert M. *The Indian Frontier, 1846–1890.* 1984; Albuquerque: University of New Mexico Press, 2003.

———. *Lone Star Justice: The First Century of the Texas Rangers.* New York: Oxford University Press, 2002.

Vanderhaeghe, Guy. *The Last Crossing.* New York: Atlantic Monthly Press, 2002.

Vezzetti, Robert B. "Steamboats on the Lower Rio Grande in the Nineteenth Century." In

Studies in Brownsville History, edited by Milo Kearney, 77–81. Brownsville TX: Pan American University Press, 1986.

Voss, Kim. *The Making of American Exceptionalism: The Knights of Labor and Class Formation in the Nineteenth Century.* Ithaca: Cornell University Press, 1993.

Waiser, William. *The North-West Mounted Police in 1874–1889: A Statistical Study.* Ottawa: Parks Canada, 1979.

Walden, Keith. *Visions of Order: The Canadian Mounties in Symbol and Myth.* Toronto: Butterworths, 1982.

Wallace, Jim. *A Trying Time: The North-West Mounted Police in the 1885 Rebellion.* Winnipeg: Bunker to Bunker Books, 1998.

Wallerstein, Immanuel. "World-Systems Analysis: The Second Phase." *Review* (Fernand Braudel Center) 13, no. 2 (Spring 1990): 287–93.

Webb, Walter Prescott. *The Great Plains.* 1931; Waltham MA: Blaisdell, 1959.

———. *The Texas Rangers: A Century of Frontier Defense.* 1935; Austin: University of Texas Press, 1965.

Webber, Jeremy. "Compelling Compromise: Canada Chooses Conciliation over Arbitration, 1900–1907." *Labour/Le Travail* 28 (Fall 1991): 15–57.

Weber, David J. *Foreigners in Their Native Land: Historical Roots of the Mexican Americans.* Albuquerque: University of New Mexico Press, 1973.

Weir, Robert. E. *Beyond Labor's Veil: The Culture of the Knights of Labor.* University Park: Pennsylvania State University Press, 1996.

Weiss, Harold J., Jr. "'Yours to Command': Captain William J. Macdonald and the Panhandle Rangers of Texas." PhD diss., Indiana University, 1980.

Whiteside, James. *Regulating Danger: The Struggle for Mine Safety in the Rocky Mountain Coal Industry.* Lincoln: University of Nebraska Press, 1990.

Wilkins, Frederick. *The Law Comes to Texas: The Texas Rangers, 1870–1901.* Austin: State House Press, 1999.

Wishart, David, ed. *The Encyclopedia of the Great Plains.* Lincoln: University of Nebraska Press, 2004.

Woodcock, George. *Gabriel Dumont: The Métis Chief and His Lost World.* Edmonton: Hurtig Publishers, 1975.

Woodman, Lyman L. *Cortina: Rogue of the Rio Grande.* San Antonio: Naylor Co., 1950.

Worster, Donald. *Dust Bowl: The Southern Plains in the 1930s.* New York: Oxford University Press, 1979.

———. "Two Faces West: The Development Idea in Canada and the United States." In *One West, Two Myths: A Comparative Reader*, edited by Carol Higham and Robert Thacker, 23–45. Calgary: University of Calgary Press, 2004.

Wrightson, Keith. *Earthly Necessities: Economic Lives in Early Modern Britain.* New Haven: Yale University Press, 2000.

Wunder, John R., ed. *Working the Range: Essays in the History of Western Land Management and the Environment.* Westport CT: Greenwood Press, 1985.

Young, Elliott. *Catarino Garza's Revolution on the Texas-Mexico Border.* Durham: Duke University Press, 2004.

Young, John D., and J. Frank Dobie. *A Vaquero of the Brush Country: The Life and Times of John D. Young.* 1929; Austin: University of Texas Press, 1998.

Zlatkovich, Charles P. *Texas Railroads: A Record of Construction and Abandonment.* Austin: Bureau of Business Research at the University of Texas, 1981.

Index

Page numbers in italics refer to illustrations.